"A pioneering book, a truly inspired revelation, and a gentle guide to the deepest terrain of our own souls. A remarkable, often astonishing document . . . probably the first book to describe the overall path of consciousness development from a Christian perspective."

—Ken Wilber, from the Foreword

Praise for *Putting on the Mind of Christ*

"In this era of spiritual books that promise their readers enlightenment and wealth in seven easy steps, it is encouraging to see a book that reminds us that true spiritual development is neither easy, safe, nor comfortable. No ego gets out of this alive, thank God."

—Bo Lozoff, author of *It's a Meaningful Life—It Just Takes Practice*

"Such thought offers the hope that we can, in the light of today's more subtle science, re-discover ourselves as responsible beings in a meaningful world. Without such a reality, preaching values and morals can be but sound and fury."

—T. George Harris, consulting editor for *Psychology Today;* founding editor of *American Health* and *Spirituality & Health* magazines and the PBS series *Bodywatch*

"A spiritual book about a simple path. When practiced with courage and perseverance, it can bring one to the highest level of consciousness. I recommend *Putting on the Mind of Christ* to spiritual seekers everywhere."

—Gerald G. Jampolsky, M.D., author of *Love Is Letting Go of Fear*

Putting on the Mind of Christ

the inner work of christian spirituality

Jim Marion

HAMPTON ROADS
PUBLISHING COMPANY, INC.

Cover design by Grace Pedalino
Cover art by PhotoDisc

For information write:

Hampton Roads Publishing Company, Inc.
1125 Stoney Point Road
Charlottesville, VA 22902

Or call: 434-296-2772
FAX: 434-296-5096
e-mail: hrpc@hrpub.com
www.hrpub.com

If you are unable to order this book from your local
bookseller, you may order directly from the publisher.
Quantity discounts for organizations are available.
Call 1-800-766-8009, toll-free.

Library of Congress Catalog Card Number: 00-190081
ISBN 1-57174-357-X
10 9 8 7 6 5 4 3 2 1

Printed on acid-free paper in the United States

DEDICATION

This book is dedicated to the memory of
Michael John Marion (1946-1998)

ACKNOWLEDGMENTS

First, I want to thank my parents, James P. Marion and Joan Durkin Marion, for the example of their lifelong dedication to God and the things of God, to their family, and to each other. I want to thank my sisters, Jeanne Marion, Ann Marie Scalea, and Kathleen Gagne, for their constant support. Jeanne was especially helpful in spending many hours carefully reading and editing the manuscript. I want to thank David DuBois for his advice on the process of publishing. I want to thank my editors, Frank DeMarco, Richard Leviton, Rebecca Williamson, and all the others at Hampton Roads who had faith in this work and immensely improved the presentation. I want to thank Ken Wilber for his beautiful foreword and for taking the time out of his tremendously busy schedule to study and endorse a book by someone he has never even met. I want to thank Barbara Marx Hubbard, Gerald Jampolsky, M. D., Bo Lozoff, and T. George Harris for their wonderful endorsements. I want to thank the hundreds of friends and "worthy opponents" who have been instrumental in bringing me deeper and deeper into God-awareness. Finally, I want to thank and express my undying gratitude and affection for two mentors whom I now call friends, and without whom my path to God-realization might never have been successful, Teresa of Avila and John of the Cross.

PUTTING ON
THE MIND OF CHRIST
The Inner Work of Christian Spirituality

But the Counselor, the Holy Spirit, whom the Father will send you in my name, will teach you all things, and remind you of everything I have said to you.

John 14:26

TABLE OF CONTENTS

PART V
SPECIAL PROBLEMS FACING THE
CHRISTIAN ON THE PATH TO THE
KINGDOM OF HEAVEN

PART VI
FURTHER REACHES OF THE
KINGDOM OF HEAVEN

FOREWORD

By Ken Wilber

Putting on the Mind of Christ, The Inner Work of Christian Spirituality is a remarkable, often astonishing document. Its author, Jim Marion, claims that "it is the first book to clearly describe the entire Christian spiritual path." This initially sounds rather grandiose, and yet, after carefully studying this book, I am inclined to agree with its author. This probably is the first book to describe the overall path of consciousness development from a Christian perspective. As such, it is a stunning achievement.

In a sense, however, this claim is much less grandiose than it sounds. For by "the entire path," Jim Marion means one that includes the basic stages of spiritual development described so beautifully by the great saints and sages, plus the psychological stages of development only recently discovered by modern developmental psychologists (such as Jean Piaget, Jane Loevinger, Robert Kegan, Lawrence Kohlberg, and Carol Gilligan). Thus, a truly complete path would, as it were, combine the discoveries of both the ancient sages and the modern psychologists, and by definition, that more comprehensive or complete map of development has only been possible in the last few decades.

Jim Marion is one of the pioneers in applying this more integral understanding to the Christian spiritual path. In doing so, Jim draws on my own work in a very fruitful fashion. In several books, I have attempted to develop a "master template" of overall consciousness development, based on sources ancient and modern, eastern and western, using each of the numerous systems to fill in the gaps left by others. (For my latest presentation of this master template, the reader might consult *Integral Psychology,* Shambhala, 2000.) But I have generally presented only the barest skeleton of this master template, and invited researchers to fill in all the rich details using their own traditions. Marion has done this brilliantly for the Christian tradition, adding his own original, creative, and profound insights along the way.

Jim Marion is not saying that past Christian saints did not possess a complete spiritual path. The point, rather, is that only recently have some of the stages of this overall path been clearly investigated and identified. By explicitly drawing on this modern research, the overall path of consciousness development can be more clearly mapped, and thus the spiritual path itself can be better understood in all its many dimensions, an understanding that will help even more souls grasp the timeless truths of the Christian revelation. The Holy Spirit continues to speak to us, even in this moment, and thus it increasingly makes the path itself more clearly revealed and understood, easing us along it all the more lovingly.

Putting on the Mind of Christ, The Inner Work of Christian Spirituality, is just such a further help for all those seeking to understand the full dimensions of the Christian path to the Kingdom. As such, it is a pioneering book, a truly inspired revelation, and a gentle guide to the deepest terrain of our own souls, where there awaits, as there has through all eternity, Christ as Source and Suchness of this and every world.

INTRODUCTION

Putting on the Mind of Christ, The Inner Work of Christian Spirituality, is the first book to clearly describe the entire Christian spiritual path. Step by step, from the consciousness of infants, children, and adolescents, *Putting on the Mind of Christ* leads the reader to the consciousness that Jesus called the Kingdom of Heaven—the highest level of human spiritual development. Citing the New Testament, Christian spiritual classics like St. John of the Cross' *Dark Night of the Soul,* and my own inner experience, the book seeks to demonstrate that Jesus' teaching and his death and resurrection were meant to show us the way to this inner kingdom.

For the Christian, the follower of Jesus, the Way to the Kingdom of Heaven (higher consciousness) is Jesus Christ himself (John 14:6). More specifically, it is "to allow God to transform us inwardly by the complete renewing of our minds" (Rom. 12:2), so that, with St. Paul, we can honestly say, "We have the mind of Christ" (1 Cor. 2:16). This "putting on of the mind which was in Christ Jesus" (Philip. 2:5), that is, the Christ Consciousness, is the goal of the Christian spiritual path. This book seeks to describe that path. It seeks to serve as a map to the Kingdom of Heaven.

This book, therefore, is concerned with the development of human consciousness. It is only in recent years that the general public has begun to realize that the development of consciousness on this planet did not come to a halt with the arrival of the human being. It has now become clear that consciousness, at least within human beings, continues to develop. Though consciousness itself is non-linear, in our world of spacetime consciousness (or awareness) it can be said to grow in a step-by-step manner, beginning at birth and continuing throughout a person's lifetime. The end of this inner growth is full spiritual maturity. This book describes that growth in the context of the Christian spiritual tradition.

It is also only in recent years that the various steps or "stages" of growth in human consciousness have begun to be systematically mapped. The science of psychology, particularly transpersonal and other "higher-level" psychologies, has been attempting to map the growth of consciousness in adults. Other psychologists, following the pioneering work of Jean Piaget, have continued to study the growth of consciousness in children. Putting the work of these two groups of scientists together, you get a fairly adequate map of human inner development from birth to well-functioning, even creatively-functioning, adulthood.

But there is still something missing. Contemporary psychology has not yet incorporated into its maps of human inner growth the full spirituality of the West's Christian tradition which, for two thousand years, has had *inner* spiritual growth as its primary concern. In particular, the spiritual teachings of Jesus and of the Christian saints and mystics have generally not been appreciated and incorporated. This has happened for a number of reasons, two of crucial importance. First, the spiritual teachings of Jesus and the saints have not been understood. Second, those teachings involve levels of human consciousness beyond that of even psychologically well-adjusted, creatively-functioning adults. No modern psychology map of human development goes beyond the vision-logic level (chapter 8). The psychic, subtle, causal and nondual are not even recognized as real, yet it is of these upper levels that Jesus and the saints speak (chapters 9 to 17).

It is the purpose of this book to show how the Christian spiritual tradition both complements and completes the work of the psychologists. The book is divided into six parts. Part 1 examines the nature of the Kingdom of Heaven, the level of consciousness that Jesus preached was the goal of human spiritual development. Part 2 examines, one by one, the seven levels of consciousness of the human personality through which the Christian grows towards full spiritual maturity.

Part 3 examines the nature of, descent into, progress through, and resurrection from what St. John of the Cross called the "Dark Night of the Soul." This is the central mystery in the evolution of human consciousness on this planet, the very mystery that Jesus enacted for us by his crucifixion and resurrection. Part 4 examines the two levels of consciousness of the Christian who has realized, in Christ, his or her own divinity. The first of these levels is that of the Christ Consciousness; the second is the nondual vision of the Kingdom of Heaven on Earth.

Part 5 explores several serious conceptual obstacles that typically confront contemporary Christians as they attempt to "put on the mind which was in Christ Jesus" (Philip. 2:5) and come into the Christ Consciousness and, later, into an awareness of Jesus' Kingdom.

Finally, Part 6 discusses the Kingdom of Heaven as it is usually understood, the after-death heaven of the Communion of Saints, as well as the eventual arrival of the Kingdom of Heaven on Earth.

To assist the reader by giving a context for many of the assertions made later in this book, that is, to help the reader "know where I'm coming from," I am taking this space to offer a short autobiography. I am, simply, an American mystic who has followed the Christian spiritual path since childhood. By "mystic" I mean nothing exotic. I mean a person of prayer and meditation who has been blessed by God with a certain amount of psychic ability, the ability to "see," "feel," and sometimes "hear," beyond the spacetime world we ordinarily perceive with the physical senses.

I was born in 1945 to very devoted Christian parents in a small coal-mining town in northeastern Pennsylvania. In that small town, where I lived for my first six years, nearly all of life revolved around the activities of the parish church. I was constantly in church for Sunday services, weddings, funerals, church fairs, and parish school events. I had what I can now, looking back, see as my first serious religious experience in that church on a Good Friday when I was about four years old. It left me with a deep devotion to Jesus Crucified, one of the many titles by which Jesus is honored.

I attended parochial schools in that town and later in Buffalo, New York, and Baltimore, Maryland. I attended religious high schools in Baltimore and Boston, Massachusetts. I had religious "conversion" experiences at the ages of 7, 11, and 15. Each conversion was a born-again experience, meaning an ever deeper inner commitment to the spiritual path. After the first, at the time of my first communion, I developed a great devotion toward Jesus' Mother Mary. At the second, at age 11, I vowed to dedicate my life to the service of God, to pray privately for at least an hour or two a day, and, to the best of my powers, to become a saint; i.e., the best and most loving person I could be. Immediately after the third conversion, at age 15, I entered a Catholic monastery where I remained for the next seven and a half years. This third conversion was probably my first real "mystical" experience. I was swept up in a highly altered and exalted state of consciousness for several days. Afterwards, I could never again see the world as "ordinary" because, from that point on, I knew by experience that the invisible spiritual world was every bit as real as this material one.

My first three years in the monastery were among the happiest years of my life. The monastery was in a rural area, the property bordering on a large lake. As monks, we kept silent most of the day and all of the night. We ate most meals in silence. We had no radio, television, magazines, and, of course, it being the 1960's, no video games or Internet. We were allowed to listen to records on Saturday nights but I often skipped these recreations and spent the time meditating in the chapel. I didn't feel I had to do this. I wanted to. I simply loved prayer more than noise. Prayer filled me with an inner bliss that mere music couldn't touch. We meditated at least two hours every day in addition to all the other more formal religious services. Studies were hard. Sports activities were both mandatory and demanding. Friendships made were solid and lasting. Inwardly I was "high" on God for days on end (a stage in the spiritual life I will describe later in the book). I loved the silence and I loved monastic life.

About three and a half years into this idyllic existence, God lowered the boom. I was plunged into what St. John of the Cross, the famous Catholic mystic, calls the "Dark Night of the Senses" (which I describe later in the book). There were no more "highs." It was no longer possible to do oral prayer. I couldn't force myself to read a spiritual book. Meditation was an arid desert. I felt aching and empty on the inside. Spiritual things seemed revolting to me. But I kept meditating and carried on with my studies and other activities. I told no one what I was feeling inside.

Then came the trials that are typical of this "night." A teacher who misunderstood me punished me severely for no apparent reason, depriving me of a holiday the other students had. My best friend left the monastery. Another teacher took a dislike to me, and though I had a very good voice, excluded me from the choir when a record was being made. But these trials were nothing compared to the next three years. There was one severe interpersonal conflict after another. One new classmate didn't speak to me for three years and tried to turn all my friends against me. Another teacher tried to have me thrown out of the seminary because I spoke up and objected when he was ridiculing a classmate in the classroom (he did succeed in having me publicly humiliated). The hostility and rage that I evoked from this priest so terrified me that I lost ten pounds in a week and developed an ulcer almost overnight. One of my best friends was thrown out of school, for petty reasons. My wrist was broken on the soccer field and my arm put in a smelly cast for months. I was often exhausted and depressed.

We were put under a spiritual director (a priest charged with guiding us, both in everyday monastic life and in inner spiritual development) who was a tyrant, albeit a petty one. He subjected us daily to countless indignities. I lobbied hard to have him replaced and eventually he was, but not before two of my classmates had nervous breakdowns. Our priest-teachers were themselves in turmoil, some leaving to get married immediately after the close of the Second Vatican Council in 1965. Some priests turned to drink. That situation got so bad that sometimes only the students showed up in chapel to fulfill the monastic observance, including the daily chanting of Matins from 2 a.m. to 3 a.m. Our formerly idyllic existence had turned into a nightmare.

One of the things the Dark Night of the Senses does is to bring previously denied contents of the unconscious to the surface. So, on top of all this, I found myself having to cope with feelings of homosexuality. One spiritual director to whom I went for advice told me that, since I had homo-sexual feelings, I was to break off all contact with my five best friends. I did and had to tell them why. They thought it absurd because not one of them was gay. Soon thereafter, almost as a reaction to the priest's poor advice, I began to fall deeply in love with a classmate. This was a hideously frustrating and agonizing business for me both because he was "straight" (and so didn't reciprocate my feelings) and because neither of us had any intention of breaking our vows. This trial lasted four years. During that period I had taken my vows (poverty, chastity, obedience) from a sense of duty to God, yet I felt nothing. After three years of all this—with two more to come—I was numb on the inside.

Thank God I had read St. John of the Cross. So I understood this spiritual passage. I stuck with it, kept praying, kept meditating, kept loving all as best I could, and kept forgiving those who caused me difficulties. It turned out I chose correctly.

After five years of this I was worn out. I was so thin I looked like a scarecrow. I also began to realize that my own consciousness had grown well beyond many of my teachers, many of whom were stuck at the "mythic level" of consciousness (see chapter 6) or, at best, at a rationalized mythic level (see chapter 7). Because of the chaos in the monastery where I was then living, a group of us appealed to higher religious authorities for help. At an assembly of the religious community, I made a plea that our spiritual directors from then on be older men who knew something about the inner spiritual life. There were a few of these men in that religious order, few and far between I'm sorry to say. All the students were punished for my "insolence" by being disinvited to the rest of the assembly. But the next year we were given a genuine spiritual director.

A few of us also asked for psychological testing to see if we were "crazy," or if the environment was causing the chaos we felt. It turned out to be overwhelmingly the latter. Soon, most of us ended up leaving the life we had loved and into which we'd invested the whole of our youth. To say this was painful is putting it mildly. For me it was like a wrenching divorce. The Catholic Church in America has yet to recover from the mass exodus of seminarians in 1965-1970. Nor, I expect, will it recover until it first, by an institutional death and rebirth, recovers its own spiritual health.

It took me two full years to heal from the emotional traumas of the previous four years; in other words, it took two years for the inner work of the Dark Night of the Senses (see chapter 10) to be completed. During that time I worked for a Wall Street investment bank in New York City and became active in civil rights, anti-war, and political activities. I worked in a minor capacity on Robert F. Kennedy's presidential campaign in 1968. I went to

Memphis, Tennessee, by bus to help complete the march that Rev. Dr. Martin Luther King, Jr. had organized on behalf of the garbage workers in the days before his assassination. I went to Ebenezer Baptist Church in Atlanta, Georgia, and paid last respects to Dr. King early on the morning he was buried. I was allowed to be alone at the open casket in prayer for several minutes. I did a short stint with the Peace Corps, and then pursued divinity studies for a year at an interdenominational Protestant seminary where I came to have friends from several Christian denominations. I taught Sunday school at a Presbyterian church, and attended services at Episcopal, Methodist, Lutheran, and churches of other Christian denominations.

Finally, on a lovely day in May, 1970, when some friends and I were attending a rally for the Black Panther Bobby Seale at Yale University, I experienced another inner transformation. This was the entrance into the subtle level of consciousness (see chapter 11). I experienced this transformation as a significant and freeing spiritual experience. To use the words of John of the Cross, I felt as though "liberated from a cramped prison cell."

During graduate school I also worked on a U. S. Senate campaign, the same campaign President Clinton was to join when he returned later that year from his studies at Oxford University. By then I'd decided to go to law school. I got my law degree from Boston University and began a public policy career in Washington, D.C. Later I served in minor capacities in the Carter administration. I've also worked for the Congress on Capitol Hill. Over the years I've held a number of positions in both the executive and legislative branches of the Federal government.

Six years into my public policy career I began, internally, to undergo the spiritual passage St. John of the Cross calls the "Dark Night of the Soul." That passage, and other spiritual passages which occurred later, are described in detail later in this book. I am still living and working in Washington, D. C.

This book, therefore, is the result of many years of spiritual practice, experience, and study. The time has come for me to begin sharing with others my experience and the insights God has given me. I offer this book to God for the spiritual health of the whole Christian Church, and for the spiritual healing and advancement of all who are trying to follow Jesus into the Kingdom of His Father.

BOOK ONE

PART I
THE KINGDOM OF HEAVEN

Chapter 1

WHAT JESUS TAUGHT ABOUT

THE KINGDOM OF HEAVEN

A proper understanding of what Jesus meant by "the Kingdom of Heaven" is essential to Christian spirituality. The Kingdom of Heaven was the central theme of Jesus' preaching ministry. By the "Kingdom of Heaven," Jesus meant a particular level of human consciousness, not a place to which Christians are destined after death. Unfortunately, most church officials and theologians today do not understand Jesus' concept of the Kingdom.

Using Mother Teresa and Jesus as examples, we can see that the two chief characteristics of the nondual consciousness of the Kingdom of Heaven are a lack of separation between God and humans and a lack of separation between human beings.

For any Christian serious about spirituality, a proper understanding of the Kingdom of Heaven is essential. In fact, the most critical spiritual mistake we Christians normally make is in failing to understand what Jesus meant by the phrases "the Kingdom of Heaven" and "the Kingdom of God." This mistake is so basic because, once made, it can throw our spirituality off on the wrong track for the rest of our lives, with unfortunate consequences that we may realize fully only after our deaths.

Most Christians believe that the Kingdom of Heaven is a place and that, if we lead virtuous lives, we will enter this Kingdom of Heaven after we die. Many Christians today find encouragement for this belief in the dozens of books that have appeared over the last twenty years telling of the "near death experiences" (NDEs) of people who have almost died and then recovered. These documented experiences seem to clearly indicate that, after death, we will go to a place filled with love, light, peace, and joy, the place we Christians normally refer to as "heaven."

The vast majority of contemporary Christians, however, are not the least upset that astronomers have yet to locate a physical place called "heaven." That is because most of us do not believe that "heaven," our promised after-death home, is to be found anywhere in the dimension of space-time. Most of us believe that heaven, though a place, is somewhere in another, non-physical dimension.

There is nothing wrong with these beliefs. There is an after-death place of love, light, peace, and joy that is properly called heaven, and leading virtuous lives will certainly help us get there. I will return to a discussion of these aspects of heaven (and the Christian belief in the resurrection of the body) in part 5 of this book. Where we Christians have made a costly mistake, in terms of our own spiritual growth, is in thinking that this after-death "heaven" is the Kingdom of Heaven Jesus dedicated virtually all of his preaching ministry to tell us about. It is not. Though Jesus acknowledged that an after-death heaven existed, Jesus devoted his preaching, not to that heaven, but to a Kingdom of Heaven that he said was here and now, near, "at hand" (Mark 1:15).

The principal message that Jesus brought to us was the Gospel or "Good News" of the Kingdom of Heaven. Matthew, the author of the earliest Gospel, begins his account of Jesus' public ministry with these words: "From that time Jesus began to preach his message, "Turn away from your mistaken thinking, because the Kingdom of Heaven is at hand.'" (Matt. 4:17). By "at hand" Jesus meant "here," "right in front of our faces," "in our midst." A few verses later Matthew writes, "Jesus went all over Galilee, teaching in their synagogues, preaching the Good News of the Kingdom, and healing people from every kind of disease and sickness" (Matt. 4:23).

In the Sermon on the Mount, Jesus described the type of people who inhabit the Kingdom of Heaven, namely the meek, the merciful, the peacemakers, and the pure in heart (Matt. 5:1-10). He told us that we should "seek first" the Kingdom of Heaven (Matt. 6:33), that is, that the realization of the Kingdom of Heaven should be the principal goal of every Christian's life. And he promised his immediate disciples that some of them would not die until they had actually seen the Kingdom (Matt. 16:28).

But the single most important thing that Jesus taught about the Kingdom of Heaven was that "The Kingdom of God is within" (Luke 17:21). The Kingdom of God or Heaven that Jesus preached up and down the land of Israel, day in and day out, throughout his entire ministry, is a Kingdom that you and I can find and see *only* by going deep *within* ourselves. There is *no other way* except by going within to get to the Kingdom Jesus preached. No other way. In the Lord's Prayer, the only prayer Jesus personally instructed us to say, he taught us that it was our responsibility to pray every single day that the *inner* Kingdom of Heaven he preached about would come into existence for all of us right here on this Earth (Matt. 6:10).

Jesus told many parables about what this Kingdom of Heaven was like, a Kingdom of Heaven he himself saw, and lived in, every day of his public ministry. And he promised that those of us who truly sought this Kingdom within ourselves, forsaking all else to do so, would surely realize the same vision, not after death but in this life.

For Jesus, therefore, the Kingdom of Heaven was something that could be realized by each and every one of us right here on Earth. It was a Kingdom that could actually be "seen," not with our physical eyes, of course, but with the inner eye of understanding. The goal of the spiritual life, Jesus taught, was to "seek first" this inner vision of *this* world. Once we, while here on Earth, have realized within ourselves the vision of the Kingdom, he said, "all else will be added," including, of course, admittance to the heaven after death (Matt. 6:33). But first, he taught, before there is any question about entering the after-death heaven, the Kingdom of Heaven here on Earth has to be realized by going deep within ourselves. The goal of Christian spirituality, the spirituality that Jesus himself preached, is for each and every one of us to *personally* be able to see the Kingdom of Heaven within, that Jesus saw. It is for us to go deep enough within our own psyches to find out for ourselves that what Jesus preached was true.

The Church (and by "Church" I mean virtually all of the Christian churches and communities, Protestant, Catholic, and Orthodox) has never sufficiently emphasized the importance of Jesus' words about the Kingdom of Heaven being within ourselves. Instead, for centuries, the Church has emphasized our responsibility to lead virtuous lives so that we will be allowed to enter, not the Kingdom of Heaven about which Jesus actually preached, but the non-physical heaven after death.

What we Christians hear most when we attend church, therefore, are sermons about morality: the thoughts, words, or deeds that the particular Christian denomination or preacher believes (based on the Bible or the reasoning of "moral theology") that we should or shouldn't think, say, or do. Secondly, we usually hear pleas to attend church, join the choir, tithe, undertake charitable or social justice activities, and otherwise participate in the external observances, rituals and activities of the local church. In other words, we Christians hear much the same things that the religious Jews of Jesus' day heard in the village synagogues from the Pharisees (the lay preachers) and in the Temple in Jerusalem from the Sadducees (the priests). We normally hear very little, however, about the *inner* Kingdom of Heaven Jesus wanted us to see and experience for ourselves.

Though some Christians may disagree with the preacher, minister, priest, bishop, or pope about this or that moral teaching or interpretation, there is nothing inherently wrong with the preaching of morality in church. In Western societies, after all, religion (after the input of parents and the assistance of the schools) has traditionally been assigned, and has itself taken on, the role of teaching and preaching the cultural and moral values of the society, especially to our children. It should be no surprise, therefore, that our clergy spend a great deal of their time and energy explaining and defending (and often criticizing) societal values and the societal institutions that incorporate and enforce those values.

But very little of this moral preaching and teaching is of any significant help to us in *personally* realizing the inner Kingdom of Heaven. None of it helps us to *transcend* this world and its values (no matter what those values happen to be) so as to enter, with Jesus and within ourselves, the inner spiritual experience of that Kingdom.

Jesus wept over Jerusalem because the leaders of his own religion had not understood or accepted his message about the inner Kingdom of Heaven (Luke 13:34). Instead, the blind leading the blind (Matt. 15:14), they continued to emphasize external observances (like fasting and the washing of hands) and moral rules and regulations over the inner spiritual core of religion. Rather than follow the narrow path within that Jesus pointed out, they insisted on following the wide path of moral rectitude that their society honored, one that afforded them the first place in the synagogue, access to political leaders, and an assumed right to the allegiance and donations of the people (Matt. 7:13-14).

But their wide path of external law and observance, though crowded and fully approved by society (the Pharisees, at least, were much respected by the Jewish people), led nowhere in terms of *inner* spiritual growth because the narrow path to the *inner* Kingdom of Heaven was sorely neglected. So much so that, as Jesus observed, very few of the people who followed these leaders were even able to find the true inner path. The same is true of Christianity today.

Why has this happened? Why has the Kingdom of Heaven within ourselves that Jesus preached been so sorely neglected and even ignored? It has happened for one simple and obvious reason: the vast majority of our Christian elders, ministers, priests, bishops, popes, and other teachers, just like the religious leaders of Jesus' time, have themselves not yet grown enough spiritually to "see" the Kingdom Jesus saw. They do not yet experience this world the way Jesus experienced it. They have not yet themselves put on the mind which was in Christ Jesus (Philip. 2:5). They cannot preach about the Kingdom of Heaven to others because, though they may have dedicated many years to the spiritual path, they do not yet see or understand it themselves.

These leaders include those who, without their own inner realization of the Kingdom, have allowed themselves to be looked upon by the world as spiritual authorities. Like the Sadducees and the Pharisees of Jesus' own religion, these leaders emphasize what they *can* see: the external aspects of religion and morality, the worldly aspects. Some are even primarily concerned with religion's grossest material aspects, the numbers baptized or converted, the dollars contributed, even the size of the congregation, church building, or denomination. Others mistakenly think and preach that the essence of what Jesus taught was political and social reform (though some suppose the reforms should be of the political left and some of the right). But none of this has anything to do with the inner Kingdom within our psyche that Jesus died to tell us about.

In making these observations, which are largely those that Jesus himself made about the religious authorities of his own Jewish religion, I am not implying that Gospel-based principles (to the extent understood) should not be applied to the affairs of this world. In fact the glory of Christianity, unequaled by any other religion, has been the gradual historical unfoldment of such principles throughout first Western society and now the entire planet. It is in large part from Christianity and its Gospel-based principles that have eventually come freedom from slavery, universal education, liberal democracy, the free market economy, social welfare programs, the movement for universal health care, and labor protection laws and unions. It is a tremendous achievement. But these advances are nothing compared to what could have been accomplished in the last two thousand years if the message of Jesus about the inner Kingdom of Heaven had been understood and heeded.

What then is this Kingdom of Heaven, the vision of *this* world that the mind (consciousness) of Jesus "saw"? First of all and most importantly, *The Kingdom of Heaven that Jesus saw so well is a vision of this world that sees no separation (duality) between God and humans.*

Jesus of Nazareth, a human being like ourselves, a lowly carpenter from a nondescript town, nevertheless managed to realize and "see" that he and the God of Israel, the God of Abraham, Jacob, and Isaac, were *one*. He "saw" with his everyday mind (consciousness) that he was completely united to the God that everyone else merely thought they should worship. "The Father and I are one" (John 10:30), said Jesus. And he also said "He who sees me sees the Father" (John 14:9). He saw his own complete union with God despite all physical and other appearances of "separateness" to the contrary, and despite all the Pharisees' and Sadducees' theological theories to the contrary.

Not only did Jesus see this truth for himself, but he saw that this essential non-separation from God was also true for the rest of us. And he actually had the courage to go about the land of Israel telling everyone that this was the case. He asked us, "Do you not know that you are gods?" (John 10:34-35). In fact, it was because he had the nerve to "make himself equal to God" that the religious authorities,

7

threatened that their own authority with the people was being undermined, handed him over to the Romans to be killed (Luke 22:71).

With his inner vision of the Kingdom of Heaven Jesus saw this unity of himself with God so clearly that he was able to create as God creates, by simply speaking his word. By speaking his word he healed the sick, multiplied fish and loaves of bread, and even raised the dead. Because he saw and lived in the Kingdom of Heaven while on this Earth, Jesus was fully aware of the fact that, though he was a human being just like us, he was also a divine being, the image and likeness of God in the fullest and deepest sense.

In Aramaic, the language Jesus spoke, the phrase "Kingdom of Heaven" or "Kingdom of God" means "God's sovereign presence." Just like Adam and Eve before the Fall, Jesus walked always in God's sovereign presence. He wanted us to do the same.

Second, *The Kingdom of Heaven that Jesus saw so well is a vision of this world that sees no separation (duality) between human beings.*

Jesus saw there was no separation between himself and any other person, again despite all physical appearances of separation to the contrary. He saw *every* other person as himself (Luke 6:31). In fact, Jesus did not see other persons as "others" at all. He saw all human beings (and indeed the whole created universe) as part of himself. And this applied to *all* human beings, not just those of his own Jewish religion, and not just people who were considered, according to the norms of his society, as morally good.

Unlike the Pharisees (the name "pharisee" means a "separated one") Jesus constantly went out of his way to emphasize this all-inclusiveness, this universal (or "catholic" in the non-sectarian sense of the Christian creed) aspect of his no-separation vision. He deliberately praised the faith of the pagan Roman centurion as superior to many in his own religion (Luke 7:9). He did the same in the case of the pagan Canaanite woman (Matt. 15:21-28). Jesus deliberately spoke at length with the Samaritan woman even though, in his culture, men almost never discussed serious matters with women, and even though Samaritans were considered heretics and therefore shunned by orthodox Jews (John 4:7-26). He deliberately told the story of the good Samaritan who, unlike the priest and the other Jewish religious officials, showed himself the true neighbor to the man robbed and beaten along the road (Luke 10:30-37). And, to the constant scandal of the morally separatist and righteous, Jesus made a habit of associating with people, such as tax-collectors and even prostitutes, whom his society considered sinners (e.g., Matt. 9:10).

Jesus tried to teach people to take the focus off externals, i.e., the "law." Instead, he wanted everyone to look deep within themselves to where, in the inner Kingdom of Heaven, all humans are one.

It was from this great vision of no-separation (or *nonduality*) between God and humans, and between and among all human beings, that Jesus, following other great teachers of his religion, formulated his two greatest commandments, "You must love the Lord your God with all your heart, with all your soul, and with all your mind," and "You must love your fellow humans as yourself" (Matt. 22:37-39).

The last thing Jesus did before he freely went to the death and rebirth that would demonstrate for us the way to the inner Kingdom of Heaven, was to leave us, at the Last Supper, the Holy Communion of his body and blood (Matt. 26:27-28) as his legacy. He left us the Holy Communion both as a sign of, and as a way of actually bringing about by inner death and rebirth in union with him, this inner realization of our oneness, our non-separation from God and each other.

At that Last Supper he also gave us his "new commandment" that we love one another just as he loved us (John 13:34). How, then, did he love us? His love for us was based on this same no-separation (*nondual*) vision of our inner substantial union with God and each other. Jesus' new commandment, therefore, requires us to come into the same level of consciousness (awareness) of the Kingdom of Heaven, and that same kind of love, that he himself displayed.

In recent years the world has witnessed the life and passing of a great Christian saint, Mother Teresa of Calcutta. Mother Teresa too saw everyone *nondually*. She saw everyone as the same Christ, whether they were Christian, Hindu, Muslim, Sikh, Jain, Buddhist, of whatever religion, or of no religion. Representatives of all these religions, and perhaps other religions I have omitted, gathered to pay tribute to her universal love and compassion at her state funeral in India in 1997. Mother Teresa, like other great saints, not only saw, but also strove to act out in her own life, the *no-separation* or *nondual* vision of Jesus.

For Jesus and Mother Teresa the nondual vision of this world was not a matter of make-believe. They did not *pretend* that there was no separation between themselves and God or between themselves and others. They did not see and treat others *as if* they were themselves. Not at all. Rather, their inner nondual vision of the Kingdom of Heaven was such that they *actually* saw this lack of separation. They *actually* saw all persons as one with God. They actually saw all persons as themselves. In fact, it was impossible for them to see otherwise. That is because once a person's everyday inner vision (consciousness) sees this world in its nondual reality, once a person actually and habitually sees the same Kingdom of Heaven here on Earth that Jesus saw, it is an irreversible change in their everyday consciousness from which there is no going back.

If you are like me, you have heard preachers urge us to treat and see each other as Christ. And perhaps, like me, you have resolved that, starting today or tomorrow, you will see and treat other people this way. And perhaps you have discovered, as I did, that it is easier said than done. In fact, it *cannot* be done in an habitual everyday way unless a person has first realized *nondual consciousness* within himself or herself. After our own consciousness becomes nondual, we need no effort at all to see people as Christ. It is impossible to see them any other way.

In summary then, the Kingdom of Heaven, as seen and preached by Jesus, is a nondual consciousness which sees no separation between God and humans, or between humans ourselves. To put on the mind of Christ, therefore, is to experience this nondual consciousness (awareness) for ourselves. And, once we do put on the mind of Christ, we, like Jesus, will see the Kingdom of Heaven all around us here and now. We see ourselves and everyone else, no matter who they are, as divine. And we will be living in the Kingdom of Heaven right here on Earth.

Jesus, of course, did have one huge advantage over the rest of us. He was *born* with the inner ability to clearly see the nondual vision of the Kingdom of Heaven. Like all humans he probably had to go through the earlier levels of consciousness as a child, but, according to the Gospel, his everyday consciousness "saw" the nondual vision of the Kingdom by the time he finished his desert retreat, or perhaps even by the time he was an adolescent discussing religious matters with the elders in the temple (Luke 2:46-50). By adolescence Jesus had also begun to see his life's mission, as given him by the Father who guided him from within. That work was to show us the way to this same inner kingdom by word and example, especially by his death and resurrection (Matt. 20:17-19). He was to become for us, as he said, "the Way" to the inner Kingdom of Heaven (John 14:6).

If we want to follow Jesus, we have no choice but to go deep within ourselves and, putting on the same mind that Jesus had, come into the nondual, no-separation vision of the Kingdom of Heaven. I hope the rest of this book will assist in the conscious realization of that vision.

Chapter 2

THE KINGDOM OF HEAVEN—THE HIGHEST LEVEL OF HUMAN CONSCIOUSNESS

The Kingdom of Heaven is nondual consciousness, the highest level of human consciousness. There are many different levels of human consciousness. Swiss developmental psychologist Jean Piaget (1896-1980), who was a professor of child psychology at the University of Geneva from 1929 until his death was a pioneer in the study of the developing consciousness of children. His writings include The Child's Conception of the World, The Moral Judgment of the Child, *and* The Language and Thought of the Child. *Contemporary American philosopher, psychologist, and mystic Ken Wilber is the author of over a dozen books on the development of human consciousness, including* The Spectrum of Consciousness; Sex, Ecology and Spirituality; *and* Up from Eden.

The nondual consciousness that is the vision of the Kingdom of Heaven is the highest stage in the growth of human consciousness from infancy to full spiritual maturity. By the process of inner growth in spiritual awareness, a path of constant *inner realization,* we gradually come to see our own union with God in Christ so that, at the final stage of nondual awareness, God alone and his Kingdom remain.

We see, when we realize the vision of the Kingdom of Heaven, that we, like Jesus, are not *mere* human beings after all, but are now, and have always been, nothing less than immortal, unlimited, divine Spirit.

In his ministry, Jesus wanted more than anything else to tell us about the nondual vision of the Kingdom he saw. He saw a Kingdom right here on Earth in which everyone was truly and substantially "one" with God and "one" with each other. At the same time, however, he saw that this nondual "oneness" didn't take away from God's transcendence or from our own humanness or individuality.

To our human minds this sounds like a paradox: how can we and God be one (divine) and yet God remain transcendent and we remain human and individual? But Jesus' nondual vision of the Kingdom of Heaven was not a paradox. It only seems like a paradox to our limited logical way of thinking. Jesus' nondual vision was simply the seeing of what, in fact, is actually true. Jesus, however, found it impossible to describe his nondual vision in simple declarative sentences without sounding paradoxical. That is because the human mind, and the declarative, spacetime language that our human minds have created, is itself dualistic. Our minds, and therefore human language, are inherently structured on the basis of countless spacetime, logical, polar opposites.

Jesus did not say, "The Kingdom of Heaven is this" because "this" automatically excludes its opposite "that." Nor did he say, "The Kingdom of Heaven is that" because "that" automatically excludes its opposite "this." He did not say "The Kingdom is here" because "here" excludes its opposite "there." Likewise, he did not say "The Kingdom is "there" because "there" excludes its logical opposite "here." So Jesus ended up saying that the Kingdom was *"not here* and *not there"* (Luke 17:21).

Still another way Jesus got around the problem of declarative or logical language was to speak about his inner nondual vision of the Kingdom in parables, analogies, metaphors, and stories. This got around the problem of logic but made his words less clear. That left him open to constant misunderstandings on the part of the Pharisees (and millions even today) who cannot understand any truth unless it can be expressed in logical black versus white terms.

Besides this difficulty of expression, however, there is a second problem that was faced by Jesus and, since Jesus, by those Christians saints (some of whom have been called "mystics") who have followed him into the Kingdom. Even when the vision of the Kingdom of Heaven is clearly expressed in poetic or metaphorical language, readers or listeners are still going to be unable to clearly understand that vision unless they too have already realized nondual consciousness! That is because we cannot understand a level of consciousness above our own by simply reading or listening to the words, to someone else's description of that level. To clearly understand a level of consciousness, we actually have to live at that level ourselves and "see" the world from that level ourselves.

This problem of understanding the words of persons at higher levels of awareness is why most Christian theologians, preachers, and church leaders have such a hard time (if not an impossible one) trying to interpret the Christian mystics or trying to compare the Christian mystics to those of other religions. They constantly misunderstand and misinterpret these mystics because they themselves do not have a high enough level of spiritual consciousness to see what the mystics are talking about. Even more importantly, it is why, after two thousand years, most of these theologians, preachers, and church leaders still do not understand Jesus and his Kingdom.

Let me try to show the chasm or "space" between different levels of consciousness (and how persons at different levels actually see this world differently) by citing examples of a child's growth in consciousness from one level to another. The examples, based on the work of the renowned child psychologist Jean Piaget, are taken from books by philosopher-psychologist Ken Wilber. Here is an example involving a glass of water and a second, taller empty glass. Wilber writes:

> If you take [very young] children, and, right in front of their eyes, pour the water from a short glass into a tall glass, and ask them which glass has more water, they will always say the tall glass has more, even though they saw you pour the same amount from one glass to the other. They cannot 'conserve volume.' Certain 'obvious' things that we see, they do not and *cannot* see—they live in a different worldspace. No matter how many times you pour the *same* amount of water back and forth between the two glasses, they will *insist* the tall glass has more. . . .
>
> If a few years later . . . you repeat the experiment, the kids will always say that both glasses have the same amount of water. They can hold volume in their mind and not be confused by its displacements. They have an internal *rule* that automatically does this. . . . And, if you show them a videotape from the earlier period . . . they will deny it's them! They think you've doctored the videotape. They simply cannot imagine somebody being so stupid as to think the tall glass more water.[1]

Here is a second example:

Three children of different ages are given the same test. One child, the youngest, still thinks in a magical way and has not yet developed thinking skills. Piaget calls this child "preop," meaning the stage just *prior to* (or *pre-*) the ability to do mental operations. The second youngest child, whom Piaget calls "conop," has learned to think, but only in *concrete* ways. The child still can't handle abstract concepts and principles. The third and oldest child, an adolescent, whom Piaget calls "formop," can think abstractly and understand universal principles, i.e., can do *formal* mental operations. All three children are separately presented with five glasses

---

[1]Ken Wilber in *A Brief History of Everything*, Shambhala, Boston & London, 1996, pp. 175-176.

that contain colorless liquids. Three of the glasses contain liquids that, if mixed together, will produce a yellow color. The children are asked to produce a yellow color.

> The preop child [the child with the lowest level of consciousness] will randomly combine a few glasses, then give up. If she accidentally hits upon the right solution, she will give a magical explanation ('The sun made it happen'; 'It came from the clouds').
>
> The conop child [a child with concrete mental consciousness] will eagerly begin by combining the various glasses, three at a time. She does this concretely; she will simply continue the concrete mixing until she hits upon the right solution or eventually gets tired and quits.
>
> The formop adolescent [the child with abstract mental consciousness] will begin by telling you have to try all the possible combinations of three glasses. She has a mental plan or formal operation that lets her see, however vaguely, that all possible combinations have to be tried. She doesn't have to stumble through the actual operations to understand this. Rather she sees, with the mind's eye, that all possibilities must be taken into account.[2]

You will notice in the above example that the information given to each of the three children is the same. All the physical parts of the experiment are identical and all three children heard the same words. It was the children's degree of inner understanding or consciousness that was different, an understanding (as the example shows) that normally progresses in an evolutionary or "developmental" way as the child grows in age. Only the child with the highest level of consciousness was able to solve the problem.

The same thing occurs among Christians, even among those who faithfully read and meditate on the Bible or study the "mysteries" set out in the Christian Creed. Some, depending upon how spiritually developed their awareness

---

[2]Ken Wilber in *Sex, Ecology, Spirituality, the Spirit of Evolution*, Shambhala, Boston & London, 1995, p. 232.

is, understand more than others. It is the degree of inner understanding, the level of consciousness, not the assumed meaning of the words (information), that counts.

St. Augustine, making this point, said that the "outer" meaning of the Scriptures was the "silver," but the inner meaning of the Scriptures was the "gold." St. Thérèse of Lisieux (1873-1897), to give just one example of continual consciousness growth at even a high stage of spiritual development, said she was forever getting new insights and understandings from the Scriptures as her inner awareness continued to grow. There would be no need for us to "truly seek" the Kingdom if we assume, as some Christians apparently do, that we already fully understand Jesus, the Gospels, and the Creed. We don't.

With respect to Jesus, how many times have we heard people say (for example, film makers who make movies about Jesus or theologians who write about him) that "Jesus was a human being *just like us,* so *therefore* he must have thought in this or that way" (usually meaning with the same level of consciousness as the film maker or theologian)? Such film makers and theologians don't understand that there are different levels of human consciousness. True, Jesus was a human being like us, but, though he perhaps knew less than one tenth of the *information* possessed by a college student today, his level of consciousness far exceeded that of today's greatest, but merely intellectual, geniuses.

This discussion, I hope, gives us an idea of how hard it was for Jesus to make himself understood by the lower-conscious Jewish priests and lay preachers. He even had problems being understood by his own disciples, though the disciples, poor fishermen as most of them were, were themselves great souls who came to Earth to help Jesus in his mission.

That the fishermen Jesus chose to be his disciples were advanced in awareness is shown by many Gospel passages. When Jesus asked the disciples, "Who do you say I am?" Simon Peter answered, "You are the Messiah, the Son of the Living God." Jesus then responded, "This truth did not come to you from any human being, but it was given to you directly by my Father in heaven" (Matt. 16:15-17). What this exchange shows is that Simon Peter, though an uneducated fisherman, was spiritually (consciously) evolved enough to be not only open to the voice of the Father within himself, but also accurately receptive to the inner messages of the Father. The consciousness of Simon Peter, therefore, was at least at the level of the psychic consciousness (see chapter 9) and probably higher. (See also Matt. 14:29 for Simon Peter's initial success at walking on water.) Similarly, all of the disciples, even during Jesus' ministry, were sent by Jesus to heal people and cast out the emotional or mental illnesses called "demons" (Luke 9:1-6). They could not have been successful in this had they not attained at least the psychic level of awareness.

When Jesus preached to the multitudes, he was like the older or oldest child in the examples earlier trying to convince the younger child or children of the truth, one the younger ones found it impossible to consciously see. Nor would Jesus have it much easier if he came to teach among Christians today. The vast majority of us, including our Christian leaders, can't see the inner Kingdom of Heaven now any more than the Pharisees and Jewish people were able to see it then.

Jesus, who thought and "saw" at the very highest level of consciousness, the nondual level, was constantly aware of this problem. Again and again, he talked about people who had "ears to hear but could not hear" and "eyes to see but could not see" (e.g., Matt. 13:13,15); similarly, he talked about "the blind leading the blind" (Matt. 15:14). It is why he expressed himself one way for the general public (in parables) and more explicitly in private to the more spiritually advanced disciples (e.g., Luke 8:10). Even the disciples were often unable to see and understand. Apparently, it was only during the inner spiritual events we commemorate at Pentecost that the disciples' eyes were fully opened and they at last completely understood.

The communications barrier for Jesus and those saints who have realized the nondual awareness of the Kingdom of Heaven has been a terrible problem because the gap between nondual consciousness of the Kingdom and the consciousness of the ordinary Christian or church official is enormous. It is a vastly wider gap than that between the children in the examples cited earlier.

Many saints "solve" this problem by not even trying to express the vision of the Kingdom in words. They stay silent, content to *be* rather than to speak. Our word "mystic" comes from the Greek verb *muo* which means "I am silent." St. Thérèse of Lisieux, though she did in the end write an autobiography, summarized her spiritual realization by saying she had learned that "My vocation is [to be] love."

Other saints have concentrated on privately teaching a small group of intimate students following Jesus' example of giving special and (to us) secret instructions to his disciples (Matt. 13:10-11). Still others, like Mother Teresa, express the vision principally by their loving and compassionate actions while, in words, stressing the two great commandments of love of God and love of neighbor.

Finally, a few mystics have tried to express the vision of the Kingdom in words and, like Jesus himself, some have found themselves in serious trouble with the religious authorities for doing so. Some genuine Christian saints have gotten the same treatment from Christian church officials that Jesus got from the Pharisees and Sadducees. Over the centuries, many were condemned, and some were even put to death.

Probably the clearest written account of the nondual vision from a Christian saint is contained in the writings of the medieval Dominican priest Meister Eckhart, a successor to St. Thomas Aquinas in the chair of theology at the University of Paris. Unfortunately, some of his writings, taken out of context and, as usual, misunderstood by cardinals and other Church leaders, were condemned. Nor, because of this condemnation, has he ever been officially recognized as a saint.

Meister Eckhart is still not understood even by theologians who have themselves not entered the Kingdom. The theologian and professor of historical theology Bernard McGinn calls Eckhart "ever-elusive." McGinn has done a first rate job in editing, for the *Classics of Western Spirituality* series, two volumes on Eckhart (the first with Edmund Colledge). In the second volume, *Meister Eckhart, Teacher and Preacher,* he selected a number of Eckhart's works for inclusion, noting that, "Each of these illustrates one or more of the most essential themes of Eckhart's speculative thought."

In calling Eckhart's thought "speculative," McGinn apparently assumes that Eckhart's level of consciousness is the same as that of most theologians, i.e., rational level (see chapter 7), and that Eckhart's theology, which he also calls "difficult," might be laid bare by more scholarly study. But Eckhart's "thought," for the most part, is not speculative. Eckhart is not doing theological theorizing. He is simply reporting and describing the world *as he sees it* at the level of nondual consciousness, the level of the Kingdom of Heaven. There is only one way to understand Eckhart: to go within oneself until one too can "see" the world as Eckhart, and Jesus, saw it. We will hear more about Meister Eckhart in later chapters of this book.[3]

My point in this chapter is to clearly point out that there are different levels of human consciousness, different levels of spiritual understanding, and that the nondual vision of the Kingdom of Heaven is the highest level. There may be some who will say that these assertions about different levels of awareness or consciousness are the type of "gnosticism" (schools of thought that held it took a special

---

[3]Bernard McGinn, ed., *Meister Eckhart, Teacher and Preacher,* Paulist Press, New York, 1986, pp. 2,4,5.

"knowingness" to fully understand Jesus and the Scriptures) that was rejected by the Church in the early Christian era. They are not.

While I agree with the gnostics that it takes a high level of knowingness (consciousness) to understand Jesus and the Scriptures, I reject those gnostic beliefs that were rejected by the early Church (such as the ideas that matter is evil, that Jesus was not truly human, that Jesus didn't have a human body, that Creation was a "falling away" from grace into matter, that Satan is an evil God co-equal with the God who is good, etc.). If the idea of levels of human awareness or knowingness *per se* were heretical, then we would have to classify as heretics all developmental psychologists and the entire Christian tradition of spiritual writers from St. Dionysios (circa A. D. 500) to St. John of the Cross (16th Century) to the Twentieth Century's Evelyn Underhill, all of whom recognize developmental stages of spiritual awareness through which the Christian must pass on the way to realization of union with God.

Even in our own society, it is still not generally understood that people (except perhaps children) have different levels of awareness. Though many transpersonal and other pioneering psychologists now know differently, most politicians and other societal leaders generally assume that everyone has the same level of consciousness. This is a dangerous assumption given the life and death urgency of many problems facing the human race.

Some social leaders think that the "information superhighway" of the Internet's world wide web will save the world because everyone will have more and more information with which to make enlightened choices. A few hours wandering through virtual chat rooms, where discussions are often little more than schoolyard brawls, should be enough to convince most people that information alone will do nothing to improve the human race if the level of human consciousness and spiritual understanding does not grow. In fact, superior information or technology in the hands of spiritually undeveloped persons is generally a dangerous thing. To give one example, consider Hitler's use of the radio, by which he used this then-new technology to stir up and control the German masses with his mesmerizing, spellbinding speeches. It is essential, therefore, even from a secular perspective, that people be assisted not just in getting more information, but in moving to higher and higher (or deeper and deeper if one prefers) levels of inner personal awareness.

This is especially important for the Christian church. It is vitally important because the only essential purpose of religion is to accelerate growth in consciousness. People do not need religion to develop laws or ethical approaches to problems. Legislatures, courts, and ethical experts drawn from the various professions, can do that. Nor do they need religion to operate hospitals, soup kitchens, schools, and social welfare programs. Government and private charities can do that. People do not even need religion to grow in spiritual awareness. They can and do grow in spiritual consciousness by learning from the wealth of experiences (often difficult and challenging ones) that life brings them.

What people need religion for is to *accelerate* growth in consciousness, to speed up our normal snail's pace growth in spiritual awareness. All the "technologies" of the Christian religion, the New Testament, prayer, Bible study, preaching, fasting, music, Holy Communion or Mass, healing services, chanting, rituals, almsgiving, monasteries, convents, pilgrimages, meditation, icons, and sacraments, have only one purpose—to accelerate people's growth in consciousness upwards and eventually into the nondual vision of Jesus' Kingdom. In the past at least, the Church's technologies have usually been essential for a Christian to realize the Kingdom of Heaven in his or her lifetime.

Christians would benefit enormously if our contemporary Christian leaders were able to skillfully and knowledgeably assist them in attaining higher levels of awareness. Isn't that more important than spending enormous amounts of time, energy and money on politics, social work, or even ethics?

In addition, many contemporary Christian leaders, sometimes even consciously and often because they themselves feel inadequate to the task, have been turning over the essential spiritual work of religion—the healing and growth of consciousness—to psychiatry and psychology. This is not only an abdication of religion's reason for being but, at the present time, is often a serious practical error. Many, if not most, contemporary psychiatrists and psychologists erroneously believe the human mind and spirit can be reduced to, and explained by, biochemistry. Others make a god of the ego. And still others strive to help the "patient" adapt to a society that is itself unbalanced. Whatever their many legitimate achievements, these sciences are not yet developed enough to be entrusted with the sacred task of healing the consciousness of Christians and raising them beyond materialism and rationalism into the Kingdom.

The Church, unless it is content to lose its reason to exist, must be the principal means that Christians can use to accelerate their growth in consciousness to Jesus' inner Kingdom. Otherwise, Christians, seeing that the salt has lost its flavor (Matt. 5:13), will go elsewhere, as in millions of instances they are already doing. Christians are in as much need of genuine spirituality today as ever in the past. Many, as Mother Teresa often noted about the Christian West, are spiritually starved. Only a reconcentration of the Church on its essential spiritual mission can provide Christians with the spiritual "food" they desperately seek.

I turn now to the question of mapping the path to Jesus' inner Kingdom of Heaven.

Chapter 3

MAPPING THE PATH TO THE

KINGDOM OF HEAVEN

The traditional Christian spiritual "maps," beginning with the three-fold map of St. Dionysios, the early Christian saint who divided the Christian spiritual path into the purgative, illuminative, and unitive ways, are inadequate. These maps do not account for the evolution of human consciousness in children, adolescents, or even in the average Christian adult. The traditional maps, understandably, also fail to take into account the mapping of human consciousness growth by modern psychology. In place of the traditional maps, I propose a nine-stage map based upon the work of twentieth century consciousness pioneers such as Jean Piaget, Jean Gebser, and Ken Wilber.

Throughout the centuries various Christian authors have attempted to map the spiritual path to the inner vision of the Kingdom of Heaven. The mapmakers necessarily had to base the maps they drew on their own experience. And, since they generally did not realize that different human beings begin the spiritual path at different levels of awareness, the mapmakers generally assumed that their experience could be duplicated by others.

The most traditional of these Christian maps was drawn by St. Dionysios about 500 A. D. St. Dionysios (actually a pseudonym for an author whose real name is unknown), following an even earlier tradition mentioned by St. Clement of Alexandria in the second century, divides the path into three stages of inner growth: "purgative" (purification from the grossest forms of egotism and selfishness), "illuminative" (the breaking in upon the person of greater spiritual insights and understandings), and "unitive" (union with God). St. Dionysios, however, proposed a second five-stage map based upon what he saw as the five levels of "prayer": vocal prayer, mental prayer, the prayer of recollection, the prayer of quiet beyond thought, and the prayer of union with God.

The anonymous author of the fourteenth century Christian classic, *The Cloud of Unknowing,* wrote that Christian spiritual development "seems to progress through four ascending phases of growth, which I call the *Common,* the *Special,* the *Singular,* and the *Perfect.*"[4] The sixteenth century's St. Teresa of Avila, in her masterpiece, the *Interior Castle,* divided the path into seven stages of consciousness or "mansions." Her friend and contemporary, St. John of the Cross, divided the path into five stages, that of the beginning "contemplative," the Dark Night of the Senses, an intervening period of progressive spiritual illuminations, the Dark Night of the Soul, and finally, union with God. The English Anglican Evelyn Underhill, early in the twentieth century, roughly followed St. John's five stages but began at an earlier point on the path than he—with what she called "the awakening of the transcendental consciousness" in a "conversion" experience.[5] There have been many other attempts at mapping with any number of different stages.

---

[4]Anonymous, *The Cloud of Unknowing*, edited by William Johnston, Doubleday, New York, 1973, 1996, p. 45, emphases in original.
[5]Evelyn Underhill. 1910, 1990, in *Mysticism*, Doubleday, New York, p. 176.

There are two basic problems with these traditional maps to the Kingdom of Heaven. First, all of them have been partial, mapping only portions of the spiritual path. For example, they have generally ignored the growth of consciousness in children, adolescents, and sometimes in the ordinary Christian adult. With respect to adults, the mapmakers have assumed that all Christians (or at least all religiously dedicated Christians) begin the spiritual path at more or less the same level of consciousness as themselves (and so can be expected to duplicate the mapmaker's experience).

St. John of the Cross, for example, begins his account of the spiritual path at the level he calls the "beginning contemplative," a stage already well past the place in consciousness where most Christians dwell. Evelyn Underhill starts earlier than John but admits that her beginning "conversion" experience usually happens to people who are already deeply religious, and is well above the level of the normal evangelical conversion experience of being "born again." St. Teresa's account begins at about the same high level as John's. The American Catholic laywoman Bernadette Roberts starts her account, which admittedly is only an attempt to describe her individual journey, at an even higher level (she begins with the Dark Night of the Soul). Meister Eckhart talks about only the two highest levels, union with God and nondual identity with God.

Second, the older maps, obviously, could not take into account the huge amount of scholarship that has been done by modern developmental psychology in mapping the levels of growth in human consciousness from infancy to highly functioning adulthood.

Thanks almost single-handedly to the work of Ken Wilber, these two problems in mapping the spiritual path have been substantially addressed in recent years. Wilber has done a massive amount of study of both developmental psychology and the traditional spiritual writings of both East and West. In his recent works, which are written in a predominantly scholarly vein, he has presented an overall outline of the spiritual path from start to finish as well as many of its details.

The fundamental structures of human consciousness do not vary from one historical period to another. The stages through which human consciousness progresses to what Christians call union with God and, afterwards, the inner non-dual vision of the Kingdom of Heaven here on Earth, are the same now as they were for the early Christians. In philosophical terms, this never-changing structure of human consciousness development has been called "the perennial philosophy" for that reason: it is indeed perennial or unchanging.

Nor do the basic structures of human consciousness growth, which are universal, vary from West to East. Human beings are the same everywhere. The same nine stages and structures, as Wilber demonstrates, are to be found, for example, in the Roman philosopher/mystic and spiritual master Plotinus (a teacher for St. Augustine and many Church Fathers) as in the Buddhist philosopher/mystic and spiritual master Nagarjuna.[6]

Wilber bases his classification of the levels of human consciousness on the work of both psychologists and mystics (both Christian and non-Christian) with contributions from philosophy and other disciplines. He divides the spiritual path into nine stages, each corresponding to a separate level of consciousness. He says that each of these levels could be broken into substages, but, for the purposes of his books (and this book), nine stages will do.

Wilber warns that the nine stages are not to be understood as neat little boxes. First, the levels of consciousness can overlap to some extent; for example, one level can begin before another has completely finished (though, in my experience, the "break" between levels is often noticeable

---

[6]In this book I am reserving the term "spiritual master" for persons of non-Christian traditions who have realized either the eighth (causal) or the ninth (nondual) levels of human consciousness described later in part 4. In Christianity it is inappropriate to talk of any "master" except Jesus.

and discrete). Second, beginning with the development of the human mind, we can "repress" parts of our consciousness that we don't like (usually sexual and aggressive feelings) and these parts of ourselves can remain "stuck" at the lower levels (where they drain our energy so much that they, unless cleared up later, can prevent our advance to the highest spiritual levels).

Third, a person can pass to the next grade of consciousness without *full* mastery of the grade below. Only basic competence at one level of consciousness is normally required before going to the next level. Fourth, things can go wrong at every level, beginning with psychosis (the worst form of mental illness) at the first level. Generally, the earlier things go wrong, the more time and trouble it takes to remedy the situation later. Finally, as Jesus pointed out, the path can get difficult, misunderstood, and controversial the farther one's own consciousness begins to go beyond the level realized by one's family, community, co-religionists, and culture (Luke 14:26). His experience on the cross shows this.

In the following chapters, I will make substantial use of Wilber's ground breaking work. I hope this book will help to give his map of the spiritual path a wider audience. Though I would have preferred a different name for a least one of the levels, I will use Wilber's terminology for the nine levels, which he himself took in part from the German/Swiss philosopher Jean Gebser. Gebser finished a monumental comparative study of civilization, *Ursprung and Gegenwart*, in 1953. His book, which describes the consciousness of various historical eras and cultures, was published in English in 1985 by Ohio University Press under the title *The Ever-Present Origin*.

I am adopting the Wilber/Gebser terminology because I believe that one of the most serious obstacles to explaining and mapping the spiritual path is that spiritual terminology has been, and largely remains, a Tower of Babel throughout the world (Gen. 11:1-9). I have no wish to contribute further to the confusion.

In addition to describing the development of individual consciousness from the consciousness of the infant to the highest mystical state, Wilber discusses the historical development of consciousness by the human race. Using the work of Gebser and the German philosopher Jurgen Habermas,[7] among others, Wilber asserts that the human race as a whole has already passed through three levels of consciousness, the archaic, the magical, and the mythical (see chapters 4, 5, and 6) and is now into the fourth level of consciousness, the rational (see chapter 7). Wilber observes that people at each level of consciousness actually "see" the world, this world, differently, and what they "see" determines the type of culture, laws, and institutions they create with their particular worldview. When the mass of humanity (or even merely the dominant leadership) moves to a higher level of consciousness, practically everything changes in the surrounding culture as the old forms and institutions crumble and new forms attempt to take their place. This is what has been happening for the last century at an ever accelerating pace.

I will make use of this aspect of Wilber's work to show how the Judeo-Christian tradition has been influenced (and has played a part in) various cultural shifts in consciousness. I will also at times make observations about what I believe the future may hold both for human culture in general and for Christian spirituality in particular.

---

[7]Jurgen Habermas (1929-), is a German philosopher associated with the Frankfurt school of critical theory. His books include *Knowledge and Human Interests, Moral Consciousness and Communicative Action,* and *Theory of Communicative Action.*

PART II
THE SEVEN LEVELS OF CONSCIOUSNESS OF THE HUMAN PERSONALITY

Chapter 4

THE ARCHAIC CONSCIOUSNESS OF INFANTS

The archaic consciousness of infants develops through two essential spiritual passages: First, the infant's differentiation of its own body from that of the mother, and second, the later differentiation of the infant's emotions from those of the mother. Critical spiritual principles can be drawn from these two passages, principles that will apply throughout the spiritual path. For example, each level of consciousness will be less egocentric than the last, and each new level will find the mind of the person freer and freer of the limitations of matter.

There is a parallel between the consciousness of the infant and the consciousness of early "Stone Age" peoples.

Individual Consciousness Development

The first level of human consciousness is the *archaic* and normally lasts into the third year of an infant's life. Archaic consciousness is primarily a physical (and later emotional) level of consciousness, one ruled by sensations and impulses. The infant's consciousness is at first so attached to physical matter that the infant is unable to distinguish between its own physical body and its mother's. Freud called this stage the state of "primary narcissism" (original self-centeredness).

The infant's first spiritual task, beginning about the fourth month, is to clearly realize that its own physical "self" is separate from, first the mother, and then from all other physical beings and objects. Gradually, based upon its own experience, the infant comes to realize that, much as it may narcissistically (self-centeredly) wish things to be otherwise, its physical reality is quite distinct from that of other physical beings and objects. And so, based on this experience that each of us had as tiny infants, we already come to the first three principles which will govern the spiritual path from start to finish:

(1) All growth in consciousness is a process of inner realization.

(2) All inner realizations are the result of personal experience "meditated upon" in some fashion.

(3) All growth in consciousness is a lessening of self-centeredness, a "death" to the old self-centered way of looking at the world and a simultaneous "rebirth" into a less self-centered way of seeing things.

It is by such continual "baptisms" into death and rebirth that the Christian will grow spiritually at every level. We are reborn again and again, with Christ leading us on, until we realize the ninth level of consciousness, the Kingdom of Heaven here on Earth.

Around the age of eighteen months, the child gradually begins to make a second separation. The child gradually realizes that its emotions are separate from the emotions of its mother and other people. This spiritual passage involving the emotions is less physical than the first passage, which involved the body, and the third passage (the emergence of mind) will be less physical still. And so we come already to the fourth major principle governing the spiritual path:

(4) As a person's consciousness goes up the spiritual ladder from level to level, the person's consciousness becomes less and less attached to (i.e., stuck in or defined by) physical matter.

There is nothing wrong with physical matter, of course. Matter, which is simply solidified energy, is as much Spirit as anything else. Nor would there be any *human* spiritual path without matter as its foundation (after all, if my body gets sick and dies, that, for me, is the end of the path). But matter is the least conscious, i.e., least aware, part of who we are. Most of mainstream science has yet to affirm that consciousness or intelligence is inherent in, and underlies, all energy, including the solidified energy we call matter, but many of the leading quantum physicists are now aware of this truth. Matter (molecules, atoms, and subatomic particles) have a slight amount of innate Spirit, intelligence, and "awareness" of surroundings, but, compared with mind for example, matter's amount of "awareness" is minuscule.

For human consciousness, therefore, to remain more or less stuck in or defined by matter, or to have our spiritual vision constricted by matter's limitations, would be a spiritual disaster. All along the spiritual path our consciousness will need to struggle to break freer and freer from matter's heavy inertial "downward" forces while at the same time remaining securely grounded in that same matter.

A child who fails to establish clear emotional boundaries between the self and others can end up as an adult afflicted with narcissism (a severe emotional disorder in which the person projects his or her own feelings outward onto everyone else, not realizing that other people have their own feelings) or as an adult afflicted with a borderline personality (in which the person constantly sees himself or herself as victimized by others and takes little or no responsibility for his or her own problems). So it is critical, for the infant's future basic emotional health and spiritual progress, that the infant succeed in making this second spiritual transition. Once this emotional differentiation is accomplished, the two spiritual passages of archaic consciousness are complete.

Cultural Consciousness Development

With respect to human culture in general, many believe that the average and dominant "worldview" of Stone Age peoples was that of archaic consciousness. These ancient ancestors of ours *felt* themselves to be part of nature and lived accordingly. They lived primarily by sensation and instinct, which were probably developed to a very high degree. For example, they probably could "sense" danger in the jungle (or any physical danger) much better than we who have let such ancient abilities go unexercised.

They did not "see" themselves as part of nature like a contemporary environmentalist might. This is because they had not yet developed the mental ability to "see" (in the sense of understand) much of anything. Rather, their connection to nature, like all else, was a part of immediate sensory/emotional experience. They therefore had no real "culture" as we would understand the word today.

Chapter 5

THE MAGICAL CONSCIOUSNESS OF CHILDREN

Magical consciousness is the level of consciousness of the young child ages 2 to 7. The magical thinking typical of this level includes the "polytheistic" world of gods, demons, fairies, and other creatures that inhabit the young child's inner world. A child at this age is often unable to distinguish between the contents of its mind and those of the external world. The child's consciousness is still egocentric and believes the outside world revolves around the self.

Magical consciousness was the general level of consciousness in the polytheistic, animistic, tribally-organized ancient world.

Individual Consciousness Development

At about the age of two, another spiritual passage begins in earnest. The infant's mind begins to emerge as something separate from its physical/emotional being. Though the beginnings of mental life, the emergence of "images," might have begun as early as the seventh month, the use of symbols (including language) begins about age two. The child then develops a magical consciousness, the second level of human consciousness. Magical consciousness is one in which the child cannot clearly distinguish between its own emerging mental images and symbols and the external world. Magical consciousness will usually last until it is replaced around age seven.

The renowned child psychologist Jean Piaget noted that the child at this stage will develop magical *beliefs*. For example the child may believe that "the sun and moon follow us, and if we walk, it is enough to make them move along; things notice us and obey us, like the wind, the clouds, the night. . . ."[8] The child will believe that the sun and the moon are alive and that they obey the child's order to follow him or her because the child wants them to do so. The child egocentrically thinks of everything in terms of its own "I." "If we ask . . . which of two people walking in opposite directions the sun would prefer to follow, the child is taken aback and shows how new the question is to him."[9]

Often the child will confuse the name of a person (or a picture of a person) with the reality of a person. They might have the magical belief that tearing up a person's picture might actually hurt the person. They might believe that saying the right "magic words" will cause the rain to fall or stop the thunder. When they play hide and seek they think that, because they cannot see you (their head being hidden) you cannot see them (even though their legs and feet are sticking out from their hiding place). Thus, they see everything from their own egocentric point of view.

In terms of moral development, the child learns what is considered good and bad or right and wrong in its particular culture or society. But this is not at all the learning of moral principles or laws. It is purely a matter of reward and punishment, a sensing of what makes Mommy and Daddy happy and what makes them angry or disappointed.

---

[8]J. Flavell in *The Developmental Psychology of Jean Piaget,* Van Nostrand, Princeton, NJ, 1963, p. 285, as quoted in Wilber, ibid., p. 212.
[9]H. Gruber And J. Voneche, Eds., *The Essential Piaget,* Basic Books, New York, 199, pp. 134-5, as quoted in Wilber, ibid., p. 213.

Gradually the child begins to realize that its own point of view is not all there is. The child realizes that magic words don't start the rain or stop the thunder. The child realizes that hiding one's head is not enough. He or she begins to appreciate that there are other points of view besides its own. The child's self-centeredness lessens. The child, for example, learns to share. So, just as in the spiritual passages of the archaic level of consciousness, the successful learning of the magical stage of consciousness also involves a lessening of egotism with its assumed self-importance, omnipotence, and narcissism.

As I said above, this continual lessening of egotism will be the case throughout the spiritual path until, at the non-dual level, there is no egotism left and the person becomes humility as well as love. Jesus demonstrated this humility when he asserted that all that he had had been given to him by the Father; he also demonstrated it when he asked, "Why do you call me good? No one is good except God alone" (Luke 18:19). Jesus was not indulging in false modesty. He was never false about anything. He was simply stating the truth.

Cultural Consciousness Development

At the cultural level, magical consciousness is the average and dominant consciousness of most tribal cultures. Tribal members, for example, may not want you to take their picture or tell you their names, fearing that this will give you power over them. Such cultures have transcended (gone beyond) the individual to the kinship level of social organization, but that level is still tied to the physical (blood relationship). With respect to religion, this is the level of animism, the type of belief system which sees the sky, thunder, and other natural phenomena as "alive," and that believes these natural phenomena can be controlled (in one's favor) by magic words and ceremonies.

Chapter 6

MYTHIC CONSCIOUSNESS—PRE-ADOLESCENCE

Mythic consciousness is the level of consciousness of the child from about age 7 to adolescence; it is the first of the mental levels. It is the consciousness of the child's emerging mind or ego. The child at this level believes that the "God in the Sky," much like its parents, can work every sort of miracle to meet the child's needs. It is a conformist, law-and-order level in which everything in the child's parochial world is seen as the "true" and the "best." The child learns to define itself by conventional rules and roles and sees its self-worth in following these "laws" and in behaving properly. Until recently, the mythic level of consciousness has been the dominant level of consciousness in all the world's "universal" religions, including Christianity.

Individual Consciousness Development

By the age of seven, the child's mind begins to grasp and understand general rules. He or she realizes that the word "dog" refers to all dogs, the abstract "class" of dog, not just the family pet or the particular picture of a dog in the storybook. The child also begins to realize the importance of specific cultural roles, such as mother, father, boy, girl, teacher, police officer, doctor, minister. The child moves into mythic consciousness, a view of the world in which concrete and definite rules and roles become supreme, a level of consciousness (if all goes well) that will normally last until adolescence.

This is a conformist "law and order" stage of development. What Daddy and Mommy *say* is right or wrong is what *is* right or wrong. Not only that, but Daddy and Mommy are the greatest and wisest parents in the world. They become, in fact, the true "gods" of the child. If Daddy and Mommy belong to a certain religious denomination, race, color, ethnic group, income level, political party, etc., these become the "correct" and "true" ones, often the *only* true ones, all others being inferior or false. One's nation is typically seen as the greatest in the world, blessed by God beyond all others, a nation that should always, like one's parents, be honored and obeyed ("My country right or wrong"). Nor does it do much good to preach "tolerance" and "diversity" to a child at this stage. The child usually has no way of understanding what we are talking about.

Great confusion can arise for the child if he or she directly encounters such "diversity" in the form of the concrete practice of an opposing "law" or "rule." The teacher—another "god"—may say something directly contrary to what the parents have been concretely doing or telling the child (the parents may smoke cigarettes while the child hears in school that cigarettes are bad and kill people who smoke them), or the child's playmates (the peer group being still another "god") say that some other religion (or style of haircut or brand of sneakers) is the only true, correct, and approved one.

The child's inner world at the mythic level of consciousness is populated by a great many "gods." In addition to the concrete external gods of parents, teachers and peer group, the child may also have Santa Claus, the Easter Bunny, and a host of other fairies, ogres, angels, and devils. These external gods will treat the child kindly and supply the child with what it wants (or not hurt the child in the case of the "bad" ones) *provided* the child is "good," that is, follows whatever concrete rules and roles he or she has been schooled to follow. Later, the Christian child will more or less combine all these gods (angels and devils perhaps excepted) into the one true Christian God who lives in the "sky" or "heaven."

Having (for the most part) left the world of magic behind, the child no longer believes that it can make the world do what it wants by uttering a magic word. But the child believes these outside gods, beginning with the parents, do have the power to do so. These gods, and later the great Christian God in the sky, can miraculously rearrange the world to meet the child's every need and want. The child learns to pray, understanding prayer as petitioning the great Christian God in the sky to work miracles on the child's behalf, to get the child whatever it wants, and to relieve the child of anything that bothers him or her. If it would take a miracle to turn broccoli into ice cream, the child has no doubt that God can do it—and that God exists primarily to fulfill the child's narcissistic wants.

The child uses his or her emerging reason to reinterpret the previous magical world. Religious myths and symbols, therefore, are now understood in a concrete, literal, "rational" way: God actually did create the world in six days; the three wise men did follow a star to Bethlehem; and Mary gave birth to Jesus, not as other mothers do, but in some sort of "miraculous" fashion.

At the mythic level of consciousness the child is "good" if the child follows the rules, and "bad" if it breaks them. The child learns to see his or her own intrinsic self-worth in terms of these external rules and roles, and in terms of pleasing these external gods. The rules and roles, therefore, are taken with deadly seriousness. This is fine as far as the child is concerned, because the child sees them as the true and correct rules and roles, taught by parents, teachers and ministers who are the smartest, in a country that is the best, following the Christian religion, the one true way to please the one true Christian god.

Note that the child does not have to be *told* that Christianity is the one true religion. The child simply assumes it. The child *assumes* that everything in its immediate cultural environment is the only true way to do things and the only true way to think. The child cannot think otherwise at this stage. The mythic level, despite the emergence of the child's mind and the shifting of the child's self-centeredness from the individual to the immediate culture, is still an egocentric level. Tolerance and understanding for other points of view and behaviors, and compassion for people who hold these views and practice these behaviors, is not possible for a child (or adult) with mythic consciousness. Nor can they see any good reason for attempting such tolerance because, for them, this would be a betrayal of their external God, the God whose rules and roles define their self-worth.

Because the child's worth as a person is seen in terms of them, the roles and rules are aggressively defended. Other children who follow different rules, have different behaviors, or are otherwise "different," must be mocked and strenuously opposed because they threaten the child's sense of self (the reason for countless schoolyard snubs, brawls and other cruelties).

For the adult Christian whose consciousness has not progressed beyond the mythic level of consciousness, it is important to convert the whole world to the one true Christian religion (and to make sure that governments enact laws that agree with what the believer has been taught are "Christian" morals) because, in the end, this is the only real way the mythic believer can safely secure his or her own righteousness. This requires the elimination, by conversion or otherwise, of all "others" because all such "others" are seen as threatening the mythic believer's externally defined sense of worth. A mythic Christian cannot rest until the whole world thinks and does as he or she has been schooled as a child to think and do.

The Christian adult who is stuck in mythic consciousness will see the followers of other religions (or "isms" such as Marxism or feminism) as "evil" and probably headed for hell. If someone dies for Christianity (a martyr), the Christian God will bring them straight to "heaven" (mythic-level Muslims, as we know from accounts in the newspapers, think the same). According to mythic consciousness, it is all right for the mythic believer to try to commandeer the police powers of the state (as was done in the Middle Ages) to impose one's belief system on others, and to punish those who believe otherwise. After all, it is for the others' own good that they submit to the "truth" as the mythic believer assumes the truth to be. It may even be all right at times to kill people of other religions (or even other denominations of Christianity) to "save their souls." Christians with mythic consciousness, unfortunately, have done a lot of such killing over the centuries. The Crusades, the inquisitions, the conquest of the Americas, the pogroms against Jews, and the Thirty Years War between Protestants and Catholics are a few examples. Millions died in these conflicts, usually calling upon God (their God) to defeat those they thought were enemies of that God.

People at the mythic level are psychologically incapable of thinking "globally." They usually neither think about, nor *care* about, such matters as the global environment, health, financial condition, or population. They are normally centered upon their own financial, familial, ethnic, sectarian, and nationalistic concerns (e.g., they vote based primarily on "what's in it for me or my group?"). Anything universal, e.g., the United Nations, does not concern them. If they happen to think about the United Nations or another "universal" religion, they are very likely to see it as a threat to themselves, their values, and their group.

If this mythical level consciousness sounds familiar, it should, because: (1) all of us went through this level during a period of childhood that we can still remember; (2) parts of most Christian adults' consciousness are usually still stuck at this level, often re-emerging in times of crisis; and (3) a large number of Christian adults, including many Christian leaders, not having heeded St. Paul about putting away the things of a child (1 Cor. 13:11), are still predominantly stuck in the rigidities and separatism of mythic consciousness.

I am not saying that mythic consciousness contains no truth. Every level of consciousness contributes its own truth. But it is an incomplete and distorted version of the truths one can see at the higher levels of spiritual growth. And, most importantly for the Christian, it is far below the level of consciousness Jesus had and wanted us to have.

Cultural Consciousness Development

At the cultural level, mythic consciousness has been the dominant and average consciousness of believers of all the world's great "universal religions," including Christianity. For example, the truths of the Christian Creed, the basic summary of our beliefs, are all expressed in mythic terms.

These great religions were (are) "universal," but, only in the sense that anyone of any race or nation could belong to the religion and be saved, *provided* they agreed to the rules and roles (usually structured in a rigid patriarchal hierarchy) and accepted the mythology. All this reflects a rather crude *materialistic* understanding of the "universality" that all such religions claimed (claim).

In the secular arena (to the extent that sacred and secular institutions were separated in the mythic era), mythic consciousness produced the great empires, all of which would have liked to conquer the whole world, a similarly materialistic notion of universality. We saw the last of these empires only in the twentieth century.

Mythic consciousness, however, was a great step forward from the world of tribes because you did not need to meet the even more materialistic requirement of blood kinship to belong. Anyone could be converted and belong. True, it was far below the level of consciousness that Jesus and his disciples preached. But most Christians, even in the early Church, were incapable of understanding Jesus except in a mythic way. They *thought* mythically and *saw* the world mythically. So Christianity, despite what Jesus and his disciples said and wrote, was soon reduced to the level of mythic consciousness and, for the most part, has stayed that way, at least at the popular level, for most of these last two thousand years.

Chapter 7

RATIONAL CONSCIOUSNESS

Rational consciousness, the second of the mental levels, is the dominant consciousness of the present age and is the level of consciousness more or less attained by the average adult in contemporary society. In today's world, the passage from mythic into rational consciousness is the primary spiritual task of adolescence. Teenagers encounter severe difficulty when their Christian denominations do not understand this passage and sometimes attempt to keep adolescents at the mythic level of understanding. There are a number of ways to assist young people to navigate this spiritual passage; for example, by teaching them a scientific meditation technique and the rules for prayer.

Individual Consciousness Development

In our society the dominant level of consciousness is the fourth, the rational. In order to be successful in our society, a child normally has to develop an ability to reason beyond the concrete (conventional) rules and roles of the mythic level. The child has to learn to handle abstract ideas and grasp universal principles. This spiritual passage of death to mythic consciousness and rebirth into rational consciousness usually begins at adolescence. As the level of rational consciousness dominates our society and its institutions—science (hard and soft), government, finance, media, universities—it is likely to be the highest level of consciousness many adolescents will realize in their lifetimes.

The rational level of consciousness is now so familiar to almost any well-educated person that there is little reason to describe it here. Rational consciousness brings with it the ability to think abstractly, to understand general statements and principles (e.g., the principle that "all human beings are created equal") and to think and write in accordance with the rules of logic. The ability to understand mathematics or any other science is dependent on having a rational level of awareness.

It is also useful to realize that the rational level, like all levels, has many gradations. A person who thinks at the lower rational level, for example, is a person who thinks in clichés. He or she has few original thoughts or insights. Rather, there is a platitude offered for every occasion. Or he or she is always asking, "You know what I mean?" To be polite, most people answer "Yes." But the true answer is that, not only don't you know what he means, but he doesn't either. He or she hasn't developed the ability to think clearly enough to be able to articulate what he or she wants to express. We sometimes meet this level of rationality in church when the "sermon" is an endless string of Bible quotes, given out as platitudes, with no coherent point evident either to the congregation or the preacher.

A higher level of rationality is reached, for example, by many college graduates. Some of these, however, equate intelligence with using big words. So-called "bureaucratese" is one example. Bureaucratic memos are filled with big words, many used inappropriately, and many used when simple words would do. Other people at this level use words that sound nice (or sound clever) but have no clear meaning.

Next we have people who are genuinely interested in abstract concepts, and whose minds are learning to fully grasp them. They are making an effort to expand their minds enough to comprehend mathematics, law, philosophy, or physics. Some of them fall prey to ideology. One system of thought captures their minds to the exclusion of others. They have made great progress in being able to grasp a logical system of thought. But they haven't yet been able to transcend the logical boundaries of any such necessarily limited system. Finally, there are people who have mastered the rational level of consciousness. They can think clearly, logically, with creativity, and without getting caught up in any doctrinaire "ism." Our society is blessed with a great many of these gifted persons.

In order for the teenager to be reborn into rational consciousness, the teenager must die to the mythic worldview, which can be an extremely painful process for teens who love God, but who belong to Christian denominations in which the leadership itself has not yet been able to successfully complete this transition. These denominations often try to get teenagers to "confirm" their belief in a literal understanding of the Christian myths, or to assent to the myths even if the teenager has no rational understanding of them.

These denominations also often require the teenager to reassert Christianity's *exclusive* possession of the keys to the Kingdom of Heaven, and to rededicate themselves to the concrete, *materialistic* rules and roles of mythic level religion. For example: girls may be required to let go of any calling to be ministers or priests because Jesus and the twelve apostles were *physically* male (even though the Kingdom of Heaven, where Jesus lived even here on earth, is neither male nor female [Gal. 3:26]); both boys and girls may be taught that every exercise of one's sexuality, even if otherwise permitted, must be open to *physical* procreation; and gay teens may be forbidden to express their sexuality for as long as they live, because such expression is seen as *physically* and emotionally unnatural by others.

However well-intentioned these teachings may be, they do a serious spiritual disservice to our teenagers.

Indeed, insistence upon adherence to a mythic understanding of God and religion is directly contrary to the work the Spirit is trying to achieve. In acting in this manner, these Church leaders play the role of Simon Peter when Jesus called him Satan (Matt. 16:23), when Peter tried to persuade Jesus not to follow his inner calling for fear it would lead to Jesus' rejection and death. These church leaders make a similar mistake in refusing to allow the teenager's consciousness to die to the mythic worldview in response to the movement of the Spirit within. The restrictions on sexuality are especially troubling because sexuality, when exercised with reverence and awareness, is designed by God to be the most powerful natural "technology" for growth in consciousness ("natural" as contrasted with specially designed spiritual technologies like rituals and meditation).[10]

In some Christian denominations, "confirmation" includes a "laying on of hands" by a bishop, presumably because, in the early Church, bishops were recognized as being more in touch with spiritual power (the Holy Spirit), and as knowing how to transmit this power as Jesus and his disciples did (Luke 13:13, Acts 19:6). In the early Church this spiritual event or initiation was called the "Baptism of Fire and the Holy Spirit" (Acts 1:5, 2:1-4, 8:14-17). It was meant to complete the inner work begun by the baptism by water. Today, putting aside the genuine faith and pure intentions often involved, the rite of "confirmation" is often a hollow gesture in which little if any spiritual energy is transmitted

---

[10]Many teenagers, depending upon their level of inner development, may be ready to move beyond rationality to begin exploring higher, more transcendent levels of awareness. In the past, many cultures and religions have channeled the sexual energy of young adults—by the use of drums, chanting, and other ritual music, as well as drugs, such as alcohol, tobacco, and peyote—to explore the psychic realm. Our rational level culture simply tries to suppress (usually unsuccessfully) these avenues. So we are left with sex, drugs, rap, and rock n' roll—but without the guided transcendent experience.

(and teenagers know it's hollow). Either the bishop is not in touch with spiritual power (the Holy Spirit), or, if he or she is in touch, the bishop lacks the knowledge and ability to transmit that power. Nor, assuming this were generally possible, are the teenagers properly prepared inwardly to receive such a baptism. I describe two levels of this Baptism by Fire and the Holy Spirit (which in the early Church was both administered and received in what today we would call an "altered state of consciousness") in some detail later in the book (see chapter 15). The American mystic Lawrence Richardson describes his own Baptism by Fire and the Holy Spirit (by the laying on of hands) on his Internet website.[11]

With respect to rules of behavior, most teenagers have already absorbed years of preaching about conventional morality and social values (rules and roles) from church, parents, teachers, politicians, the media, and even from athlete "role models" and the characters on television dramas. What they need now is not more of the same, but practical and conceptual assistance in moving into the level of rational consciousness and into a rational spirituality.

The development of reason will allow the teenager, for the first time, to analyze and even criticize the conventional rules and roles of the society (including religion) with which the teen has been schooled (programmed) during the years of mythic consciousness. It will allow the teenager's imagination to envision possible worlds, different worlds with different values, and (he or she normally hopes) possibly better, more sensible worlds. This ability to creatively envision an alternative and better future is one of the things that the spiritual level of rational consciousness is designed by God to accomplish.

The development of reason, for the first time, will bring the teenager's consciousness to the level of the truly universal, to a global perspective not limited by membership in any particular family, tribe, race, or mythic belief system (any "ism"). For example, the teenager will learn that the rational

---

[11]Lawrence Richardson's website address is www.chrmysticaloutreach.com

laws of science, which are encountered at this level, are not limited to any particular religious, ethnic, racial, or other separate group of people. They apply universally. At the level of reason the teen for the first time has the psychological capacity to think globally and be concerned about global problems. In terms of religion and spirituality, the development of reason will allow the teen to begin to understand *universally* applicable spiritual truths, such as those taught by Jesus, and to distinguish those universal truths from the merely sectarian and cultural "wineskins" in which those truths have often been enclosed (cf., Matt. 9:17).

In making the transition from mythic to rational consciousness, Christian teenagers will normally try their best to "rationalize" the Christian myths. In this they are not alone. Most of the Christian clergy and most seriously Christian adults have developed a more or less "rationalized" Christianity for themselves. That is, they use reason to try to interpret the Christian myths and/or they emphasize the more rational aspects of Christianity, such as moral teachings and denominational regulations. In doing so, they follow in the tradition of those past Christians who had advanced to the rational level of consciousness (and often beyond). These include the early Church Fathers, many of whom were highly educated in the schools of the Roman Empire, St. Thomas Aquinas, and the Protestant reformers. Like these noted predecessors, these teenagers often try to interpret the myths, as best they can, in the light of reason. The myths they are unable to interpret (e.g., Jesus' descent into hell or the Virgin Birth) they generally ignore, and, by and large, no one seems worse off on that account.[12]

---

[12]Given the place of myth in the history of Christianity, it may never be possible to jettison the myths altogether. Nor might that be wise. As symbols, the myths not only resonate fruitfully within the human psyche, but they may also contain truths that are still unknown or not fully understood. They may indeed, no matter how far humanity progresses in spiritual understanding, never lend themselves to full rationalization.

Many teenagers are unable to translate the myths into rational understandings and some do not bother. It is too much trouble to make mini-Church Fathers out of themselves, especially since, unlike in the time of the Church Fathers, Thomas Aquinas, or the Reformation, the dominant culture awaiting them as adults is rational, not mythic. So they drop out, often returning to church only years later when they feel they need assistance in teaching their own children the social rules and roles that are now sometimes called "traditional" or "family" values. Others may never return, thereafter calling themselves atheist or agnostic, by which they usually mean unbelievers or skeptics about the existence of the mythical Christian God in the sky.

To the mythic believer, these teens and future adults have "lost the faith." But the only faith they've lost is in the imaginary God of children, and in teachers who would continue to saddle them with mythic consciousness (cf., Matthew 18:6). By abandoning such a God and such teachers, they have actually grown spiritually into a higher level of consciousness, one closer to the mind that was in Christ Jesus. Like Jesus, they have become more tolerant, less judgmental, more compassionate, more inclusive, less fearful, less aggressive, and more universally loving. Like Jesus, they have more faith in the action of the Spirit within their psyche and in life itself than those who worry about being punished by God for breaking the moral and other rules of their denomination or society. They have more faith in the Spirit which, though unseen, directs all of life (Heb. 11:1), and less in the religious practices, rules, and roles that can be seen. Like Jesus, they have let go of the arrogance and self-importance of the exclusively "saved," a self-importance that manifests even today in aggressive moral crusades of one type or another.

How can we help teenagers make the transition from mythic to rational consciousness? For one, we can explain, if they haven't already figured it out, that the God in the sky, who performed a much needed psychological function for them as children, was a mythic and, for them now, inadequate understanding of God; we can explain that they now need a more adequate and rational understanding. (Nevertheless, for important emotional reasons to be discussed later, we can help them by encouraging them to continue addressing God in an intimate fashion, as Jesus did, as their loving Father or Mother.)

We can also assist teenagers by introducing them to the rational arguments for God's existence that have been made by the philosophers. But even more importantly, we can help them by telling them that the God who lives deep within themselves is much more magnificent than the sky God they are now leaving behind. Within themselves, if they go deep enough, they will find a totally nonjudgmental, loving, and merciful God, a God who does indeed know how many hairs we have on our heads and about the fall of every sparrow (Matt. 10:29-30), and a God who, in fact, runs this universe from A to Z, human free will notwithstanding.

We can also help them by teaching them the science of prayer, following the rules Jesus and his disciples laid down.[13] There is probably no better example of proper petitionary prayer, for example, than the methodology of contemporary science, including medical science. The scientist sets out, for example, to find a cure for a disease. He or she has no doubt, that is complete single-minded faith, that (1) an answer exists to his prayer, and (2) her mind is fully capable of finding that answer. The scientist then works very

---

[13]If the reader wants to learn these scientific rules of prayer, there are in the United States many Christian Science, Science of Mind, Divine Science, Unity, and metaphysical churches that teach the basics. There are also a number of "new age" books that explain the laws of prayer and manifestation as set out in both the Old and New Testaments. The best and most powerful prayer, of course, is prayer "in Jesus' name" (John 16:23-24). Prayer "in Jesus' name," however, does not consist in uttering Jesus' name like a magical talisman. It means praying as Jesus did, by the same methods. In the passage from John cited above, it means, above all else, praying with the same consciousness that Jesus had, the Christ Consciousness (see part 4).

hard, asking question after question, always trying to ask the right question and the right follow-up question. The scientist puts mind, emotions, and will into the search. Then, after working hard and "putting it out to the universe," so to speak, the scientist knows how to "give it a rest," to trustfully "let go." Finally, as was expected all along, the answer is revealed, sometimes in a dream, sometimes in a daydream on the commuter bus, and sometimes by sudden inspiration in the shower—all times at which the scientist has allowed his or her self to be open and receptive to receiving the answer.

Another rule of prayer is that to successfully manifest a cure for a disease or something more tangible like good grades, one uses "will" not "will power." The latter is force. Force sets up an equal and opposite counter-force that frustrates the seeker's goal. The difference between will and will-power can be seen by contrasting the mental frames of mind of the successful dieter and the failed dieter. The successful dieter uses no force. He or she just "does it." And "it" is not a crusade against food or fat or sweets, but a positive, step-by-step series of choices and actions that are pro-health or pro-slimness.

We can also help teenagers by teaching them that, in petitioning God, they are actually contacting that part of themselves that is divine, and motivating themselves to manifest in their lives what they desire. They, by their own inner growth in consciousness, must claim their own divinity, their own co-creatorship with God, so that, as joint heirs with Jesus of the Kingdom (Rom. 8:17), they will themselves know how to manifest on this Earth not only what they need, but true abundance (John 10:10).

We can help them too by advising teenagers that the prayer of thanksgiving is often a more effective form of prayer than the prayer of petition. Jesus sometimes used the prayer of petition (e.g., Matt. 6:11) though he used it not because he thought it necessary but so others would understand that the Father within himself was the source of his power (John 11:42). He preferred prayers of thanks (e.g., John 11:41) because prayers of thanksgiving assume beyond a shadow of a doubt that God, who already knows our needs (Matt. 6:8), will meet them. A prayer of thanksgiving, even before the event desired comes to pass, is far less likely to contain doubt or a sense of lack and, therefore, much more likely to be effective.

We can help teenagers by teaching them how to make rational use of the Christian rituals. Holy Communion in particular (in those denominations that still celebrate Jesus' Last Supper) can be used to help bring about within themselves a growing inner identification with the mind of Jesus (Phil. 2:5). On this point, the pioneer psychologist Carl Jung's work on the transformational symbolism of the Christian Mass (how we can use the Mass' symbols to inwardly change ourselves) might be a good place to start.[14] We can help teenagers by teaching them as Jesus taught, that religion is a tool to be used to the extent it is useful (Mark 2:27) to develop their own consciousness upward towards the inner Kingdom of Heaven.

We can also assist teenagers by devising ways, ceremonies and rituals to support their efforts to creatively fashion a vision of *their own* future path, *their own* spiritual work in the world, *their own* vision of what they can contribute to society. I do not mean this only in an external vocational sense. That kind of help is usually given to teens, particularly to middle class teenagers, in one way or another. What I mean is something more spiritual, like the "vision quest" upon which Native American youth were sent, or like the powerful "initiation ceremonies" that other so-called primitive societies conducted to spiritually assist their young people into adulthood

---

[14]Carl Gustav Jung, 1875-1961, is regarded by many as the greatest twentieth century psychologist. He was a colleague of Sigmund Freud from 1907 to 1913 but broke with Freud because Freud tended to reduce human psychology to sexuality, whereas Jung recognized the transpersonal, spiritual realm as vital. His works include *Dreams, Answer to Job,* and *Memories, Dreams, Reflections.*

(I say "so-called" here because these simpler societies often seem to have done much better by their young people than ours does). Our Christian young people need help in finding their own inner link between who they are as incarnate souls and their future path into the world.

Perhaps most important of all, we can aid our teenagers by teaching them a scientific form of meditation, one they afterwards can use to seek the Kingdom of God within themselves. Christianity, unfortunately, has been so focused upon externals for such a long time that there is scarcely a scientific form of meditation to be found in the Christian tradition (though Jesus probably used one and instructed his disciples in it). Two I know about are "centering prayer," by the contemporary Trappist monk M. Basil Pennington,[15] and the "Jesus prayer," used by many in the Orthodox church. But except for contemplative monks and nuns, and a few denominations such as the Quakers, meditation does not play a significant role in most Christian worship.

Fortunately, the Hindus and Buddhists have developed hundreds of scientific meditation techniques and yogas which can be borrowed by Christians and pressed into service. Wilber advises, however, that some discrimination be used in selecting among the Eastern meditation techniques. Though most of the time-honored techniques have succeeded in producing genuine spiritual masters, not all of the techniques are directed towards realizing the same level of consciousness.

In general, there are three different types of Eastern meditation techniques. The first group, which aims to transmute bodily and emotional energies, includes hatha, kundalini, kriya, and tantric yogas as well as pranayama (breathing exercises). The second group deals with the high subtle regions (see chapter 11) and uses sound and light

---

[15]Among other books, Pennington has written *Centering Prayer: Renewing an Ancient Christian Prayer Form* and *Call to the Center: The Gospel's Invitation to Deeper Prayer.*

absorption and includes *Nada* and *Shabd* yogas. The third group, which has as its focus the causal and nondual levels of consciousness (see part 4), includes Zen and Vedanta practices. Wilber notes that all of these meditation techniques can bring one to the nondual consciousness of the Kingdom of Heaven, but this is both easier and more likely the higher the path one initially adopts.

If we assist our teenagers in these ways, their paths into the level of reason (and eventually beyond) will be aided immensely, for their good, our good, and the good of generations of children yet to come.

Cultural Consciousness Development

Rational consciousness dominates today's world in our universities, government, science, technology, medicine, business and finance, media and communications, and in nearly every other human institution except, in a few cases, our churches. We are now so familiar with rationality that we often fail to realize what a magnificent achievement it is for humans to operate at this level, and how long and hard was the struggle of the human race to get to this level of awareness. The United States, the first nation ever founded upon rational principles, including rational spiritual principles such as the equality of all under God, is barely over two centuries old.

But, though everyone in America and the other advanced nations must cope with the dominant rational level, not all citizens, including many religious and political leaders, truly live at that level. Millions lag at least partly at the mythic level, though fewer as the years pass and the level of education rises. In religion, that most conservative of human institutions, not only millions of adherents but many in leadership positions lag behind in the mythic level. Fundamentalist religion, in no matter what religion it is found (Christianity, Judaism, Islam, Hinduism, Buddhism), is chiefly characterized by its holding on to the mythic worldview and its exclusion from "salvation" of those who do not adhere to that worldview. (I once had a young Buddhist tell me in all sincerity that Buddhism was the one true religion, outside of which there is no salvation, a view we often hear about Christianity from mythic level Christians.)

But in the West, Christianity sowed the seed from which the rational level of consciousness arose. The lifting of human consciousness from the mythic level into the rational level has been the principal spiritual task of the two thousand years since Jesus. St. Augustine and the other Fathers of the Eastern and Western Churches; the Irish monks who preserved the ancient books and the culture of learning when the rest of Europe was overrun by tribes with magical level consciousness; John Scotus Erigena and others who reintroduced schools and learning into western continental Europe at the time of Charlemagne during the "Dark Ages"; St. Thomas Aquinas and the other great medieval university scholars; the great Renaissance thinkers like Leonardo da Vinci; the Protestant reformers; the great founders of schools for the lay public like St. Ignatius Loyola and St. Francis de Sales; and the enlightenment scientists and philosophers, many of whom remained devoutly Christian—all these played important roles in helping human consciousness make this transition.

The task has been substantially completed in the advanced countries only in the last two hundred years. Even today, Christian missionary schools are hard at work in practically all of the less advanced nations guiding their pupils in how to think and prosper in today's rational society. The world is now moving rapidly into the rational level of awareness and all our modern national and international institutions operate at that level. It is true, of course, that the Church has often dragged its feet, (e.g., in the case of Galileo), but, looked at in the long run of history, the Christian church deserves to compliment itself for a job well done.

Chapter 8

VISION-LOGIC CONSCIOUSNESS

Vision-logic consciousness is the highest of the three mental levels of consciousness. It is the consciousness of many great artists, writers, international financiers, scientists, and philosophers. Vision-logic's primary characteristics are the identification of the self with the abstract mind, and the ability to think from many different perspectives. Vision-logic consciousness is global in its interest in, and concern for, other persons. It is capable of grappling with global problems beyond the ability of any one nation or society to solve. Vision-logic consciousness, however, can also have its downside in the form of considerable inner anguish. More and more the leadership in many fields is moving to this level of consciousness. This social movement, however, is seen as threatening and is being opposed by many Christians (fundamentalists of every denomination) whose awareness remains at the mythic level.

Individual Consciousness Development

At the vision-logic level of consciousness, the self is fully identified with the abstract mind. Like great thinkers such as Albert Einstein, William Shakespeare, Thomas Jefferson, or Theodore Roosevelt, we are not only capable of abstract reasoning, but are capable of taking many different perspectives, integrating them, and putting them together in new and surprisingly creative ways.

We have learned to transcend the pitfalls of rigid mental ideologies and "isms." Our mind roams free of such limitations. Since we can see and understand many different perspectives, we may be capable of producing universally appealing works of art, music, literature, or philosophy. We may be capable of negotiating a treaty between many different nations, or putting together systems of international business, finance, or telecommunications. At this level we are not all geniuses. As always, and as is the case at every level, basic competence at seeing and integrating many mental perspectives is all that is required. As Wilber points out, even the chieftain of a primitive tribe might rise to this level by learning to handle the competing interests of tribal factions with different perspectives, or by conducting successful negotiations with neighboring tribes.

Paradoxically, as is also the case at every higher level of consciousness, we are more grounded than we were at the merely rational level. At the rational level we can become so enamored of a particular ideology, for example, that we live our lives all in our heads. This is not the case at the vision-logic level. To get to this level, once again, as is the case with all the higher levels, more of our unconscious, that is, repressed emotions as well as higher abilities, must be brought into awareness and integrated into the consciousness. The vision-logic level is the level of the integrated human personality, and will be measured as such on the standard psychological personality tests. It is the first level of consciousness at which it can be said that we have successfully integrated body, emotions, and mind.

Because this level is one of personality integration, Wilber calls it the "centaur," after the mythical beast that was half human and half horse. In terms of spirituality and the understanding of the Scriptures, at this level we appreciate the fact that the Scriptures can be read on many different levels. We will begin to appreciate and understand how the Scriptures use the mind-body symbolism employed by Jesus, St. Paul, and the four evangelists, as, for example, Jesus' constant references to "seeing" and "hearing."

At the vision-logic level we now have a global perspective. We no longer define the self in the narrow terms of race, color, national origin, sectarianly-understood religion, gender, sexual orientation, national citizenship, or belief in a particular "ism." We are all these things, but we primarily see the self as a simple human being, one of almost six billion on this planet, and see our mission as service to all. In accordance with reason's own universality, we seek the good of all humanity. As a result, we are tolerant of (and genuinely interested in) persons of other cultures, religions, and races. We appreciate other philosophies and perspectives. We see all persons as free citizens in a global society, and seek to maximize that freedom for everyone as fully as possible through universal education, planetary economic integration, global communications and environmental safeguards, increased democratization of governments, adherence to international law, and in defending the right of every human being to make their own moral choices.

So far the vision-logic level may sound wonderful, and it is wonderful in many ways. Psychologically, we are an integrated personality. Inwardly, we enjoy a great deal of freedom compared to the levels below. In terms of worldly career, at this level we usually have no problem manifesting creative employment for ourselves. We generally work at what we love to do and find great fulfillment in carrying out our visions.

But all is not rosy. The vision-logic level has also been called the "existential" level by the many modern philosophers who have described it, philosophers like Kierkegaard, Camus, and Sartre. It can be, on the negative side, a level of profound angst and inner unrest. Part of the reason for this, ironically, is exactly the above-described success of this level in terms of this world and the achievements of this world.

More and more we have "been there, done that." As a result, the world begins to lose its glamour. We have done all the things that bring "immortality" in a worldly sense.

We may have achieved great fame, may have produced immortal works of art, may have buildings and institutions named after us thanks to our financial largess as benefactors. We may have degrees and honorary degrees galore. We may have children and grandchildren, all of whom have graduated from prestigious universities. We may be on a first-name basis with celebrities and "movers and shakers" in a variety of fields of human endeavor. But we know that, nonetheless, we are going to die and that none of these "immortality projects" can undo that fact.

Even worse, even though we may expend countless hours a week working for the good of all, many of us at this level have often lost God. We know that no outside Sky God, the God that consoles many millions at the levels of consciousness below, is going to save us from disease, old age, or death. "Where was God at Auschwitz?" we may ask. For many at this level, God is dead. And we may know of no other God to replace the one that has been lost.

As a result, despite all our outside successes and achievements, we may be, and often are, in deep inner agony. We often struggle in vain to discover meaning in our lives and suffer profoundly when such meaning cannot be found. And, if things go wrong—our business goes bankrupt, our political party loses office, our spouse or children are lost to cancer or a car accident, we can fall into such depression that suicide is a danger. In spite of this angst, most of us at this level carry on, trying somehow to make this world better for our children and grandchildren.

As we near the end of the vision-logic level of consciousness, we begin to transcend the mind itself. We begin to become aware of our rationality and begin to see the mind itself and its thinking as an object. This means we are, to some extent, beginning to locate the self beyond the mind. We begin to identify the self with that part of us that transcends body, emotions, and mind, the part of self that observes these first three parts as an inner witness. The integrated human personality (body, emotions, mind) begins to be seen as a whole by this inner witness as we become more and more detached from the spacetime personality itself. We begin to move into the next level of consciousness: the psychic.

Cultural Consciousness Development

In terms of cultural evolution, the vision-logic level of consciousness lies in the future, though, in historical terms, in the not-too-distant future. Most of the people on this planet are only now moving into or trying to master the rational level. Nevertheless, in the highly educated and interconnected circles of the world, the vision-logic level is becoming increasingly commonplace. It has been said, for example, that ninety percent of history's greatest scientists are living today, and the same could be said of many other fields. Much of the planet's leadership is now rapidly moving into this level of awareness. Given the planetary scope of so many of today's problems, it is probably not a moment too soon.

Currently, people at this level are rising to the top of corporations, government, the church, finance, telecommunications, and other fields that demand not only intellectual creativity but also much practical wisdom and common sense. Often this worldly success brings with it financial rewards and perhaps fame and external power as well.

Because the vision-logic level of awareness is one of integration, the culture that vision-logic awareness will produce will be concerned with "wholes," e.g., global integration in finance and politics, holistic approaches to medicine, and systems theory in the sciences.

This movement does not overly alarm people at the rational level. By and large, they are willing to move to a global society or are willing to be led there. But it is terrifying for the millions of people still operating at the mythic level. People at the mythic level still want the world to adopt their worldview and have no intention of having their parochial perspectives, whether national, religious, racial, sexual, or otherwise being seen as one of many.

These are the fundamentalists of every sort throughout the world. They exist, often in dominant positions, in every religion and in every country. Many of them, under the direction of politicians and religious leaders who share (or exploit) their worldview, have begun an organized opposition to the emerging planetary culture (sometimes, ironically, using the latest communications technology). For these people, the world is *literally* going to the devil. More enlightened political and religious leaders throughout the world have their hands full trying to keep these frightened souls from violence. There has been violence already and there may be a lot more of it. But in the end, vision-logic consciousness will prevail. Spirit demands it. Christ demands it. For it is the Christ unfolding in history.

Chapter 9

PSYCHIC CONSCIOUSNESS

At the psychic level of consciousness we no longer identify the self with the rational mind. Instead, we identify the self with the inner witness that observes body, emotions, and mind. This inner witness is the permanent self, the part of self beyond spacetime. The permanent self has senses such as clairaudience and clairvoyance that roughly parallel the physical senses, and which are referred to in the New Testament. Persons with psychic consciousness may make use of abilities such as healing by the laying on of hands, prophecy, and speaking in tongues.

Individual Consciousness Development

The chief characteristic of the psychic level of consciousness is the identification of the self with the inner witness. The witness, which is familiar to all serious meditators, is the part of self beyond body, emotions, and mind, beyond the frontal personality by means of which we operate in spacetime. The witness, therefore, is itself beyond spacetime. The witness has been called by some the permanent self.

As we move into the psychic level of consciousness, the sixth level of human awareness, we will gradually become more consciously aware of information coming from beyond the five physical senses. We will develop what is sometimes called extrasensory perception (ESP). Extrasensory perception is normally not exotic or sensational as the media often portrays it. It is simply the ability to obtain information that the five physical senses cannot. The Christian who is able to tune in to the "small still voice within" (Ps. 46:10) is making use of ESP. He or she is developing psychic consciousness.

Often the entrance into the psychic level is dramatic, taking the form of a conversion or rebirth experience. Evelyn Underhill, who begins her map of the spiritual path at this point, calls this "the Awakening of the Self."

> All conversion entails the abrupt or gradual emergence of intuitions from below the threshold [of consciousness], the consequent remaking of the field of consciousness, an alteration of the self's attitude to the world . . . but in the mystic this process is raised to the nth degree of intensity, for in him it means that first emergence of that passion for the Absolute . . . . Those to whom it happens, often enough, are already "religious": sometimes deeply and earnestly so.[16]

Underhill's point is that the person has now awakened to the deeper part of self, the permanent part of self that transcends space and time. At this point on the path we awaken to the energies of the psychic or astral body. Later, at the subtle level, we will awaken directly to the energies of soul. From now on we are directly in touch with those parts of self that continue after death, the permanent personality. In this deeper opening a new, more intense world opens before our eyes, a world that stretches to the infinite.

At the psychic level of consciousness we may begin to open regularly to those peak experiences that are often called nature mysticism or cosmic consciousness. For example, we may be lying on the beach gazing into the sunset

---

[16]Evelyn Underhill, *Mysticism*, New York, Doubleday, 1910, 1990, p. 177.

when, suddenly, we are caught up in an awareness of oneness and unity with the sea and sun, sky and sand. For those who wish to explore this nature mysticism aspect of psychic consciousness further, there is perhaps in America no finer example of this level than Ralph Waldo Emerson (1803-82) who, along with Henry David Thoreau and others, was a founder of the "Transcendentalist" movement of the early nineteenth century.

Emerson reacted against the materialism then coming to dominate American intellectual circles with its idea that we can contact truth only through the five physical senses. He also reacted against external, materialistic religion with its reliance on rules, rituals, and other external observances. Emerson taught that, through intuition, we can contact the "oversoul," our own inner divine self and, by doing so, intuit the connection of all humans to each other and of humans with nature. Both he and Thoreau preached self-reliance, attuning to our one's inner truth, and marching to one's own "inner drummer."

The psychic or astral level, in contrast to the spacetime universe of the physical body and the physical senses (which exist in the third dimension), exists in the fourth dimension. Our astral bodies, therefore, transcend space. At the psychic level, we begin to be able to experience a knowingness that is not dependent on the five senses or on being in the same space with the person or thing that is known. For example, we may experience instant connection with the mind of another (telepathy) across hundreds of miles. We may get the feeling that our mother is going to call from a distant state, perhaps even "sensing" in advance what mother has in mind to say.

We may also begin, in the dream state especially, to have "out-of-body" experiences whereby we travel in our astral bodies to distant places, perhaps even seeing what others are doing or what is going on in those places. (The astral body has always had this ability, but now we may become consciously aware of it). If we are trained, we may begin to remember these experiences clearly or even develop the ability to astral travel when we are awake.

We may begin to develop, consciously or unconsciously, one or more of the five astral senses (the senses of the astral or psychic body) that parallel the physical senses: clairsentience (psychic "sensing"), clairaudience (psychic "hearing"), clairvoyance (psychic "sight"), psychic "smell," and psychic "taste."

Clairsentience, for example, may allow us to walk into a business meeting and sense immediately who is in charge, whether there is any tension in the room and, if so, between whom. It may allow us to take the sense of a person we have just met, to let us know if the person is trustworthy, a possible friend, a possible lover, or someone to be avoided. It may allow us to sense the spiritual energy in a church or the negative energy in a dangerous place. Jesus was a master of this ability. It allowed him, as if tuning into a radio station, to key into the hearts of others (their inner emotional vibrations) to see what they felt (Matt. 12:25).

Clairaudience may allow us to hear telepathically. It may allow a composer to hear wonderful music in his head. Clairaudience also allows the "voices" of our own higher self (the voice of conscience), our guardian angels, our spiritual masters, and our various spiritual helpers and guides to come to us more clearly. If trained and developed, it may allow us to be a medium or a channel, using our bodies and voices to bring the guidance of advanced beings (such as the saints) to others. Jesus and many saints had clairaudience. Jesus, for example, again by tuning in, could read the minds of others and hear their thoughts (Mark 2:8, Luke 5:22).

Clairvoyance may allow us to begin to see the energy bodies which surround the physical bodies of all living beings. This energy body, usually called an aura, is made up of energies that vibrate at a rate higher than the physical. Because of the importance of the aura to many early Christians, and increasingly to many seekers today, it is worthwhile to present a few general ideas about this aspect of clairvoyance.

The human aura or energy body has several layers and is much larger than the physical body. The golden halos that we see usually depicted around the heads of Jesus and the saints are a representation of the spiritual energies contained in their auras, and are an indication that, at one time at least, some Christians knew about, studied, and trained themselves to see and interpret auras. Like so much else concerning spirituality, however, this knowledge and skill is mostly lacking from today's mainstream Christianity.

The first layer of the aura is the etheric, which is basically the physical body in energy form. After a leg is amputated, for example, we can usually sense the leg as if it were still there. In doing this, we are sensing the etheric body, the principal job of which is to hold together the form of the physical body. The higher bodies (our astral bodies and "thought" bodies) are also surrounded by the etheric body (which holds all of our various forms together into a coherent whole). The geometry of this is complex, and impossible to diagram, because the physical body exists in the third dimension (spacetime), the astral body in the fourth (which transcends space), and the "thought" body in the fifth (which transcends space and time). (Some seers talk about still another body, the "causal" body, which exists at the level of the divine archetypes, i.e., the level of the soul.)

There are many energy meridians (lines) in the etheric body. Oriental medicine has made use of these energies, which can (so far at least) only be seen psychically, for at least two thousand years. Christians also make use of them when they do healing by the laying on of hands. There are also centers or whirlpools of energy usually called wheels or chakras. There are seven principal chakras: at the base of the spine, near the genitals, at the solar plexus, at the heart, at the throat, between the eyebrows, and at the top of the head. The base chakra maintains the integrity of the physical body. The heart chakra anchors the astral body. The "third eye" chakra between the eyebrows is the center of psychic sight, and the crown chakra (atop the head) connects us to God and other high spiritual beings like Jesus. Though you could make an extremely rough, and over-simplified diagram of our various bodies as if one enclosed the other (like Russian dolls that have dolls inside them and dolls inside of them), the various bodies (which are in different dimensions) actually "interpenetrate" each other.

The second layer of the human aura is the astral or psychic body, the emotional body. The astral body exists on the astral plane, the fourth dimension, which is also the plane of dreams. Dreams are astral phenomena; when we dream, we are operating on the astral plane.

With respect to the emotional body, negative emotions, relatively speaking, vibrate at very slow (heavy) frequencies while positive emotions vibrate faster and are lighter. Joy has a much higher and faster vibration, for example, than sadness or fear. Negative emotions can produce disease in the physical body because emotions that exist in the astral body generally seek expression in the physical. Positive emotions, on the other hand, generate physical well-being. In fact, our physical bodies were created this way, as a perfect expression in physical form of our astral bodies. Our souls created our physical bodies *by means of* first our "thought" bodies and then our astral bodies, using those bodies as intermediaries.

Christians are accustomed to thinking that we "have" a soul. That's getting it backwards. The soul, which is individuated Spirit, is the real "me." We, as human personalities with minds, emotions, and bodies, do not "have" souls. The soul "has" us. The soul is the eternal living reality or principle that creates, gives life to, and sustains all three bodies of the personality, the physical, astral, and thought bodies.

The next layer of the aura is the "thought" body which exists in the fifth dimension where not only space but time is transcended. (Some psychics see the thought body as the "upper floor" of the astral body rather than as a separate third body, with the emotional body being the "lower floor"). In the thought body, the vibrations are faster still. Thoughts vibrate much faster than emotions and are much more powerful.

Everything that exists or is created on the physical plane of spacetime first exists as a thought on the thought plane.

Then it exists, with accompanying emotion, in the astral plane; finally, it becomes physical. If we want to create something good in our lives, we must think about it clearly and then put some emotion into it. The higher vibrations will then precipitate like rainfall out of the astral plane into the physical plane and manifest what we want, even if it's only moving our body to get a glass of water. The art and science of this kind of manifestation is one part of the science of prayer, as practiced in the early Church, a science well known to Jesus and his disciples but again virtually absent in mainstream Christianity today. It was how, for example, Jesus multiplied loaves and fish (Matt. 14:16-21). As the sign of the loaves and fish showed, Jesus was such a master of this ability that he could literally manifest things "out of thin air" (a good description for both the plane of thought and the astral plane).

To return to our discussion of psychic consciousness, the second spiritual art and science known to Jesus and to many in the early Church was healing by the laying on of hands (Luke 13:13). This uses thought and astral vibrations, using the healer's thoughts and emotions (and any psychic ability the healer has to "pick up" and transmit the healing vibrations of higher spiritual beings) to heal the sick person's astral and/or physical body at the places the healer sees or feels are diseased. Once the patient is healed of negative thoughts and emotions, this healing will automatically heal the corresponding (dependent) parts of the physical body, provided the sick person doesn't invite the negative energies to return (Matt. 12:43-45).

If a person of extremely high vibration, (e.g., at the causal level) were to transmit his or her vibration (for example, by the laying on of hands) to a person who is vibrating at a much lower level (e.g., at the mythic level) the recipient would probably have an instant nervous breakdown, a blood pressure surge sufficient to cause a stroke, or some other such calamity. Fortunately, there are natural "circuit-breakers" that prevent such transmissions. People who "fall out in the Spirit" (lose consciousness by fainting) at the touch of a healer or at an intense spiritual exercise, do so because of the circuit-breakers. Their bodies, emotions, and/or minds can't take in the high energies beyond a certain point, so they pass out. (I am not saying that this is the only thing producing this effect. It may also be that the higher vibrations relax the person so much that this too prevents them from staying on their feet.)

The Eastern religions usually prescribe abstinence from alcohol and meat because these foods (especially meat today considering how animals are raised and slaughtered) have heavy vibrations (e.g., fear) and hinder the raising of the body's vibrations (this can cause problems if one is doing exercises that bring in intensely high energies). Jewish, Muslim and Christian traditions have had similar restrictions, which now, in the case of Christians, are more honored in the breach than in the practice.

A third spiritual art and science practiced in the early Church, but now largely lost except in some marginalized Christian churches like the Pentecostals, was that of prophecy (1 Cor. 12:8). Prophecy is also a psychic level phenomenon.[17]

Prophecy, as that term is used in Corinthians, can be used to tap into the spiritual realm—but, in my experience, only by a person whose consciousness is already at the sixth level, the psychic, and *that* type of prophecy comes through in coherent sentences the content of which is, from a rational

---

[17]Though I do not pretend to be an expert on Pentecostalism, I see it as an interesting spiritual experiment with mixed results. Most Pentecostals appear to be mythic level Christians (third consciousness level) who are attempting direct contact with the spiritual realm (eighth consciousness level) by means of the psychic level (sixth consciousness level). That is a feat if one can pull it off. Despite the purity of heart and intention (Matt. 5:8) and the genuine seeking (Matt. 7:8), however, it appears that, most of the time, the effort fails. I am not doubting that psychic level energies are "tapped into" through emotion, music and other techniques, but that appears to be all that is tapped into.

perspective, genius level. That is altogether different from the Pentecostal experience where the "messages," not mediated by even rational level development, come through largely as incoherent utterances which are then normally "interpreted" by a fellow mythic level congregant. And congregants constantly "fall out in the Spirit," because, luckily for their own mental health, their bodies, nervous systems, and consciousness cannot handle the energies from the psychic level. All the major spiritual traditions on the planet strongly advise against the development of psychic powers until one is *grounded* in the psychic level itself, and they are very wise to do so.

How does prophecy work? We have already seen how everything that exists on the physical level of existence must first exist as a thought with accompanying emotion in the astral plane. If you were able to see or sense these thought and emotional vibrations before they "rain" their physical manifestations into spacetime, you would be a prophet. The basic principle of prophecy is as simple as that.

Prophecy, as the word is used in the New Testament, is not limited to foretelling the future. It is a much broader term. It means opening our inner psychic faculties to *hear* the words, or *see* the images, sent down from the spiritual planes (including our own "higher selves" or souls) for our guidance. The early Church members constantly received these communications on behalf of each other and their communities, so much so that prophecy (today called channeling) was an integral part of worship (1 Cor. 12:8, 1 Cor. 14:22). Today, this type of prophecy is practiced by many Christian new agers and in spiritualist and metaphysical churches (the majority of whose members are Christian). By not making use of this psychic ability, and by relying principally on the reasoning mind, mainstream Christianity is handicapping itself seriously and unnecessarily and is depriving its membership of worthwhile spiritual guidance.

Speaking in tongues, which was also much practiced in the early Church, and is still practiced by some Christian denominations today, is another psychic phenomenon that makes use of the astral body (1 Cor. 12:10). I will have more to say about speaking in tongues in chapter 21.

This book does not intend to explore in detail the nature of the astral body or the astral plane. Just as the astral body is much larger than the physical body, so the astral plane is much larger than the physical universe, and both are every bit as fascinating and complex as their physical counterparts. It will take hundreds more years, in all likelihood, for the human race to master even the basics of these subjects.

As far as the spiritual path to the Kingdom of Heaven is concerned, as always, it is not necessary to master the psychic level of consciousness. Basic competence will do. Nor are specific psychic skills or specific psychic experiences (which can happen to anyone at any level at any time) important.

What is important for basic competence at the psychic level is that we, for the first time, become more interested in what happens within our own psyches than in the outside world, and that we develop the ability to accurately see and feel what is going on within ourselves. What is important is that we become what Christian tradition calls *contemplatives*, that is, serious meditators. It is not necessary for us to become *mystics*, who are contemplatives with pronounced psychic abilities.

At the psychic level, the Christian turns within in a more radical way than previously. We identify ourselves, our "I," with the inner witness who observes mind, emotions, and body, and we become skilled at watching ourselves dispassionately from the witness' vantage point. This witnessing is meditation even if no specific meditation technique is practiced. We become decisively inner directed and self-reliant, rather than relying on the advice, opinions, and values of others. We learn to listen to the still small voice within before making decisions, learning in this way to "pray always" (1 Thes. 5:17). We become sensitive to the messages of the soul or higher self.

Because the soul itself is pure spirit and formless, these messages are often transmitted to us through the symbols, sounds, and feelings of the astral plane. One of the primary purposes of dreams, for example, is to convey, symbolically, the messages of our souls in a manner that, with training, can be then consciously interpreted by our everyday conscious selves. The Bible has dozens of examples of messages from Spirit being sent by dream. In a dream, Joseph was told it was all right to marry Mary, Jesus' mother (Matt. 1:20); another dream told him to take the Christ Child and flee to Egypt (Matt. 2:13); and still another told him when to move to Galilee (Matt. 2:22).[18]

As we gain experience at the psychic level we realize that, as Jesus said, there is a vast and wondrous world within. But that does not mean we neglect spacetime and its obligations. It would be a terrible mistake to do so, because the psychic level of consciousness, like every level of consciousness, must be thoroughly grounded in the levels below, including the physical. To act otherwise would invite psychic disaster.

Normally, we actually become *more* effective and creative in spacetime. For the first time, our consciousness can see spacetime in context. For example, we can now see how everything that happens on the higher planes (thought and emotion) has enormous consequences on the physical plane, for better or for worse, and we can take this knowledge into account in everyday life. We will also see what eventually most people will come to see: the danger of constantly spewing out negative thoughts and emotional vibrations, especially fear, including over the radio, television, Internet, and other media.

These vibrations, especially when they induce mass phobias, panics, rages, griefs, vengefulness, etc., damage not only our social and political environment but also the animal kingdom and the physical environment. This is because

---

[18]For those interested in a further exploration of the subject of dreams as messages from God and one's own Christ Self, an excellent place to start is the book *Dreams, God's Forgotten Language,* by the American Jungian analyst and Episcopal priest John A. Sanford.

human consciousness is the most powerful force on this planet, greater than that of the animal and the other life forms over which we have stewardship, and greater than that of the physical Earth. Our mental and emotional "storms," therefore, have negative manifestational consequences for these other beings and for the planet itself.

Putting aside the wonders of the psychic world, if we intend to consciously realize the Kingdom of Heaven before the end of our lifetime, we are best advised not to waste time at the psychic level or get lost in all its fascinating aspects (and lost we can easily get).

There are also dangers at the psychic level, so much so that it is best not to dabble in this realm, such as with the use of Ouija boards or the unguided use of mind-altering drugs. The lower astral regions are filled with extreme darkness and negativity; they are the location of hell—in fact, there are many hells of various types, each more hideous than the last.

These regions are repulsive and psychically dangerous, and full of negative entities (thought forms, discarnate humans, and demons) that will harm you (or even take partial possession of you), given the chance. By "partial possession" I mean that if they find a damaged part of our emotional body that vibrates similarly to their own vibration, they may become magnetically attached to that part with the result that we thereafter have to contend not only with our own emotional damages but also with theirs.[19]

Some people say that the grotesque imagery and activity that have been appearing in recent years in movies, videos, and computer video games are the result of "holes" having been punched in the "veil" that separates the physical and the lower astral planes, perhaps by the use and testing of nuclear weapons, among other causes. Whatever the reason, artists with psychic ability are now more easily tapping into

---

[19]For a much fuller explanation of partial possession from a psychiatric point of view, see *Remarkable Healings* by American psychiatrist Shakuntala Modi, M.D.; Hampton Roads, Charlottesville, VA, 1997

these realms and using them to create such things as violent pornography, video games, and movies. It is an unwholesome development, and it is the dark side of the recent general rediscovery of psychic abilities and the astral realm.

In addition to the above dangers, there is a case to be made that much of what we call schizophrenia, a serious mental disorder that usually appears from late adolescence to early adulthood, is caused by psychically opening up into the astral plane (and sometimes communication with the beings who live there) *before* there is sufficient ego-development to handle these tremendous (and, for the rational ego, tremendously confusing) energies.

All the major spiritual traditions advise serious spiritual seekers not to tarry at the psychic level, but to keep moving on the path. St. Paul gave this advice to the Corinthians. These early Christians were meditating, and developing and using their psychic abilities in many ways. But they became proud, boasted of their abilities, grew jealous of each other's gifts, and neglected to keep their eyes on the still higher spiritual levels of consciousness. So Paul wrote to them:

> There are different kinds of spiritual gifts, but the same Spirit gives them. There are different ways of serving, but the same Lord is served. . . . One and the same Spirit gives faith to one man, while to another man he gives the power to heal. The Spirit gives one man the power to work miracles; to another the gift of speaking God's message. . . . To one man he gives the ability to speak in strange tongues, and to another he gives the ability to explain what was said. But it is one and the same Spirit who does all this. . . .
>
> All of you, then, are Christ's body, and each one is a part of it. . . . They are not all apostles, or prophets, or teachers. Not all have the power to work miracles, or to heal diseases, or to speak in strange tongues, or to explain what is said. Set your hearts, then, on the more important gifts. Best of all, however, is the following way:
>
> I may be able to speak the languages of men and even of angels, but if I have not love, my speech is no more than a noisy gong or a clanging bell. I may have the gift of inspired preaching; I may have all knowledge and

understand all secrets; I may have all the faith needed to move mountains—but if I have not love I am nothing. [I Cor. 12:4-5, 9-11, 27, 29-31; 13:1-2]

Paul told the Corinthians to keep moving on the path, to strive onward to come into Love, the Christ Consciousness of the spiritual level (see part 4), because otherwise their psychic gifts and practices will be in vain.

Cultural Consciousness Development

At the cultural level, the psychic level of consciousness was normally the very highest level the elite of humanity (in terms of consciousness) achieved in the ancient world. In fact, it can be said that the psychic level was the true "glory" of the ancient world. All over the world psychic oracles (normally after years of intense, difficult training) advised their governments, from the courts of the Chinese and Roman emperors and Egyptian pharaohs to the famous Oracle at Delphi in Greece and the court of the Jewish kings in Jerusalem.

There was a Jewish school for prophets on Mt. Carmel, and there were many renowned centers of psychic healing dedicated to Asclepios in Greece. Even tribal cultures revered their psychic healers, medicine men and women (shamans) from the Native American tribes to the European Celts, to tribes of Africa and Siberia.[20] The spiritual master don Juan

---

[20]With respect to these tribal cultures, Pope John Paul II asks something very interesting in his book, *Crossing the Threshold of Hope*, about their belief in ancestor worship (a belief that also applies to large elements of Chinese and Japanese society). He asks: "Is there, perhaps, in this veneration of ancestors a kind of preparation for the Christian faith in the Communion of Saints?" I used to think the same. But my study of shamanistic spirituality has convinced me that the veneration for one's deceased relatives that is prevalent at the popular level in China, Japan, and in many tribes, is actually a corruption of the ancient shamanic psychic practice (still alive in many places) of consulting on the peoples' behalf with precisely those spiritual guides with whom the Pope wants to restore communion (see, for example, the testimony of Agnes Whistling Elk in chapter 16).

Matus, the Yaqui teacher of the late Carlos Castaneda,[21] tells of the stupendous psychic achievements of Native American "sorcerers" (his word for psychics) before the arrival of Columbus. He taught Castaneda and others many psychic abilities, which he called the abilities of the "second intention." Don Juan's "third attention," he said, was the goal of his seer's path in contrast to the "second attention." I label don Juan's "third attention" the causal and nondual levels in this book. In other words, the "third attention" is seeing at the spiritual level whereas the "second attention" is seeing at the psychic level.

As we have seen, the early Christians were also keen on developing psychic abilities as part of their efforts to follow Jesus and his disciples. But it was not to last. Once Christianity degenerated into a religion operating at the mythic level, all such abilities became suspect. Many Christians regarded those with psychic powers in exactly the same way the Pharisees had regarded Jesus, as having abilities that came from the Devil (Matt. 12:24). Scarcely a hundred years or so after Jesus' death, St. Clement of Alexandria wrote:

> Another consideration shows us clearly how much of this early teaching has been lost. The church now devotes herself solely to producing good men, and points to the saints as her crowning glory and achievement. But in the older days she claimed to be able to do much more than that. When she had made a man a saint, her work with him was just beginning, for only then was he fit for the training and teaching which she could give him then, but not now,

---

[21]The late American anthropologist, mystic, and author Carlos Castaneda was born in Peru in 1925 or in Brazil in 1931 (accounts vary). He came to the United States in 1951. He studied parapsychology at Los Angeles City College and anthropology at the University of California at Los Angeles. On a field trip to Mexico he met his spiritual teacher, don Juan Matus, a Yaqui Indian, in 1960. He was his apprentice until 1965 and again from 1968 to 1971. He wrote eleven books based on the teachings of don Juan Matus, beginning with *The Teachings of Don Juan: A Yaqui Way of Knowledge* in 1968. Castaneda died in 1998.

because she has forgotten her ancient knowledge. Then she had three definite stages in her course of training—Purification [right living], Illumination [visions of the kingdom], and Perfection [the direct experience of God]."[22]

So began a long period during which mythic Christianity persecuted many whose consciousness had attained the psychic level. Tens of thousands in Europe alone, mostly women, were burned as witches. The same harshness was often applied to tribal medicine men and women wherever mythic Christianity sent its missionaries. St. Joan of Arc, whose reputation has since been rehabilitated, was one of thousands of spiritually advanced persons who were condemned and executed by Christianity.

Christianity, of course, is not the only religion that has experienced degeneration. The degeneration of the levels of consciousness as a spiritual reality into the caste system as a social reality was (and to a large extent remains) a catastrophe for Hinduism. All religious movements tend to regress after the death of their higher-consciousness founders as the religion, religious community, or other spiritual movement, is taken over by persons of lower consciousness. The lower-consciousness disciples, since they cannot understand the Spirit, always tend to emphasize the religion's forms, including its thought-forms, long after the usefulness of such forms has passed. Christianity would never have survived until now without the periodic reforms, under the guidance of Jesus, of the saints and others with higher levels of awareness. To survive until the end of the third millennium, Christianity will have to become still more adaptive in obedience to the Spirit within its adherents.

Today, just as the consciousness of many educated Christians is rapidly advancing to the fifth level of vision-logic, many dedicated spiritual seekers are advancing into the psychic level. Beginning with the Spiritualist movement of the last century, and extending into the much more

---

[22]St. Clement of Alexandria, in *The Stromata*.

broad-based contemporary new age movement, these seekers, including thousands of Christians, are contributing significantly to humanity's spiritual revival, one that will be
planetary in scope and comprehensively ecumenical in character. The new planetary ecumenism will be based more
upon the contributions that each religion and denomination
can make to the furtherance of human consciousness, and
not as much on the patching of old institutional ruptures.

It is true that there is much regressiveness in the new age
movement (sometimes a reversion to magic and a naive ide-
alization of primitive societies). There is also a large amount
of commercial hucksterism and psychic charlatanism. There
are also new agers who imagine themselves specially chosen
by God to "save the world" by means of some new revelation.

In addition, there is a fair amount of low-grade channeling, the type that sees calamities occurring everywhere with
California and New York City usually cast in the role of Sodom
and Gomorrah. There is a large undercurrent of puritanical,
anti-city, anti-technology sentiment still extant in American
spirituality. Some new agers of this type, often mistranslating
higher-level transformational energies as physical ones, seem
more interested in seeing San Francisco leveled by earthquakes
and washed out to sea than in recognizing the work of the
Spirit in the wondrous spiritual transformations that have
swept the former USSR, Eastern Europe, South Africa, and
elsewhere. I am not suggesting, however, that all predictions
of calamities be rejected out of hand; some can be genuine
prophetic warnings: Some calamities *could* happen absent sustained spiritual growth by a sufficient number of humans.

This is perhaps the best place to note that we should use
a great deal of discernment with respect to channeling. Just as
was the case in the early Church, some channeling (or
prophecy) is sounder than others. Much depends upon the
level of spiritual development of the channel and on the level
of spirit tuned into. Genuine spiritual teachers, i.e., those with
the Christ Consciousness, are not in the business of satisfying
idle curiosity. They never disrespect human freedom by telling

people what to do. Nor are they usually concerned with either world events or everyday matters except to use such events to make a spiritual point. Finally, they will never say anything incompatible with the core teachings of the great religions.

Despite all the faults that I have just listed, however, the new age movement also contains a great amount of genuine spirituality. There are thousands of serious spiritual seekers and, as Jesus said, those who truly seek will truly find (Matt. 7:7-8). There are many gifted healers, and many channellers who are genuinely in touch with the higher spiritual realms. Powerful, high-level spiritual transformations are occurring at new age events held by genuinely spiritual persons. I have personally seen a number of such transformations in consciousness and I mean genuine, permanent, spiritual conversions and rebirths, not weekend emotional "highs" manufactured through emotional and mental manipulation (as happens with some cultish commercial groups).

In the new age movement, not surprisingly, mythic Christianity has found still another enemy to fight and condemn in the name of God. Not long ago, for example, a then American Catholic Archbishop gave a blanket denouncement of the new age movement as paganism and superstition. Many Christian fundamentalists see in the new age the work of the Devil. In response to such critics, I ask, "Where are Christians who are trying to advance in consciousness to the psychic level and beyond to go for support and guidance?" Educated and spiritually serious Christians are turning to the new age largely because mainstream Christianity is not watering the spirituality of those who seek beyond conventional levels. This can be remedied, of course, if the Church itself undertakes serious and widespread spiritual renewal. I sincerely pray for such a spiritual renewal.

Chapter 10

THE DARK NIGHT OF THE SENSES

The spiritual transition between the psychic level of consciousness and the next level, the subtle, is the "Dark Night of the Senses." This is the name give to this passage four hundred years ago by St. John of the Cross (1542-91), a religious reformer and friend of St. Teresa of Avila. Considered by many to be one of the finest poets in the Spanish language, he was also the author of major works on mystical theology, such as The Dark Night *and* The Ascent of Mount Carmel.

Because my personal experience of this transition was so close to John's, (not in externals but in inner experience), and as I don't think I can improve on his description of this inner passage, I use John to describe this spiritual initiation. I follow St. John in using the "seven deadly sins" to portray the faults and neuroses of even those professionally spiritual persons whose awareness has risen to this level. The inner dynamics of this passage can be understood both in terms of modern depth psychology and in terms of metaphysical principles (for example, the existence of higher and lower spiritual vibrations). It is also important to note the advent of what the Christian tradition has called "infused contemplation" (and some Hindus call kundalini)—the infusion of energies from the higher self.

The Dark Night of the Senses constitutes the transition between the psychic and subtle levels of consciousness. The name "Dark Night of the Senses" was coined by the

Carmelite priest St. John of the Cross in the sixteenth century and has been accepted into much of the Christian spiritual tradition since that time. In one of the Western Christian esoteric traditions, this transition is called the "transfiguration" or third spiritual initiation and is the spiritual initiation symbolized by the Gospel account of Jesus' transfiguration. According to this same tradition, the first initiation is symbolized in the Gospels by Jesus' infancy narrative and is called "The Birth of the Christ" in the soul. The first initiation involves the mastery of the body and of sexual and survival (economic) urges. The second initiation, according to that tradition, is called "baptism," as symbolized by the Gospel account of Jesus' baptism, and involves the mastery (civilizing) of the emotions. Some evangelical born-again conversions may result from the taking of the first or second initiations or the experiential climaxes of those initiations.

John of the Cross is rightly esteemed because he was the first person in Christianity to clearly describe the passage from psychic to subtle consciousness. Even though I have personally experienced this passage on my own path (see the introduction), there is not much I can add to what John says. But I can place his account in the general context of human consciousness development, and translate it into language that is more understandable today.

John of the Cross begins his map of the spiritual path somewhere in the psychic level. He calls the psychic level "the state of beginners," whom he defines as "those who practice meditation on the spiritual road" but who are not yet "proficients."

A person in this "beginning" state, is by John's own definition, already a meditator, a person who has become accustomed to "praying always" with eyes focused more within than without (1 Thes. 5:17). Not only that, but the person, like John himself, has already developed his or her inner psychic senses in a manner sufficient to actually see and feel with great accuracy the work that the Spirit is accomplishing within the psyche.

John notes "that God nurtures and caresses the soul, *after it has been resolutely converted to his service* [emphasis added], like a loving mother who warms her child with the heat of her bosom, nurses it with good milk and tender food, and carries and caresses it in her arms." He says that the person begins to experience "intense satisfaction in the performance of spiritual exercises, because God is handing the breast of his tender love to the soul, just as if it were a delicate child. The soul finds its joy, therefore, in spending lengthy periods at prayer, perhaps even entire nights; its penances are pleasures; its fasts, happiness."[23]

After we have become competent at the psychic level, we begin to feel within ourselves the subtle vibrations of the next higher level of consciousness, the subtle level. Neither God nor the soul wastes time. As soon as we are competent at one level, the next transition begins.

In the Christian tradition these subtle energies are usually called "infused contemplation," with the emphasis being on the action of God (by means of the higher subtle energies); the meditator is seen as a passive recipient. In some Eastern traditions, the energies are called the kundalini, and the emphasis is on the effects these energies sometimes have on the body and emotions.

Sometimes the arrival of infused contemplation or kundalini causes great disturbance. The American mystic Lawrence Richardson reports that he first tried to learn a secret meditation/breathing technique from an Orthodox church but was turned away because he was not a member. So he learned another one from a yoga monastery. He began doing 450 of the breathing exercises a day, lasting four hours. He reports:

> The Spirit would flow into my heart and start burning and I couldn't get it to stop. The burning would proceed into my lungs and I could not take a deep breath for days, let alone do the breathing exercises. In about a week the

---

[23]John of the Cross, *The Dark Night*, Book One, chapter 1, pp. 361-2, in *The Collected Works of St. John of the Cross*, translated by Kieran Kavanaugh, O.C.D. and Otilio Rodriguez, O.C.D., ICS Publications, Institute of Carmelite Studies, Washington, D.C., 1991.

Spirit would dissipate. . . . This happened to me six times that year. . . . I had read that by adding clarified butter to one's diet it would help with the heat. So I wrote the yoga monastery. . . . The abbot called me. Quite concerned he stressed very forcefully that I was about to permanently damage my nervous system, and instructed me to cut back on my devotional routine, now! When I resigned myself to fewer breaths the problem never returned.

I also know a young person who opened up to the kundalini by the use of street drugs. In this person the "fire" burned for months, almost incapacitating the person. That person is still recovering under the guidance of a spiritual master. I have also known of several priests who, by intense spiritual exercises, opened themselves to the energies of infused contemplation. But, intellectually, for whatever reason, they were apparently unable or unwilling to let go of the rigid mythic belief system in which they had been schooled. Their inner battle between head and heart resulted in disaster. They ended up in mental hospitals after suffering nervous breakdowns. I don't think any of them has fully recovered.

The contemporary Indian spiritual master Sri Sri Ravi Shankar has introduced many Americans to a special breathing exercise that Spirit gave to him. But he prohibits people from doing the exercises on their own. They must be done in a group. I have enjoyed doing this exercise on many occasions. What often happens in newcomers to meditation is that the exercises stir up physical and emotional "stuff." I attended one session at which some people began laughing hysterically and couldn't stop. Others began crying uncontrollably. Others let out all sorts of moans and groans. This is not unusual, and it is expected to happen. So, boxes of tissues are kept on hand to handle the tears, and the exercise is *always* done under supervision, in a safe place, and only once.

In many monasteries and seminaries, infused contemplation brings on what I call the "grinny ninnies." I remember them from my own days in the monastery. People get very high on the spiritual energies and often very silly. They go about for days with smiles permanently affixed to their faces. I've seen this in Hindu and Buddhist monasteries, too. As John of the Cross notes, meditators sometimes mistake these initial highs (which traditional Christian spirituality called "consolations") for genuine spiritual bliss.

In my own case (perhaps because I wasn't using a powerful breathing technique, but more likely for reasons I will suggest in chapter 21), I experienced none of the above. I never felt any energy rushing up my spine, as some have reported, or any other disturbing phenomena. When I opened to infused contemplation at sixteen, living in a monastery, it was a joy. I relate this here because my own experience was like John of the Cross'. He too reports none of the above described problems. But these problems can be serious ones for people who have never before opened to these energies. Serious meditators and their spiritual directors, therefore, need to be prepared in case these types of things occur.

Regarding infused contemplation, the vibrations coming into the psyche from the subtle level are higher than anything we have felt before. They are exquisitely beautiful, warm, intelligent, and dazzling. We would rather pray than do anything else because we know there is nothing else that could possibly make us feel any better. Even sex pales in comparison to the energy pleasures we are feeling by means of our inner senses. The subtle energies are so delightful that we may be high on God for hours or days on end, easily praying all night, as John said.

It is not enough, however, to feel these vibrations when at prayer. To move into the subtle level of consciousness, to *live* there, is the goal the Spirit has in mind for the meditator. This cannot be done without healing and transmuting a sizable part of our deeply (and most often unconsciously) held negative emotional and mental vibrations. That is because these negative vibrations literally *weigh us down*, making us spiritually unable to advance into the higher subtle realm.

As chapter 4 noted, the higher we ascend in the spiritual life the less dense or lighter our consciousness becomes. A definite quantity of these heavy negative vibrations, therefore, must be transmuted by the incoming subtle energies (i.e., changed into a lighter and faster vibrating form of energy) for us to graduate into the subtle level. I say "definite quantity," "heavy," "lighter," and "faster" not because we can actually weigh or clock these vibrations physically, but because these physical terms are analogous to what is happening on the astral level. To give a concrete example, we feel lighter emotionally when we come out of a depression or a period of sadness or release a fear. This is the type of transmutation of energy, from a heavy form to a lighter one, that the subtle energies bring about.

Each level of consciousness has a distinct vibratory frequency. It is analogous to the frequencies of the musical scale or the colors of the rainbow. Matter vibrates at the densest frequency and possesses the least consciousness. The subtle energies, in contrast, have great inherent intelligence. They have such a great amount of inherent intelligence (as well as beauty and power) that one can properly call them "angelic."

The negative emotional vibrations are most often locked away by denial in the shadow sections of the person's astral body. There are also negative mental vibrations stored in the thought body (the higher portion of the astral body). These include beliefs like "I am not a worthy person," "Nobody loves me," "I never get a break," "Everything always goes wrong for me," etc.). This negativity will burn up like fire when the subtle energies, at first so wondrously pleasant, finally hit those dark corners of the psyche.

The subtle vibrations will reach those dark corners when the meditator finally relaxes enough, trusts the spiritual process, and lets go of fear (breathing it out, so to speak). In fact, a good capsule definition for the spiritual path is that it is a never-ending process of relaxing, of breathing in light, breathing out fear, and of coming into fear's opposite, which is love (1 John 4:18).

St. John of the Cross spends half of his account of the Dark Night of the Senses describing the spiritually weak condition of "beginners." He does a masterful job describing the neurotic egotisms and the selfishness that afflict beginning contemplatives. Beginners will only be able to clearly see their egotism in hindsight, after the inner purification is over, he says. This too is the case at every level and why one must have complete trust and faith in God and in the spiritual healing process itself. One can never see with exactness where one is going; one can only see afterwards where one has been.

Keeping in mind that St. John was writing primarily for monks and nuns, what he says is nevertheless applicable to serious Christian meditators. He says that beginners "conduct themselves in a very weak and imperfect manner." Regarding their spiritual pride, he says "their motivation in their spiritual works and exercises is the consolation and satisfaction they experience in them," and that "they develop a somewhat vain—at times very vain—desire to speak of spiritual things in others' presence, and sometimes even to instruct rather than be instructed; in their hearts they condemn others who do not seem to have the kind of devotion they would like them to have." They "do not want anyone except themselves to appear holy. . . . They want others to recognize their spirit and devotion." They search for a spiritual director "who will congratulate them and be impressed by their deeds." John further says, "they are often extremely anxious that God remove their faults and imperfections, but their motive is personal peace rather than God."[24]

Regarding their spiritual greed, John says they never have enough of collecting spiritual books, maxims, pictures, and objects. They become attached to all sorts of spiritual paraphernalia. This trait is noticeable today in the new age movement. There is a constant "collecting" of workshops, paraphernalia, and books, a constant dabbling in every sort of healing and religious tradition, a perpetual shopping for the guru who'll give one effortless and instant enlightenment. It also remains a problem in traditional seminaries, monasteries, and convents.

As for spiritual lust, John says beginners often try to get inordinate pleasure from spiritual exercises, from their attraction to spiritual persons and instructors, and from

---

[24]St. John of the Cross, ibid., chapters 1 & 2, pp. 362, 363, 364.

either indulging or fearing the impure thoughts and feelings that arise during prayer. These thoughts and feelings are to be expected at this stage as repressed unconscious emotions begin to loosen up and enter the light of awareness.

Regarding anger, John says beginners become peevish when they don't get consolations in prayer. They also "become angry over the sins of others, reprove these others . . . setting themselves up as lords of virtue" And, "in becoming aware of their own imperfections, they grow angry with themselves . . . they want to become saints in a day."[25] They also make great resolutions and get angry with themselves when they can't keep them.

Regarding gluttony, John says these beginners get such great delight with spiritual practices they go overboard and "kill themselves with penances" or "weaken themselves by fasts."[26] They become attached to pleasure in prayer and seek that rather than God. They neglect their other duties and are generally willful and stubborn.

Finally, with respect to envy and sloth, these people are sad when others progress ahead of them; they try to criticize their betters and bring them down, and they grow weary of spiritual exercises if they're not getting some kind of high out of it.

All of this egotism, John says, will never be conquered by the spiritual efforts of these beginners. That is because their spiritual athleticism is always something *they* are doing, rather than what *God* is accomplishing in them. Even at this relatively high level of human consciousness, with people who are devoted to a life for God, the seeker is still caught up in the selfishness of what John calls "these trivialities and childish ways."[27]

All this will end when the higher subtle energies encounter the person's deep seated negativities that, so far, the person has hidden even from himself. As John says, "No

---

[25]St. John of the Cross, ibid., chapter 5, p. 370.
[26]St. John of the Cross, ibid., chapter 6, p. 371.
[27]St. John of the Cross, ibid., chapter 7, p. 375.

matter how earnestly beginners in all their actions and passions practice the mortification of self, they will never be able to do so entirely—far from it—until God accomplishes it in them passively by means of the purgation of this night."[28]

When the subtle energies come in, and the Dark Night of Senses begins in earnest, the person, now able to "feel" psychic events, will often experience psychic pain, especially if her emotional woundedness is deep, and if there is unconscious resistance of which there normally is a good deal. On the positive side, this transformation will release the creative energies that have been used, up until then, to repress those parts of self the person heretofore judged against; usually parts of the self involving aggression and sexuality.

The transformation will unlock the truths, usually trapped in denial, that have to be faced and accepted. In the end, the person, having been set free by the truth, will be far better off emotionally and usually physically (John 8:32). To the extent these negative vibrations are already in the process of being cleared by manifesting in the etheric and physical bodies as disease (disease being one way to cleanse the psyche of them) the advent of the subtle energy flow may have pronounced effects upon the person's physical health, ultimately for the better. The higher energies will usually clear out the most life-threatening energies first, followed in order by the progressively less threatening ones.

I am not saying that a realization of the original causes of one's neuroses or emotional damages is necessary here as it is in psychotherapy. It is not, though a psychologically educated contemporary Christian will likely be made aware of some of these causes as the Night progresses. One of the great values of this natural psychotherapy is that the causes of the inner negativity need not even be considered any more than we'd go through last week's trash saying, "Ah, here's the remnants of Sunday dinner, and here's Tuesday's

---

[28]Ibid.

lunch." You just toss the trash and be done with it.[29] The Night surpasses psychotherapy not only because it cleanses us of even emotional damages we know nothing about, but also because it is a much more thorough-going cleansing .

But before the healing comes the pain.[30] John says the person is plunged into "such darkness that they do not know which way to turn in their discursive imaginings."[31] There is extreme aridity of spirit. Nothing the person does, including any kind of prayer or spiritual exercise, gives emotional satisfaction. There is only a deep inner anguish that is with the person twenty-four hours a day and for months on end. The aridity may also be accompanied at times by depression. But, unlike the case in normal depressions, the person is always aware that the depression and aridity are a healing work of Spirit.

I make this distinction between normal depression and the Dark Night of the Senses following John, who labels what I've called normal depression "melancholy." It could be that the normal depression experienced at the lower levels of consciousness (when the person is lacking the considerable awareness of self that the experienced meditator has) are also caused by the light the higher self is sending to the person to clear away denials and neuroses. If so, then even normal depression could be seen not so much as a disease (the view of most contemporary psychiatrists) but as a spiritual initiation meant to bring the person to a higher level of awareness.

With the advent of this Night, vocal prayer becomes almost impossible. Visualization (the contemporary term for imaginative prayer) likewise becomes almost impossible.

---

[29]I am indebted to the Hindu spiritual master Sri Sri Ravi Shankar for the trash removal analogy.

[30]There is at least one meditation technique, the integral yoga of the late Indian Hindu spiritual master Aurobindo Ghose, that reportedly is able to take a person through this level (and other levels) without the intense psychic pain. If so, it is certainly worth exploring. Other Eastern techniques (such as Zen) seem no more able to avoid this pain than the techniques of the Christian tradition.

[31]St. John of the Cross, ibid., chapter 8, p. 376.

Spiritual exercises that were once enjoyable become onerous, an ordeal, and sometimes an object of revulsion and disgust. Nor does anything else help or ease the situation.

The person is often wracked by feelings of lust, anger, and confusion as the repressed contents of the unconscious surface. John calls these "evil spirits" the spirits of fornication, blasphemy, and vertigo (confusion). For example, John says, "An angel of Satan, which is the spirit of fornication, is given to some to buffet their senses with strong and abominable temptations, and afflict their spirit with foul thoughts and very vivid images, *which sometimes is a pain worse than death for them* [emphasis added]."[32]

"At other times," he says, "a blasphemous spirit is added; it commingles intolerable blasphemies with all one's thoughts and ideas. Sometimes these blasphemies are so strongly suggested to the imagination that the soul is almost made to pronounce them, *which is a grave torment to it* [emphasis added]."[33] John is describing repressed aggression, especially aggression against religious authority (hence "blasphemous").

These two passages from John give some inkling of the spiritual damage that has been caused by the Church's repression of sexual expression and genuine self-assertion through the centuries to the point that millions of Christians hold significant amounts of repressed anger directed against their churches. Like the Pharisees of Jesus' time, the Church has often heaped up huge burdens upon its followers, burdens sometimes so oppressive that they have kept many Christians from entering the consciousness of Jesus' Kingdom (Luke 11:46, 52; Matt 23:1-36).

In the Church's defense, however, the consciousness of a mythic level person (and even more so than that of a person at the tribal-magical-animist level) is close to, and heavily conditioned by, matter and its forms. The disciplining of sexuality and aggression is a difficult issue for such persons. Only at higher

---

[32]St. John of the Cross, ibid., Chapter 14, p. 393.
[33]Ibid.

levels of consciousness do both sexuality and aggression become servants to be used in the pursuit of awareness. At the lower levels it is often the person who is the servant, with sexuality and aggression as the masters, and it is mostly persons at these lower levels that, until recently, the Church has had to serve.

John says that the third negative spirit, the spirit of vertigo or confusion, fills the person with worries and scruples of all sorts and the person often gets so emotionally upset that no amount of rationalizing, or consoling by others, is of any help.

It is true that most meditators judge their repressed negative emotions, including those involving sexuality and aggression, as "demons" and "evil." In that sense, John is merely being descriptive of their judgments and of his own as he went through this transition. It is also true that these repressed emotions are "evil" both in the sense of being unbalanced, and because they have been, up until now, the cause of the person's unconscious negativity and negative behaviors.

Further, it is true that these repressed negative parts of the self (our inner "shadow" or darkness) are sometimes magnetically linked to the energies of other dark (negative) entities that share the same low vibrations. The dark entities to which these damaged soul parts can be linked include negative thought forms, discarnate human beings who, for one reason or another, have not found their way to the Light, and perhaps even real demons (the dark angels who emanate from, and answer to, the Archangel Lucifer).[34]

But none of these—negative thought forms, negative discarnate human beings, the dark angels, Archangel Lucifer—are "evil" (see chapter 19 for a fuller explanation). They are simply negative. The Archangel Lucifer's job, as assigned by God, is to be in charge of the negative pole of Creation. From Lucifer emanate the dark forces, first and foremost fear (the true opposite of love), and then countless other negative angels (energies) who carry the negative emotions of pride, anger, lust, envy, sloth,

---

[34]For a psychiatrist's description of her encounters with these dark forces in the course of her healing work, see Shakuntala Modi, M.D., *Remarkable Healings*, Hampton Roads, Charlottesville, 1997.

jealousy, covetousness, selfishness, greed, etc. These energies are negative, but each of these emotions is essential for the evolution of human consciousness into the wholeness of the Christ Consciousness. If they weren't, God would not have created them nor would God continue to hold them in existence.

It is best to show compassion, not fear, for all the dark forces. They are just doing their jobs. Send them love and they will either be transformed into the light or, if they fear the light you send them, they will go away. The dark angels, like the angelic energies of light, are intelligent. They also each have a kernel of truth (light) at their core. That is why Lucifer's name means "light bearer." They too can be transformed into light and the truth they hold released.

Let me give a practical example. Suppose a little girl is physically abused by a man. What often happens is that part of her soul becomes so damaged and fearful because of this abuse that it splits off from her conscious awareness. The girl now has little conscious remembrance of what happened and/or of the terrible feelings that accompanied the abuse. You could say, if you wanted to picture this or speak mythologically about it, that an angel of Lucifer, a demon of fear, had seized control of that part of the girl's soul (whether or not the demon may have a separate identity of its own is not at all important). From now on, unknown to her consciously, a demon of fear is in her. But that demon is just doing its job, which is twofold:

First, the demon protects her from further abuse. You can be sure that if that little girl, even decades later as a grown woman, comes across a man with abusive energies (which is very likely since fear magnetically attracts what is feared), the fear inside her will cause her to "pick up on" the man's energies, to be aware of those energies and her own fear of them, and will perhaps cause her to flee that man. Second, by sealing that part of the girl's soul off from the rest of her psyche and conscious awareness, the demon allows the rest of the girl's psyche to function so that she can live a relatively happy life.

That split-off part, however, usually causes some problems. The hurt little girl inside the woman may have concluded that all men are abusers. Because of the little girl's fear and this unbalanced conclusion, the woman, perhaps to her great frustration, may fail whenever she tries to establish a lovingly intimate relationship with a man. The woman is also cut off from the spontaneity and innocence she had when she was that little girl. Worst of all, the woman can end up being an abuser of children herself. Research shows that child abusers in virtually one hundred percent of cases have been abused as children themselves. The worst part of denial (the inability or refusal to face our own inner pain) is that we often end up doing to others exactly what was done to us.

Eventually the soul will want to heal that dark part and reunite it with the rest of the soul. It will usually do that by making the girl or woman conscious that she has that fear, perhaps by psychotherapy, meditation, by magnetically attracting another man with abusive energies, or perhaps by exploring the feelings behind her own abusive behavior. Once the fear is conscious, the demon of fear can be thanked for its work, and the truths it held (an awareness of the energy of abuse, and awareness of what it is like to suffer abuse) can be made forever a part of that woman's soul experience. The little girl's spontaneity and innocence can also be restored, and the "lie" of the demon—that all men are abusers—can be released.

Whatever the nature of the demons one encounters during this spiritual passage, there is no need to condemn them, fear them, or run away from them. The terrible psychic pain of this transition is caused by *resistance* to unlocking these repressed parts of self, letting go of fears, and owning truths. And the length of the passage is also a result of resistance. Condemning, fearing, running away from, or fighting these demons increases the resistance and pain, and it prolongs the agony.

The meditator should stop the judgments, and look upon these damaged parts of the soul (and any negative spirits that may be attached to them) with compassion. The meditator should relax, surrender to God in trust, and simply allow the healing process to do its work quickly and with a minimum of resistance and pain. Normally, however, this is advice more easily given than heeded by the person desperate to maintain his or her social (and church) approved image of being a "good" person. As John says, the encounter with the demon is a "grave torment" and "sometimes a pain worse than death" because it is profoundly embarrassing and humiliating to the person who took pride in his or her "goodness." The last thing we want to admit is having inner demons of any kind, let alone showing compassion for those damaged parts of ourselves.

As John indicates, what is learned from this encounter with the shadow side of oneself is (1) humility, and (2) the beginnings of some real compassion for oneself and others. Up until now, at least unconsciously, we took great pride in our spiritual and creative achievements (as opposed to all those sinners, atheists, and others out there). Until now, to be honest, we secretly supposed God must be very pleased with us, perhaps, like Jesus' disciples, imagining we were already worthy to sit at the Lord's right side (Matt. 20:20-24).

The Night is a rude awakening, exposing to our conscious awareness, and often even to others, those demonic parts of ourselves we'd been schooled by parents, church, and society to keep under wraps. Having finally begun to thoroughly confront our own inner demons, we are no longer as quick to judge and look down upon others. We realize that our "goodness" is not *ours* at all, but a gift, like all else, from God who, as Jesus said, is the *only* possessor of goodness (Luke 18:19).

Before this time we were capable of real compassion only occasionally, usually, as Jesus said, only for family, friends, or co-religionists (Matt. 5:46-47). We were still incapable of compassion in an ongoing, comprehensive, universal sense. Rather we usually *pitied* others we *judged* (normally in terms of externals such as church attendance, professed beliefs, or behaviors) less virtuous or less well-off than ourselves. A prime example of this pity masquerading as compassion is the attitude of many towards gay persons, prisoners, and intravenous drug users with AIDS. Such so-called "compassion" is actually a simple-minded way of looking down upon others. Compassion as virtue, that is, as an habitually empathic attitude towards *all* persons, comes only after the Night of Senses.

In speaking of compassion, I am using both a contemporary term and the term that is the goal of Buddhist spirituality. Compassion, in the Buddhist sense and in the sense I am describing here, is identical to Christian love, the nonjudgmental, unconditional love that is the goal of Christian spirituality. The goal of the Dark Night of Senses is none other than the emergence in a person of the spiritual capacity for universal love. During this passage, our heart center, the focal point of the astral body, opens up, after having been virtually closed since childhood by a host of fears. In transforming these fears, we at last begin to know what love means, and genuinely start to love the way Jesus did.

This Dark Night of Senses can go on for years and often does. Because of all the negativity that is being transmuted by being released into conscious awareness, all sorts of negative things tend to occur in our outer lives. This is because negative thoughts and negative emotions (conscious or unconscious) *produce*, by the laws of manifestation, negative external consequences in a person's life. This has always been the case, of course, but we may now finally become *consciously aware* of the fact.

If these outside mirror reflections of our inner world are carefully examined, they will usually shed much light on the types of emotional imbalances being healed within. Perhaps they will illuminate the nature of the negative false beliefs we harbor about ourselves. So, we can work with the external to heal the internal, and vice versa, and we can use dreamwork to check our progress with respect to both. Some people will also benefit from psychotherapy during this Night. Thus, we begin to learn the art of always being aware of our thoughts and feelings in dialogue with external circumstances. This is a skill that can be sharpened by journal keeping and/or dreamwork, and one that will serve us in good stead as we go farther on the spiritual path.[35]

---

[35]Dreams occur in the astral "half-way" world between normal waking consciousness and deep dreamless sleep (when our consciousness rests in the causal/spiritual realm). Because they exist in this half-way world, dreams can be used by the higher self to communicate—by means of symbols—to

Another reason why it becomes increasingly important to discipline one's thoughts, and especially speech from this point on, is that our power to affect the outer world by thought and speech grows exponentially as we ascend the levels of consciousness (James 5:16). We must become much more responsible for watching what we think and say, lest we damage our own lives or the world itself. We need to take full responsibility for the increased voltage of our manifestational ability. Jesus, emphasizing this point, said, "I tell you this: on the Judgment Day everyone will have to give account of every useless word he has ever spoken" (Matt. 12:36). Remember how Jesus killed the fig tree by merely cursing it (Matt. 21:18-22). Great psychic power, thank God, comes to us exactly proportionate to our growth in awareness, responsibleness, and love, and is not available to those of lesser spiritual growth.

Eventually the Night will come to its natural end, and I use the word "natural" here and elsewhere for a reason. Unlike most of the traditional Christian accounts of the spiritual path, I call nothing that happens on the path "supernatural." I have long thought that the distinction between natural and supernatural (and "sacred" and "profane," "natural" and "miraculous") creates more confusion than it sheds light. There is some practical usefulness in distinguishing holy water from regular water or sacred places from the non-sacred, but there is nothing in God's universe that, in the final analysis, is not holy or sacred. If we prefer, we may call *everything* that occurs in the growth of human consciousness (or consciousness in general) supernatural, that is, the product of God's grace. Or, if we have a mental bent more like modern science and the Buddhists, we may

---

our everyday consciousness. And, as psychotherapy has discovered, dreams often portray "where we are" spiritually with far more accuracy than our everyday awareness. Dreams, for example, can let us know what issues we are working on, both consciously and unconsciously, and what fears are currently blocking us. They can suggest ways to overcome those fears, and, by changes in the dreams themselves over time, can let us know what progress we are making in overcoming the fears.

The Seven Levels of Consciousness of the Human Personality

call it all natural. Or again, following the incarnational theology of the early Church Councils, we may call it both natural and supernatural at the same time. What is not correct is to label some things and events as natural and other things and events as supernatural as we so often do; this is an error often further compounded when we mean by supernatural some sort of magical divine intervention.[36]

With the natural end of the Night of Senses, as John puts it, we will find our "house being now all stilled."[37] Our consciousness will then pop up to the next level, that of subtle consciousness, to which we now turn.

---

[36]On this point the great student of comparative religions, Mircea Eliade, writes, "The sacred is qualitatively different from the profane, yet it may manifest itself no matter how or where in the profane world because of its power of turning any natural object into a paradox by means of a hierophany (it ceases to be itself, as a natural object, though in appearance it remains unchanged. . . . If it is true . . . that the simplest definition of the sacred remains 'the opposite of profane,' it is also clear . . . that the dialectic of hierophanies tends endlessly to reduce the spheres that are profane and eventually to abolish them. Some of the highest religious experiences identify the sacred with the whole universe. To many a mystic the integrated quality of the cosmos is itself a hierophany. 'The whole universe, from Brahma down to a blade of grass is one form or another of Him,' exclaims the [Hindu] Mahanirvana Tantra." Mircea Eliade, *Patterns in Comparative Religion*, Sheed & Ward, 1958, New American Library, 1963, pp. 30, 459.

[37]St. John of the Cross, ibid., chapter 13, p. 392.

Chapter 11

SUBTLE CONSCIOUSNESS

St. Teresa of Avila has written masterfully about the subtle level. St. Teresa (1515-82), the first woman Doctor of the Catholic Church, entered the Carmelite religious community in 1536. Many years later (around 1555) she had a second religious "conversion" which eventually led her to start a reformed branch of her religious community. She was assisted in this by her friend and fellow mystic St. John of the Cross. Among her writings were her Life, The Way of Perfection, *and her masterpiece,* The Interior Castle.

After the death of the Night of Senses and rebirth into the subtle level (the constant Christian theme at every level), our consciousness feels "as if liberated from a cramped prison cell" (St. John of the Cross). The subtle level is the last level at which our self will be identified with our human personality. At the subtle level, our consciousness becomes capable of receiving direct communications from the causal level, the level of the soul. We gain immediate contact with our guardian angel (the angel of the true self), our own spiritual master, and Jesus himself. All three of these serve as messengers (angels) of the true self and guide us towards our final individuation as a human being.

If we are especially psychic, like Teresa, we may begin to hear voices and/or heavenly music, experience visions, have raptures and spiritual revelations, or experience the other subtle inner phenomena of this level. Gradually, as we become more individuated, and as we grow closer in consciousness to the level of the soul, our worldview and psychic structure will begin to unravel. We move simultaneously upward into the causal level and downward into the Dark Night of the Soul.

The subtle level of consciousness is the seventh and last level of consciousness of the human personality. It is the last level at which we understand our identity to be that of a mere human being. St. John of the Cross, in his attempt to fit his five-stage map into the older three-fold traditional map of the spiritual life, calls the level of subtle human consciousness "the illuminative way or the way of infused contemplation." That is, he sees this level as the second level of the traditional three-fold spiritual path. It is a level of human consciousness far above the consciousness of most people, a fact John acknowledges but never tries to explain.

Beginning with this chapter, John's soul companion on the spiritual journey, St. Teresa of Avila, will be added as a guide. She and John were true "soul mates." Teresa's psychic and subtle "seeing" abilities were much more developed than John's. As a result, she was able to see and feel a lot more of the various occurrences on this part of the path than he.

I wrote at the end of the last chapter that our consciousness "pops up" from the psychic into the subtle level of consciousness. This abrupt kind of shift actually occurs at every level but, as is the case at the higher levels, we now become much more consciously aware of what is happening. Often, for example, after the long years of inner preparation in the Dark Night of the Senses,[38] we emerge into the

---

[38]All of the time-frames I am giving with respect to the higher levels of consciousness are based upon my own experience, which generally parallels John of the Cross'. But it must be remembered that the Christian path generally does not use a scientific method of meditation. I believe that all of these time frames can be shortened considerably were one to be used, especially if used under the direct tutelage of an incarnate spiritual master.

subtle level in the space of an hour, a day, or a week. The Christian tradition aptly calls these transformational endings "rebirths."

We have died to the old level of consciousness, which in hindsight is seen to have presented an inadequate, incomplete, constricted, and distorted picture of the world in which we live (and of Jesus' teachings), and are reborn into a new, more expansive and finer world.[39] John of the Cross writes with respect to entrance into the level of subtle consciousness, "In this new state, as one liberated from a cramped prison cell, it [the soul] goes about the things of God with much more freedom and satisfaction of spirit and with more abundant interior delight."[40]

Whenever we are reborn into a new level of consciousness, we feel that we have finally discovered the truth. We always feel that we have finally come home. We always feel psychologically stronger and more integrated. And we always

---

[39]For many years there has been a debate among the scientists who study evolution as to whether past evolution from one level of complexity to another proceeded gradually or by sudden catastrophe. To the psychically gifted person who has developed his or her consciousness into the subtle realm (human consciousness being, among other things, evolution finally becoming aware if itself), it may be seen that evolution proceeds by a combination of both. Ordinarily, everything is gradual. After the sudden rebirth into a new level, it may (and often does) take several years to become fully accustomed to the energies at that level. For example, the very same subtle energies that caused all that commotion (when they broke through into the psychic level) now become normal. Next the person must become competent at the new level of awareness, gaining facility in the use of the insights and abilities of that level in their everyday life. God, in fact, will send them just the challenges they need to gain this competency. This too usually takes years. Finally, when competency is mastered, the energies of the next level begin to come in, ushering in the whole tumultuous (catastrophic) death and rebirth process all over again. And so it goes. The same mechanism operates throughout the evolutionary process, including that of physical and social evolution.

[40]St. John of the Cross, *The Dark Night*, book 2, chapter 1, ibid., p. 395.

wonder why we could not before see the truth of the new level, which is now obvious.

The first thing the reborn person is usually tempted to do is to write a book, or to go on the preaching circuit to tell others about this truth, just as Jesus did when he emerged from the desert. Many do so, though sometimes it might be better if they did not. Jesus constantly admonished those whom he had healed to keep silent and tell no one about what had happened to them. And one reason he did so was perhaps because he knew that the person, though healed and reborn, had lots more deaths and rebirths to go through before they could come fully into the mind of Christ. By preaching and gathering followers, instead of humbly moving on, we may end up stuck at the new level for the rest of our lives.

In being reborn at any level, we always gain a clearer, more comprehensive, freer, and detached system of beliefs, a belief system closer to the mind of Jesus and the core values of Christianity. This new belief system (which includes but transcends the old) always affords a more aerial view of the world. The people we left behind at the old level are now seen to be stuck in more materialistically based details and distinctions that do not matter to Jesus or God, their consciousness weighed down and "blinded" by the denseness of matter and its limitations. But the new more aerial view is also, paradoxically, a more grounded and down-to-earth consciousness than the one we had previously, one less caught up in preconceived assumptions, concepts, and head trips, one that is more accurate in seeing the actual world (visible and invisible) around us. All this is abundantly true of entrance into the subtle level.

Once we have consciously realized the subtle level, it will usually take some years to get accustomed to the energies at this level and become competent exercising them in our everyday life. As John says, "after having emerged from the state of beginners, the soul usually spends many years exercising itself in the state of proficients." This is usually a creative and productive period of life.

Even before entrance to the subtle level, during the Dark Night of the Senses recounted in the last chapter, we began to develop the "subtle senses," the equivalent at this level of the psychic senses at the psychic level and the physical senses at the physical. The subtle senses can detect much more rarefied energy vibrations than the prior senses, and their use brings in much finer, more delicate, and subtler shifts in awareness—hence the name "subtle level."

On entrance into the subtle level, for the first time, we are given *immediate* contact with our guardian angel, and with our personal spiritual master, who might be, for example, one of Jesus' disciples. Torkom Saraydarian writes: "It is during this initiation [the Dark Night of the Senses described in the last chapter] that the physical, emotional, and mental nature is flooded with a great light and energy. . . . This enables man to stand in the presence of his Angel and have direct communication with Him."[41] This could not happen before because our vibrations were too low to see or hear these spiritual guides regularly. The guardian angel (whom I prefer to call the angel of the true self) and the spiritual master will often begin to appear in our dreams. There is no mistaking them when they come, because they are numinous figures, meaning they shine from within by their own internally generated spiritual light.

For a person of a different religious tradition, the guides and messengers will appear differently, perhaps as buddhas to the Buddhist or prophets to the Jew, though I know of at least one Jewish mystic who, to his surprise, encountered Jesus at this level, Jesus telling him that he [Jesus] still has an assigned role to play for his people. For a

---

[41]Torkom Saraydarian in *Christ, the Avatar of Sacrificial Love*, AEG, available through T.S.G. Publishing Foundation, Inc., Cave Creek, AZ, 1994, p. 106. Torkom Saraydarian (1917-1997) was born in Asia Minor and later came to the United States. He studied with Sufis (Muslim mystics), dervishes, Christian mystics, and masters of temple music and dance. He wrote 170 books on the huge body of knowledge he called the "Ageless Wisdom."

person of no religion who reaches this level (and some do so), the guides and messengers may appear as archetypes like the Wise Old Woman, the Beautiful Young Princess, etc. The form (the astral clothing) does not matter. All function as messengers from, and archetypes of, the soul, the true self, the higher self, what the Christian calls the Christ Self.

The causal or soul energies that are entering our awareness at this level are properly called angelic. They are angelic in their function as messengers from our Christ Self, in their tremendous healing powers, and in their sublime intelligence. There are no "free floating" energies in either the visible or invisible parts of our universe, that is, energies not connected to personal beings of one sort or another. In the Orthodox Christian tradition, these angels or energies are emanations from the great personal (though nonhuman) beings we call archangels.

Although they have their own distinct spiritual existence, both the master and the angel also stand for our own soul, our true Self, or higher self, and, for the Christian, the Christ Self. For the Christian, Jesus also becomes, at this level, a personification of our true self. If we read certain Gospel passages, especially in the Gospel of John, in which Jesus speaks *as the Christ* (i.e., from the level of the Christ Consciousness), these passages contain surprising new meanings and depths if we substitute, where Jesus says "I" or "me," our own true self. For example, "Whoever loves his father or mother more than me is not worthy of me" (Matt. 10:37), "Believe in God and believe also in me" (John 14:1), "Whoever accepts my commandments and obeys them, he is the one who loves me" (John 14:21), and "You cannot bear fruit unless you remain in me" (John 15:3).

The same dynamic operates with respect to Jesus if we unite with him in Holy Communion. Each reception of Holy Communion becomes an opportunity to visualize ourselves as being more transformed into our divine Christ

Self. Jesus, speaking as the Christ (our own Christ Self), said "I am the Bread of Life . . . . Whoever eats it will not die" (John 6:48, 50). By interiorly incorporating this "bread" more and more as our own identity, we begin a rapid inner transformation in identity from human to divine. At the subtle level, our inner identification with Jesus as Christ comes ever more quickly into fulfillment.

It is at the subtle level that we begin our final individuation, the process by which a person becomes spiritually and psychologically whole, unique, and full of inner beauty. We take the final steps in the creation of ourselves as friends of Jesus (John 15:15), joint heirs with Jesus of the Kingdom (Rom. 8:17), integrated and complete human beings who unite all the male and female parts of ourselves into one divine Christed whole (Eph. 2:14, Gal. 3:26). All the guides and messengers are sent to help us accomplish this task (Col. 1:16).

If we are the type who does not pay attention to dreams, the spiritual guides will find other ways to communicate. We may experience waking dreams, that is, visions. The spiritual guides may also communicate telepathically, so that we begin to hear their voices in our heads. We may experience raptures by being caught up in the sublime energies breaking through from the level of the soul. We may see synchronicities in our daily life (positive or negative), or experience profound new insights of every sort (what Teresa calls "intellectual" visions). There is practically no end to the types of psychic, subtle, and pure intuitional phenomena that may occur at this level as the soul's way of knowing—pure intuition or knowingness—begins to become operative in us.

In her masterpiece, *The Interior Castle*, beginning with Mansion Six, St. Teresa describes many of the subtle phenomena one may encounter. As Wilber says:

> Teresa . . . gives clear and classic phenomenological descriptions of so many of the subtle-level apprehensions: interior illumination, sound, bliss, and understanding

beyond ordinary time and place; genuine archetypal Form as creative pattern (not mythic motif); and psychic vision going all the way to pure nonverbal, transverbal, subtle intuition.[42]

The subtle level of consciousness begins with peace after the commotion of the Dark Night of the Senses, and remains largely peaceful for several years while we gain experience and competence at this level. Eventually the peace begins to break down under the onslaught of all these new inner phenomena. The soul energies coming in from the causal level start breaking up our psychic structure and belief system, and once again our emotional balance (or what we took to be balance) begins to be seriously disturbed.

Both John of the Cross and Teresa describe the transition in considerable detail. As always, John will usually be the best guide for Christians who are only moderately psychic while Teresa is the best guide for the mystic. Wilber again on Teresa:

> Teresa is positively brilliant . . . in distinguishing the agonies of the soul in its higher mansions or stages from those emotional problems that [often simultaneously] characterize the lower faculties. She clearly distinguishes, for example, three types of "inner voices"—those of the "fancy" or "imagination," which can be hallucinatory and "diseased" she says; those that are verbal, and may or may not represent true wisdom (for they may also be deceptive and "diseased"); and those that are transverbal altogether, representing direct interior apprehension. [43]

Though many Christian saints have had to go through this territory with almost no earthly assistance since there were (and are) hardly any Christian spiritual masters around to help them, the Buddhists wisely insist that it is imperative

---

[42]Wilber, ibid., p. 298.
[43]Ibid.

for persons at this level to have a living human master to keep an eye on them. Otherwise, especially if we are very psychic, we may wonder sometimes if we are losing our minds.

There are dangers at this level. For example, the remaining dark parts of the self (which John calls the "roots" of the person's negativity) can easily be projected outward into visions of the type called "hallucinations" and "diseased" by Teresa (and called devils or bad angels by John). Inner voices can also be infected with negativity, so much so that we must be extremely careful channeling spirits at this juncture or some very negative and unbalanced messages can come through. The horrendous visions of St. Anthony of the Desert probably occurred at this level, usually referred to as "Satan disguising himself as an angel of light." It is about this level that the Buddhist masters warn their disciples in no uncertain terms, "If you see the Buddha on the road, kill him." John of the Cross says, "This is the stage in which the devil induces many into believing vain visions and false prophecies." It is the healing and illuminating action of the subtle energies within that principally matters, not the phenomena that may or may not accompany them. These can be a danger to the extent they are infected by the demonic dark forces of negativity.

As we get closer to the level of the soul two things happen. On the negative side, the phenomena are likely to accelerate, becoming more de-centering and upsetting. On the positive side, our spiritual guides will step up their efforts on our behalf. The result is that, as our consciousness gradually ascends to the next level of consciousness (the causal level, Christ Consciousness), we also begin a simultaneous descent into a spiritual crisis the like of which we have never before experienced, into what John of the Cross calls the "Dark Night of the Soul" and the late Buddhist spiritual master Chogyam Trungpa Rinpoche called the realm of "hell."[44] This simultaneous ascent and descent can take several years and usually accelerates in intensity as it does. With it, the transition beyond identification with the human personality has begun in earnest.

---

[44]Chogyam Trungpa Rinpoche (1939-1987) was eleventh in the Tibetan Buddhist line of Trungpa tulkus, teachers of the Kagyu lineage. He was head of the Surmang monasteries in eastern Tibet. He fled Tibet in 1959 and came to the United States in 1970. He founded the Naropa Institute in Boulder, Colorado and over 100 contemplative centers worldwide. He was especially gifted in expressing Buddhist teachings in the language of the West. His books include *Shambhala: The Sacred Path of the Warrior, Cutting Through Spiritual Materialism,* and *The Myth of Freedom.*

PART III
THE DARK NIGHT OF THE SOUL

Chapter 12

THE NATURE OF THE
DARK NIGHT OF THE SOUL

The Dark Night of the Soul is the central mystery in the evolution of human consciousness on this planet. A principal purpose, and perhaps the primary purpose, of Jesus' Cross and Resurrection, was to act out for us this death and rebirth, which Jesus called the "Sign of Jonah." The Dark Night and one's resurrection from it constitute what the New Testament calls the "Baptism of Fire and the Holy Spirit;" for the Christian, it is the one sacrament or sign necessary for salvation. We enter the Dark Night understanding ourselves to be mere human beings, sinful and mortal, but we come out of this profound spiritual passage with the realization of our sinless, immortal divinity. The sufferings of the Dark Night are intense, and have four principal causes.

The Dark Night of the Soul constitutes the transition from the subtle to the causal levels of human consciousness. It is the transition during which our identification of ourselves as human personalities finally gives way to the realization of our divinity. The name "Dark Night of the Soul" was given to this transition by St. John of the Cross in the sixteenth century and has been in general use within the Christian spiritual tradition since then.

The Dark Night of the Soul is the central mystery in the evolution of human consciousness on this planet. I use the word mystery deliberately for, although this chapter and the next three will examine the Dark Night in detail, there are elements of the Night and the perceptions it brings that defy definitive explanation. Once human consciousness begins to move beyond the boundaries of the human personality (and, by definition therefore, beyond spacetime and spacetime language), the multidimensional world that begins to come into view can only be glimpsed "through a glass darkly" as St. Paul said (1 Cor. 13:12).

This does not mean that there is no clarity of truth. Just the opposite is the case, for many truths are now seen with great clarity. But there are aspects of these realms that remain mysterious. I say this lest anyone think that in the following pages I am reducing the mystery to mere psychology or in some sense secularizing it (as many, incorrectly, accuse the Buddhist masters of doing). In defense, I must say that our sense of awe with respect to Jesus, the Self, the Universe, and with All That Is Just As It Is, grows exponentially as we come into these levels. Awe, wonder, and amazement constantly occur in these realms and are indeed the fuel that keeps us striving ever onward to God, despite the terrific dangers and obstacles.

The death and rebirth of the Dark Night of the Soul is what separates humans who think they are mere mortal human beings from those who know they are divine and immortal. We enter the Dark Night of the Soul thinking that we are sinful, fallen, and in need of salvation, and emerge knowing that we are, and have always been, sinless and saved. Emergence in rebirth from the Dark Night of the Soul, therefore, conquers both death and sin, as St. Paul testified (1Cor. 15:55-56). The Dark Night of the Soul is the ultimate Baptism of Fire and the Spirit which John the Baptist said Jesus would manifest for us (Matt. 3:11).

Christian baptism by water is the precursor and a psychologically appropriate symbol of the inner spiritual baptism of this Night, just as John the Baptist's baptism by water was the precursor of Jesus' baptism into his death and resurrection. The Dark Night of the Soul, therefore, can be understood as the true baptism that is the only necessary Christian sacrament for salvation.[45] As such, the Dark Night is the only necessary sign that Jesus came to show us: the Sign of Jonah (Luke 11:29-30).

One may ask why we, having climbed the spiritual ladder to this point, now have to undergo the profound suffering of this Baptism by Fire and the Spirit. There are four reasons. The first is intellectual and has to do with our realizing who we truly are. The Dark Night is necessary because, despite all that has gone before, despite years of Bible reading, prayers, and church attendance, despite reading mountains of spiritual books, and despite the years of meditation, we still don't have a clue as to who we really are.

If we are asked who we are, will still say our name is Mary Jones or John Smith. We will say we are of a certain gender, race, nationality, religion, age, occupation, and sexual orientation. We will say we are a mother, a father, a sister, a brother. We will say we have an IQ of such and so, are an extrovert or introvert, or have a degree in x or y. In short, we still identify who we are as defined by our personalities. We even suppose that our spacetime defined personalities are the part of us that is eternal, and that our personalities will live beyond the conclusion of our earthly lives. We further suppose that our thoughts, free will, and creativity originate

---

[45]A sacrament is a ritual that both symbolizes and results in inner spiritual growth. Traditionally, there have been seven Christian sacraments: Baptism, Confirmation, Holy Communion, Penance (Confession, Reconciliation), Holy Orders, Matrimony, and Extreme Unction (Last Rites, Anointing of the Sick). Some Christian denominations recognize all seven, some less than seven. Some recognize only one—Baptism. But virtually all of the denominations recognize Baptism as the only sacrament essential for salvation.

from our personalities and are its thoughts, its free will, and its creativity. In all these things we are mistaken.

We are still seeing God, the Devil and other people as distinctly separate from ourselves. We may acknowledge, when asked, that God lives within us, but we may picture God within ourselves as if God were an extra but invisible appendix, in us but separate from us. As John of the Cross says about persons at this level, "They still think of God and speak of him as little children, and their knowledge and experience of him is like that of little children, as St. Paul asserts (1 Cor. 13:11)."[46]

You may ask: how can this be? I put aside the *concept* of a separate "outside" God and a separate "outside" Devil way back at the rational level of consciousness. I have meditated on Jesus and the Gospels for years and years. I have read books written by saints and other enlightened persons a hundred times over. I know intellectually that I am really an immortal soul, not a personality. So how can I still not see?

The answer brings us to the second reason for the Dark Night, the purification of the emotions. Emotions are our most human attribute, often acknowledged as such even in science fiction, such as the classic *Star Trek* in which the android Data perpetually seeks an understanding of human emotions, which he lacks. Our watery planet is the planet of the emotions, of the heart, of the path to love. All of us have incarnated here for one reason only: to learn how to love, to love as Jesus did. This cannot be done as long as our emotional bodies are not thoroughly purified by the death and rebirth of the Dark Night.

As long as we are harboring deep within our psyches the "roots" of emotional imbalances, our consciousness cannot help but engage in projection. We project our repressed good parts outward onto our parents, our leaders, our lovers, and, most importantly, onto God. Likewise, we project our repressed bad parts outward onto others and,

---

[46]St. John of the Cross, ibid., chapter 3, p. 399.

archetypically, onto the Devil. It can't be helped. Even the staunchest atheist is subject to this psychological dynamic.

In America, the seemingly endless obsession of otherwise intelligent people (e.g., on talk shows) with the president is classic projection. Catholics often behave in the same manner towards the pope and Britons towards the queen. First, people give away their own power to someone else, usually a parental authority figure, unconsciously hoping that person will "save" them in some way or at least give meaning to their lives. Then, because people *always* resent those to whom they've surrendered their own power, and because no person, authority figure or not, can ever successfully carry the projections of others, the same people usually end up despising and endlessly running down the authority figure when the "parent" fails them by not living up to their unrealistic expectations. The whole business is extremely dysfunctional and, in many instances, can become dangerous. We cannot claim our own divinity and realize the Christ Consciousness or the Kingdom of Heaven as long as we continue to give away our own power, by projection or otherwise, to any guru, magisterium, or any other authority outside ourselves. That is why Jesus said, "Do not call anyone here on Earth father, because you have only the one Father in heaven" (Matt. 23:9).

The Dark Night of the Soul will thoroughly rid us of our projections. By means of the Dark Night, can we finally own all of these outside projections, both demonic and godly. In the process we finally become psychologically whole and our entire vision of the world and of ourselves, changes profoundly as we then see both for the first time without projections.

"But why," you may ask, "does the suffering of the Dark Night have to be so horrendous? How can there possibly be so much emotional imbalance still remaining in me after decades of spiritual and healing practices, and especially after the years of purification of the Night of Senses? After all, psychological tests showed conclusively that I was a very integrated personality way back in the fifth level of consciousness, that of vision-logic." St. Teresa tried to answer this question but she did not succeed in finding the answer (beyond saying that the suffering is afterwards seen to have been worth it). She wrote:

> You will . . . ask why the soul doesn't conform to the will of God since it is so surrendered to Him. Until now it could do so, and has spent its life doing so. As for now, the reasoning faculty is in such a condition that the soul is not the master of it, nor can the soul think of anything else than of why it is grieving, of how it is absent from its Good, and of why it should want to live . . . everything torments it . . . the soul sees that it is like a person hanging, who cannot support himself on any earthly thing; nor can it ascend to heaven. On fire with this thirst, it cannot get to the water; and the thirst is not one that is endurable but already at such a point that nothing will take it away. Nor does the soul desire that the thirst be taken away save by that water of which our Lord spoke to the Samaritan woman. Yet no one gives such water to the soul. Oh, God help me! Lord, how you afflict your lovers! But everything is small in comparison to what You give them afterward. It's natural that what is worth much costs much.[47]

The third reason for the great suffering of this Night is a surprising one for most Christians, though not for the majority of the world's believers. What one must remember is that we are not dealing here with the integration or individuation of the personality. We are dealing here with integration and individuation at the level of the soul.

Much, if not most, of the emotional imbalances and other sufferings of the Dark Night originate from parts of the person that are beyond the personality, that is, beyond the boundaries of the individual personality. I will discuss this matter further in a separate chapter (see chapter 21). It is

---

[47]St. Teresa of Avila, *The Interior Castle*, Mansion VI, chapter 11, sections 5 & 6, pp. 423-424, in *The Collected Works of St. Teresa of Avila, Volume Two*, translated by Kiernan Kavanaugh, O.C.D., and Otilio Rodriquez, O.C.D., ICS Publications, Institute of Carmelite Studies, Washington, D.C., 1980.

enough for now to say that our present personalities are not the only incarnate personalities that our souls have created in their earthly quest towards realizing their individuated divinity. There have usually been many, many others, and much of the emotional and other suffering encountered in the Dark Night originates from those other unseen parts of our souls.

The fourth reason for the psychic suffering of the Night is also transpersonal. The Christian in the Dark Night, like Jesus on the Cross, is allowed to participate in the redemptive work of the Christ (Col. 1:24). That is, we take into our psyche, as we move through the transpersonal planes of consciousness, a measure of the world's negativity, and we transmute that negativity back into the basic stuff of the universe—consciousness/love. Contrary to what we have supposed up until now, neither the light nor the dark parts in the depths of our psyche are fully confined (in a walled-off sense) to our individual personalities. The light within us is connected to the light of other beings of light and to the positive energies of the universe in general, and the negativity within us is connected with the negativity of the universe in general and with the darkness of other beings properly called demonic or angels of darkness.

Once our consciousness moves beyond the boundaries of the personality we can encounter straight-on these angels of light and darkness. From the former come tremendous light, healing, consolation, insight, and assistance, but from the latter can come what Wilber calls the "subtler *pathological* states of what can only be called Kosmic terror, Kosmic evil, Kosmic horror."[48] At times the latter encounters can be terrifying in the extreme.

In the life of Jesus as a human personality this confrontation with the demons is symbolized by his encounter with

---

[48]Ken Wilber, *A Brief History of Everything,* p. 211, Shambhala, Boston & London, 1996. Wilber uses a "K." He says he does so because today, when people talk about the "cosmos" or "cosmology," they are almost always referring only to the physical universe. Wilber emphasizes that these terrors come from beyond the physical dimension.

Satan (the Tempter) in the desert before he begins his public ministry. In Buddhism the confronting of these demons (just prior to enlightenment) is symbolized by Siddartha Gautama (who became the Buddha) being accosted by Mara (the Tempter) as he sat meditating under the fig tree.

One Western Christian esoteric tradition calls the Dark Night of the Soul the "Crucifixion Initiation" (the Fourth Initiation according to their map of the spiritual path) because the Dark Night is the initiation, the baptism, that Jesus, in the fullness of time (Rom. 5:6), came to Earth to existentially act out for us in the physical by his death on the Cross and subsequent Resurrection. This tradition says that the Gospel Crucifixion/Resurrection narratives may be read as a psychological parable of what a person goes through in this initiation or transition. When you read the Gospel Crucifixion narratives with this in mind, they can be a revelation. Take, for example, the images of Teresa "hanging" between heaven and earth (like Jesus on the Cross, Matt. 27:35), and her rending description of spiritual thirst (again like Jesus on the Cross, John 19:28). In both these examples what Teresa experienced internally paralleled what happened to Jesus externally. We will see many other such parallels as we go along.

Because Jesus alone was chosen by God to act out in the flesh for us, in the fullness of time, this central mystery in the evolution of human consciousness on this planet of the heart, Jesus is properly seen as the Lord of History. Jesus alone, using his own human body, enacted in the flesh what we have to do internally. By his Cross and Resurrection Jesus graphically symbolized for us humanity's death to the mankind of Adam (humans understood as fallen, sinful, separate, and mortal) and rebirth into the realization of our divinity (humans understood as being in substantial, sinless, and immortal union with both God and each other)(1 Cor. 15:45-49, Rom. 5:14-17). For this the name of Jesus will be eternally honored (Philip. 2:9-11).

With respect to the future history of humanity on this planet, the completion of the current phase of human history (the "Second Coming" of Christ, Matt. 24:30) will arrive when humanity, *as a whole,* is baptized by means of this Dark Night. This means humanity's letting go of its understanding of humanity as separate from God and its rebirth into the realization of the Christ that all of us already are. When all humans realize their own divinity a new phase of life will begin on earth.

I personally believe that God has "scheduled" this event to occur sometime during (perhaps at the climax of) the Age of Aquarius, the symbol for which is a young man carrying a water jug. It was this same young man whom Jesus' disciples, on his instructions, followed into the Upper Room where Jesus gave us his legacy, the Holy Communion (Luke 22:10-20). The Age of Aquarius will see the fulfillment of this Holy Communion between humans and God, and between each one of us.[49] By the end of the Age of Aquarius, if all goes well, humanity may live as the manifestation of the Christ on Earth.

---

[49] I am indebted to David Spangler for this insight into the significance of this Scriptural account.

Chapter 13

PRELUDE TO THE DARK NIGHT—
BREAKTHROUGH TO THE CAUSAL LEVEL

To help the reader understand some of the higher and more difficult parts of the Christian path to higher consciousness, I switch to an autobiographical mode. I hope that by sharing my own experience I will make it easier for the reader to follow the stages of this spiritual transition. I describe my personal struggle, as a Christian, to reconcile my denomination's insistence that same-sexual expression is sinful with the inner promptings of my higher self to exercise my sexuality. I review my decision to obey this inner guidance, and the consequent reopening of my emotional and psychic centers; further, I recount many of the spiritual visions, voices, revelations, and other phenomena I encountered at this level, and my breakthrough into the causal level.

As I recounted in the introduction, my consciousness popped up into the subtle level during the spiritual experience I had on the green at Yale University in 1970. I experienced this transformation as a significant and freeing spiritual experience. To use the words of John of the Cross, I felt as though "liberated from a cramped prison cell." This experience marked the definitive end of the Dark Night of the Senses.

After that day I lived at the subtle level for about seven years. I did not call it the subtle level, or call it anything for that matter. I found myself to be an integrated, happy, and productive person. During those seven years I was basically content with life. I attended law school, got my law degree, and began an exciting career in public service. I got several promotions, bought a home, and formed many wonderful friendships. My work was creative, well-paid, and meaningful because I was able to be of service to a great many people. If anything, I was a workaholic in my efforts to serve others and maximize my career.

I had discontinued regular church attendance as well as any formal practice of meditation. Like most Christians, I'd never been taught any scientific meditation method even though I'd been in seminary for seven years. But I had become a "natural meditator," one focused more within than without. Since my self was identified with the inner witness, I kept an observant eye on my thoughts and feelings and constantly tried to break through whatever I felt were inner constrictions into greater freedom. The breakthrough from the inner "cramped prison cell" into the subtle level had been so liberating that I worked hard to keep freeing myself from all fears and limitations.

In the meantime I was so engaged in my life's new work that I'd pretty well forgotten the various psychic and perhaps a few subtle experiences that I'd had before and during the Dark Night of the Senses. I was closed down psychically. All my focus went into my intellectually demanding career. I had also closed down emotionally after the totally frustrating love affair I described in the introduction (and a similar law school friendship that proved just as hopeless). I didn't want to go through pain like that again. And I still believed, as I had been taught, that same-sex sexual expression was morally wrong. I also feared, realistically for those times, that any such expression would ruin my image, my relationships with friends and with my devout family, and sabotage my rapidly unfolding political career and ability to be of service to others.

But, shortly into my new career, I began to be moved from within to begin exercising my sexuality. For all the reasons given above I resisted mightily (and successfully) and concentrated on my work. I kept up this resistance for three years.

God's grace—the Holy Spirit—then intervened strongly and directly. I was given the realization that all love, including same-sexual love, necessarily comes from the God who *is* Love (1 John 4:8). I was also given the realization that the only way for me to experientially come into my true self, which I understood to be the same as my Christ Self, was to accept my sexuality. Those church authorities who would prevent me from coming into my true self, like Simon Peter when he tried to steer Jesus from his mission, were *for me* occasions of sin (Matt. 16:22-23). An "occasion of sin" is a Christian term that most Christian readers will understand. Christians would consider visiting a bordello, for example, as putting oneself in an "occasion of sin," a place where the person has a good chance of succumbing to temptation. Here I am saying that even listening to these teachers would have been, for me, an "occasion of sin" because it would have seriously tempted me not to follow my inner guidance.

Finally, I was given to realize that, to achieve my long-held goal of experiential union with the God of Love, I had to let go of my fear that exercising my sexuality would somehow offend God. This is because I knew from the Scriptures that fear (not hate as many suppose) is the true opposite of love (1 John 4:18).

If I wanted to follow Jesus into love, therefore, I felt I had no choice but to let the fears go. So I set out to conquer them, putting my trust, not in visible and human church authorities and their rationally constructed theology, but in the unseen God who directs, from within us, the process of life itself (Heb. 11:1).

As soon as I began exercising my sexuality, I immediately opened up again both emotionally and psychically. Though for me a little sexual experience went a long way, the more I exercised my sexuality, the more open I became.

I began to see and feel the incoming subtle and causal energies. I found myself more moved to renew my formerly intense quest for union with God. Once again I found myself passionately interested in spirituality, psychology, and religion, and started attending church again regularly.

An argument can be made that, from the point of view of spirituality, it is sexuality, not marriage, that is the true sacrament, or effective sign, of God's union with us, and of ours with each other. According to some biblical scholars, Jesus appears to have made precisely this point (Matt. 19:12). The exercise of sexuality *always* has a powerful spiritual (inner psychological) effect. It is precisely *because* sexuality is so spiritually powerful that, however playful the encounter, it is best exercised with reverence and awareness. To do otherwise risks getting badly burned.

Marriage, on the other hand, though it usually contains sexual union as its psycho-spiritual core, has no inner psychological effect *per se*. In many cultures, including medieval Christendom, children have been married to distant spouses they have never even met. Marriage is primarily a legal, contractual matter having to do with such material things as property rights, inheritance, legal responsibility for child rearing, taxation, and immigration rights. The role of the Christian Church as the "defender of the traditional family" is largely a cultural phenomenon, perhaps originating after the tribal conquest of Europe when the Church took upon itself the task of bringing the tribal peoples from the level of magical consciousness upward into the mythic and later the rationalized mythic.

In my case, due in no small measure to the reopening of my heart energies by sexual experience, my inner spiritual experiences immediately grew in intensity. For a year or two, whenever the name of Jesus came up in a hymn at church, I was so profoundly moved that I found myself unable to continue singing, instead lapsing into a silence filled with intense longings and yearnings for Jesus, my Beloved. (This was an example of subtle level affectivity.) Another time, hearing the Gospel in which Jesus promises living water to the Samaritan woman, I was overwhelmed by the sensation of myself being inundated with these living waters (John 4:7-14). Still another time I looked about in church and, instead of seeing other people, I saw each person as a burning bush of the type Moses saw on the mountain. I realized I was seeing the Fiery Light of God (Christ) within, the core reality of each person (Ex. 3:2-4, Deut. 33:16). (This was an example of subtle level seeing.) I started noticing the powerful numinous figures in my dreams and began faithfully to follow their instructions.

Thinking of what Jesus had said to the rich young man, I once again applied for the ministry, resolving once more to leave all for God (Matt. 19:16-21). But later I had a dream in which, while I was at a church service, the Christ Child appeared next to me in the pew and said, "Don't you find this terribly boring? I'd rather go swimming."

I knew enough psychology to understand that water represents the subconscious, and that swimming would mean exploring the subconscious layers of the psyche. The message was that, for me at least, Jesus did not care about external ministries and observances, the forever crying out of "Lord, Lord," but cared very much that I do God's will by going deeper within my psyche (Matt. 7:21). I withdrew my ministry application the next day. Later I found out the official in charge of admissions had judged me morally unsuitable anyway because of the sexual activity.

I began to keep a journal and often found myself writing all night, many times moved to rapturous love for God, and just as often dissolved in tears. I wrote for about fifteen minutes one time, but, when I "came to" and looked at the clock, ten hours had passed (an example of subtle level rapture). Many times I was listening to music for hours at a time, but when I "came to" I found that neither the radio nor stereo had been playing. The music, usually a wondrous mixture of every sound from rock music to Beethoven, had been coming from within. (This was an example of subtle level hearing.)

Another time I went to a church service at which a great many church leaders were present. Thinking of what Jesus had said about the mother hen and her chickens, and realizing how much these high officials of the New Jerusalem[50] resembled the high officials of the Old, I started to cry (Luke 13:34-35). I continued to cry uncontrollably throughout the service (Luke 19:41).

There were negative experiences as well, magnetized into my life by the action of the incoming light in stirring up my buried dark side. One time I got involved with a person who seemed nice. It turned out that person operated a ring of prostitution. A crazy person followed me into my house one day, scooped up all the change I'd been saving in a bowl, and, with hardly a word, exited the house. I came across so many unsavory characters in one way or another that I became quite paranoid about meeting anyone.

Several times negative spirits woke me from sleep, filling the room with frightful energy. I was terrified at these visitations. Some years later I was told these spirits may have been people who had died, gotten lost in the etheric plane, and failed to make the transition into the light. These souls apparently saw my own astral body aflame, crackling like a bonfire, and full of magnetism (as it is at this stage), so they'd come hoping I would lead them to the light. Unfortunately, the poor souls got a rude reception. I practically threw them "bodily" from the room. I redoubled the sincerity of my nightly prayers to the angels for protection, as otherwise I would have been too scared to go to sleep.

During this time, I was also given visions of various hells, one more loathsome than the next, and of the poor

---

[50]The metaphor "New Jerusalem" can be used in several ways, including, as here, referring to Christianity as the successor to Judaism. The Pilgrims, for example, thought they were founding a "New Jerusalem" in Massachusetts. And President Reagan alluded to America as the New Jerusalem with his reference to the "shining city on a hill" in his now-famous 1974 speech to the first Conservative Political Action Conference.

souls who, by their own thinking and deeds, had trapped themselves in those awful places. Often I was given visions of this world as though seen from the other side, as if through God's eyes. In these visions I was shown how everything in the world, down to the smallest detail, positive and negative, operates with absolute perfection under the direction of a multidimensional intelligence so awesome that there is no way to describe it.

For example, one time I went to a convenience store around midnight. While in the store, in a flash, I was shown the life history of everyone in the store as well as how they had come to be in that place at that particular time. I understood how perfect the choices of all had been, and how even casual conversation between the patrons had, in a sense, been preordained from all eternity and perfectly and exactly fostered God's purposes for each person there. Even this description of the vision, however, fails to do it justice. I saw so much so fast of how God's supreme intelligence permeates even a perfectly mundane experience that I was thrilled, staggered, and humbled.

By means of these visions, I realized how we create everything in our lives down to the smallest detail or event, and that, putting aside all judgments of fault or blame, we must all take responsibility for all of our creations, whether thought, word, deed or omission. I was given the general laws governing the manifestation of physical things and events out of the energies of the higher planes.

On occasion my adventures took me into what many people might call the "sexual underworld," a place of unconventional sexuality, drug-dealing, prostitution, heavy alcohol use, and other socially condemned practices. But I learned much in that world. I was given to see (sometimes with great exactness, as from God's viewpoint) that what Jesus said about many prostitutes and sinners entering the Kingdom of Heaven before the righteous is as true today as it was when Jesus spoke (Matt. 21:31). In the "underworld," I met people who trusted life enough to allow themselves to experience the extremes of this world. These people were truly "hot," or truly "cold," to use Jesus' words, and sometimes both (Rev. 3:15-16). Some, reminiscent of the woman who anointed Jesus' feet, had learned, by the very experiencing of such extremes, to "love much" (Luke 7:47).

True, the path of these unconventional, marginalized people is a dangerous one that often proves fatal. But, as Jesus said, this path can be, and often is, a much faster path to the Kingdom than the safe, lukewarm, socially approved, avoid-all-risks-and-risk-factors path many Christians follow. We can grow in awareness (and love) just as fast by being "cold," by resolutely exploring our dark sides, as we can by being "hot," resolutely exploring our light sides. Either way, as Jesus said, is preferable to a mediocrity which results in little or no growth in awareness. Exploring the dark side is not a path to be recommended, but it is a reality to keep in mind, especially in dealing with human beings society has judged against.[51]

All this and lots more went on with increasing intensity for three years. I found it difficult to do my high-powered job, the demands of which had also increased. There things took a sharp turn for the worse. A new, paranoid regime was installed at my workplace. I knew this was an outer reflection of my own paranoia now coming to the surface to be cleared. But this realization was little comfort when the new bosses began the systematic dismantling of projects and

---

[51]Today there are many Christians who are exploring the Native American spiritual path, a path that is basically shamanistic. Some are dabblers; some merely incorporate certain practices, such as sweat lodge ceremonies, into their Christian or eclectic paths; a very few are drawn to actually follow this path. With respect to the last, if you find the traditional Christian path of John of the Cross scary, you may want to think twice about the Native American path. That path, as outlined for outsiders in such books as Carlos Castaneda's and Lynn Andrews', often contains practices and experiences that would make your hair stand on end. The ancient shamanic paths, from which the Christian path was long ago derived, are often dangerous in the extreme.

policies I had worked on for years. Increasingly, I felt called to resign but, worried about money, I held on. Finally, in the fourth year of this process, I did resign.

No sooner had I let go of my career than I was guided to consult the books of John of the Cross and Teresa of Avila. I was still feeling guilty about sex and my on-again off-again church attendance, and I was also feeling the terrible inner misery and worthlessness that people usually feel at this level. So I was astonished to see that what I was feeling agreed with the feelings John of the Cross described in *The Dark Night of the Soul* on no less than 38 separate points.

John of the Cross goes on at great length about how wretched the person feels at this level *despite* whatever visions, insights, or other positive things happen. The person feels "so unclean and wretched that it seems God is against them and they are against God." Also, "individuals feel so far from all favor that they think . . . there is no one who will take pity on them" so that they cry out with Job, "Have pity on me, at least you, my friends, for the hand of the Lord has touched me." [Job. 19:21][52]

I saw the essence of my state clearly set out in Mansion Five of St. Teresa's *Interior Castle*. I was overjoyed because, having let go of the mythic level Sky God twelve years previously, I was often bereft, feeling that I had lost God. I still believed in God, trusted God, and prayed to God, but who or what God was I did not know, and neither could I feel anything I could have labeled God.

After reading John and Teresa I remembered the Dark Night of the Senses of a dozen or so years earlier and how I had relied on John for guidance. What gave me so much hope and joy was the confirmation from Teresa and John that I had not lost God, lost my way, or fallen off the spiritual path, but that, somehow, over the intervening twelve years, God had guided me to make my way into the Dark Night of the Soul.

---

[52]St. John of the Cross, ibid., p. 402, p. 403.

I decided immediately that union with God must be once again, as it had been for so many years when I was young, my absolute number one priority. Teresa's account was especially encouraging to me (now unemployed and with no steady income) because Teresa said that, after Mansion Five, there was only one more mansion to go through before reaching the goal of union with God (Mansion Seven).

I decided to seek spiritual direction. I consulted two religious men: one of whom had written a book on psychology and spirituality and the other of whom had a reputation for giving spiritual direction. But, when I met with them, it was clear neither understood what I was talking about. One thought I was merely going through "some kind of depression." I crossed off consulting with mental health professionals. I knew traditional talk therapy would have been useless and I wasn't going to allow myself to be put on any drugs.

I was thrown back on my own. This is to be expected in the Dark Night, and is specifically mentioned by Teresa. The person at this stage is in the process of claiming and owning his or her divinity. The spiritual guides will guide, as will a living spiritual master, but under no circumstances is anyone (and God sees to that) going to do the work for you. Whether you sink or swim is up to you. I redoubled my efforts, often doing spiritual exercises and meditating throughout the night. I studied John and Teresa's accounts, but then I put the books aside. It was not the time for reading but for hard work on myself.

Not long afterwards, while I was attending church on Good Friday, Jesus himself appeared to me in a vision.[53]

---

[53]John of the Cross writes that, even if Jesus appears to a person at this level, it is more likely an angel than Jesus himself. He is making in a different way the same point I am making in saying that one's guardian angel, Jesus, and other spiritual beings, though they have their own identities, are appearing here in an angelic function, that is, as messengers from, and representations of, the person's own soul or Christ Self.

Jesus said to me, "Do not be afraid. I go before you always. Come, follow me, and I will give you rest." These words of Jesus had the intended effect. I now knew with certainty that I was on the right track. Though, if I had paid more attention than I did to the day on which the vision had occurred, which was Good Friday, I might have had an inkling of what lay ahead.

How did I know that the vision was genuine? All I can say is that, if a vision "happens" to you, you know it. There is absolute certainty conveyed with it. There are, nonetheless, some rules of discernment. For example, the words and images of genuine visions, as contrasted with products of the imagination, impress themselves indelibly. This is also true of genuine visions received while dreaming. Unlike ordinary dreams and products of the imagination, a true vision is never forgotten and the truths conveyed in it are as if permanently "carved" into a person's mind. A true vision will also be spiritual in content and will never deviate from the core spiritual truths of religion.

Soon after the vision of Jesus I was offered an easier job. That helped me financially for a while. But my inner turmoil was such that, six months later, I could not manage even that, and once again, I had to resign. With no income, I could only hope the Night would end soon.

Then, two days after Christmas, while I was doing chores around the house, the "heavens" inside myself opened up and a loud voice said, "You are my beloved son in whom I am well pleased." I was astonished at hearing this voice and mortified by the content of the message (Matt. 3:17).

Coming some nine months after the vision of Jesus, this was my first real experience with God the Father. At least one Western Christian esoteric tradition apparently has a lot to say about the role of Jesus and other spiritual entities at specific levels of consciousness, and about specific mystical experiences, such as this one, the timing and content of which, according to that tradition, is not by chance. That tradition holds that here, at the fourth or Crucifixion Initiation (by their map), the person has finally become totally identified with Jesus as his or her own Christ Self. The person now, as he or she enters the causal level of consciousness (the Christ Consciousness) is given direct access on an ongoing basis to the communications of the Father. (This is similar to coming into the subtle level, when the person is given direct access to the Guardian Angel, their spiritual master, and, if need be, Jesus himself.) This, they say, is a principal meaning of the statement attributed to Jesus (speaking as the Christ) that, "No one comes to the Father except through me" (John 14:6).

By the "Father" that tradition means a still higher spiritual realm called the monadic plane, which seems to be their name for what I call the Kingdom of Heaven, that is, the level of nondual consciousness. What seems most interesting to me is that I heard the exact words reported in the Gospel as heard by Jesus *before* I had even heard of the Western esoteric tradition, and *before* I had a clear awareness that there were such things as levels of consciousness. In other words, these things can happen whether one knows the theory behind them or not, and it happened to me despite the fact that, consciously, I had never heard of such a thing happening to anyone except Jesus.

The direct experience of God the Father, I now know, meant that I was close to breakthrough into Christ Consciousness. But I didn't know that then. I had no idea how long this sort of thing would go on. Another six weeks went by. Then I had a dream: I was a passenger in a car and, all of a sudden, the car drove straight up into the air at top speed. Terrified, I jumped out the window, grabbing the top branch of a tree. Trembling, I climbed down to earth. (The dream meant that my resistance to the breakthrough was almost over.) The next evening there was no escape. As I read a book by the American Episcopalian nondual mystic Alan Watts, my consciousness suddenly took off and zoomed upwards into the causal plane. Breakthrough, at last.

During this great experience, which lasted four days, my life passed before my eyes in a flash and I saw that my life up until then had been perfect, even its sins. This astonished me, though I was getting used to being astonished. In a sense, my life was "over" at that point, certainly my life as a mere human personality.

As Gary Zukav says in his wonderful book, *The Seat of the Soul,* one of the reasons our soul creates a particular human personality is to heal emotional damages incurred during the earthly learning experiences of other of its created personalities. If a person works hard by spiritual practices and in everyday life (by replacing fear with love, vengeance with forgiveness, jealousy with supportiveness, etc.), he or she can literally finish the assignment early. The person is then eligible to be "called" to the next level of consciousness and invited to take the required initiation; no one takes a spiritual initiation without such an invitation, but the invitation is always given to those who are ready. In the process, the rest of the damages are transmuted and healed. As Jesus said, if we pay a small part of the debt, God, our loving Father, cancels the rest (Matt. 18:27). As tough as the Dark Night is, therefore, it is essentially an exercise in mercy.

Because of this experience and the understandings I was given by the Holy Spirit, I believe that mercy is a fitting name for this material universe. And the divine Mother Mary, under her mythic title of Mother of Mercy, is an apt symbol for that universe. I realize that there are many Christians who would much rather not have Jesus' mother acknowledged as divine. But the Catholic Church continues to develop its Marian mythology and theology under the guidance, I believe, of Mary herself. If Mary, as many Christians propose, were to be acknowledged as Co-Redemptrix (or Co-Redeemer) and as Mediatrix of All Grace, those titles, when added to those of Mother of God and Immaculate Conception, would make her divinity plain to see. It would also illuminate the divinity of the material universe for, Mary, as Mother or *Mater*, mythologically represents matter. [54]

Besides the life review, many other things happened to me during this event, and many spiritual insights were infused into me. It took a week to get grounded again. During that time I went to a college basketball game with a friend. I had a difficult, even comical time of it, because I was seeing the whole world in dazzling astral colors, more brilliant and striking than colors normally appear on Earth. But, after a week or so, I was back to "normal."

After this experience, I thought I was home free. I knew my consciousness had definitely entered into what Christians have traditionally called the Unitive Way and what I am calling in this book the causal or soul level. I figured the Night was over and started making plans to resume my life. But, unknown to me, all that had happened up until then was mere warm-up. It had been only the *ascent* to the causal level and simultaneous *descent* into the Night, not the actual Dark Night of the Soul itself.

---

[54]What the Catholic (and Orthodox) churches still need to do, in my opinion, is to start translating some of that Marian mythology into practical actions, for example the ordination of women priests, an area where many other denominations are substantially in the lead. Whatever the supposed effect upon ecumenism, which too often seems a defensive circling of wagons against the future, Mary was indeed every bit as divine as Jesus and saw the Kingdom of Heaven as well as he. It is just that, in terms of our admittedly patriarchal Christian mythology, she is not properly addressed as "Christ" because there can be only one Christ, one Only-Begotten Son (see chapter 18).

Chapter 14

DEATH ON THE CROSS OF INNER CONTRADICTIONS AND THE DESCENT INTO HELL

Shortly after breaking through into the causal level, my consciousness was plunged into the Dark Night of the Soul. Bernadette Roberts, an American contemplative housewife and mother (who begins her spiritual autobiography at this point) is a helpful guide here. I compare similar experiences of Teresa of Avila, John of the Cross, and Bernadette Roberts with my own, and I note how the Gospel crucifixion narratives were deliberately constructed by Mark, Matthew, Luke, and John to symbolize the inner spiritual events that take place during this Night.

A couple months after my breakthrough into the causal level of consciousness, as I sat writing at home, a sea of heavy darkness descended upon me. The darkness, though I did not know it then, had been uprooted from the unconscious parts of my astral body by my now total openness to the powerful new light of the causal level. The darkness had come in from the unconscious depths of my soul's other incarnations. The darkness had also come in from that part of the world's negative collective unconscious that vibrated at the same dark heavy level as my own soul's repressed negativity. None of this I knew at the time, only now. In Matthew's crucifixion narrative, this darkness is symbolized by the darkness which fell upon and covered Jerusalem for the three hours that Jesus hung on the cross (Matt. 27:45). All the "roots" of my buried dark side, to use John of the Cross' word, were now fully exposed to the light, their deep sufferings and pain brought into conscious awareness.[55]

It is at this point that the contemporary American Catholic laywoman Bernadette Roberts begins her account of her spiritual path. Bernadette, imitating John of the Cross, cites in the first sentence of her book, *The Path to No-Self,* the traditional three-fold map of the Christian spiritual path: the purgative, illuminative, and unitive ways. Next she assumes (wrongly) that John's efforts to fit his experience into these three parts was successful and constituted an accurate map of the whole path: the Night of Senses as the purgative way; the period between the Nights as the illuminative way; and the unitive way following the Dark Night of the Soul. But, when she tries to fit her experience into John's version, it doesn't work. She has to admit she's never experienced either the Dark Night of Senses or the period between the Nights (the subtle). Finally, she gives up and starts her story where, in fact, it started: at the beginning of the Dark Night of the Soul.

It is amazing Bernadette felt and saw as much as she did as she went through this part of the spiritual path. I say this

---

[55]I expect the same thing probably happens at entrance into the subtle level. That is, the definitive move of the consciousness into that level may occur before, not after, the Night of Senses. If so, the experience of "popping up" into the subtle level that I have earlier described marks the completion, rather than the beginning, of the transition. This may well be the case at all levels so that every transition between levels has a definite beginning and end. One would have to systematically track people as they progressed to map the process with certainty. This mapping may be the most important scientific endeavor of the century to come, during which the science of spirituality may take the place held by theology in medieval times—as the foremost of the human sciences.

because, by her own report, she had an enormous amount of emotional blockage in her "third eye," the center of psychic and spiritual vision. All through the Dark Night she had great psychic pain in that center and that area seems to have completely healed only a couple years before she entered the Kingdom of Heaven, the level of nondual consciousness (see chapter 17). At that time her psychic powers finally opened up, but by then, seeing no use for them, she chose to shut them down.

Bernadette's account begins when she is seventeen years old and apparently living in a convent. Here is her account of the descent of the darkness:

> I had been reading in the garden when I felt an invisible film, or thin veil, come down over my head, and shroud my mind. Instantly, I knew something had happened, but no idea came to mind, nor was there any other response. Swiftly and decisively, all had been done in silence; yet, however simple and innocent its quiet descent, this act was, in effect, terrible and awful—the Almighty had simply lowered the boom.[56]

In my case, two months went by, then I had a dream in which my guardian angel, a being with great beauty and power and with blazing blue eyes, said "Goodbye." He also said, with a dazzlingly beautiful smile of the deepest love, compassion, gratitude, and satisfaction, "I'll see you later, upstairs." This dream comforted and terrified me. It comforted me because it indicated that, despite the overwhelming darkness I was feeling, I was still on the right path and had somehow evoked the compassion of God and the angel. But it terrified me because I thought the dream might mean I would soon die. Indeed, I felt like I was about to die even though my common sense and my inner knowingness told me that physical death was not imminent. The departure of the guardian angel marks the completion of the individuation

---

[56]Bernadette Roberts in *The Path to No-Self,* Shambhala, Boston & London, 1985, p. 27.

process at the level of the soul. Torkom Saraydarian, a devotee of one of the Western esoteric traditions, writes, "The
most interesting thing that happens at the Fourth Initiation
is the departure of the Guardian Angel. . . . The One Who
guided the steps of the Initiate since the individualization
[as a human soul] now departs giving him a chance to delve
deeper into the mystery of his own Self."[57]

Next I was led to encounter two persons. One was a
street hustler and the other a very spiritually evolved person.
Both, unknown to me or even to themselves, harbored
strong negative feelings towards me. Ironically, it was the
spiritual person who had the energies most antagonistic to
me.[58] The energies of these two people began to "zap" me.
When a "zapping" of this sort is done deliberately by a black
magician, a person who uses psychic powers for negative
purposes, it is called a psychic attack. It can totally debilitate
a person (see the comments of Agnes Whistling Elk later
on). In my case, it was not deliberate, but, rather, deliberately scheduled by God to help, not hurt.

Warned by inner psychic alarms, I fled first from one of
these people and then from the other. This was a classic subtle
level test of energy discernment. We find the motifs of this initiatory test in many of the ancient myths. One has to wonder if
they were just "myths" or if they came out of the actual experiences of the adepts of the ancient mystery schools, and were,
like Jesus' parables, told as stories to the uninitiated. Conversely,
one also has to wonder, given what a psychic initiate experiences
in this passage, whether the Gospel Crucifixion/Resurrection
narratives are not historical, as I am presuming, but a psychological parable and, if so, what sublime intelligence created that

---

[57]Torkom Saraydarian in *Christ, The Avatar of Sacrificial Love,* 2nd edition, 1994, AEG, available through T.S.G. Publishing Foundation, Inc.,
Cave Creek AZ, p. 106.
[58]It had to do with the experience of other incarnations of our souls
together in ancient Greece before the time of Jesus. My other incarnation had been very cruel to that person's incarnation in that life.

parable? My belief is that both are true, the history and the wondrous parable. To me that is most awesome of all.

When I let go of these two people in the space of two weeks, it was the last emotional straw. My psyche could no longer take the strain. One sleepless night it shattered into what seemed like a million pieces. The literature of the Zen tradition has much to say about this critical point on the path. Like the path I followed, but by different means, the path of Zen seems to increase psychic strain to the point that the old psychic structure, held together by the paranoid ego, finally snaps and collapses. As Jesus said, "a house divided against itself cannot stand" (Luke 11:17). And he also said the wheat and weeds (the positive and negative aspects of our personalities) have to grow together until the very end, and only at the harvest can the weeds be separated out and burnt (Matt. 13:28-30, 40). My story had now entered the harvest time, and the weeds, which had played their legitimate part in the individuation of the soul, were about to be transmuted by spiritual fire.

With this psychic shattering I was plunged into the depths of the Dark Night of the Soul. The psychic pain of this was so extreme I thought I was dying. Much the same happened to Teresa. She appears to have been zapped by the unconscious negative vibrations of another person who had spoken a word to her about death's delay. Here is her account in Mansion Six, chapter 11:

> Well, here is what happens sometimes to a soul that experiences these anxious longings, tears, sighs, and great impulses that were mentioned . . . but they are all nothing in comparison with this other experience I'm going to explain. . . . While the soul is going about in this manner burning up within itself, *a blow is felt from elsewhere (the soul doesn't understand from where or how). The blow often comes from a sudden thought or word about death's delay. . . . I said "blow" because it causes a sharp wound. . . .* It isn't felt where earthly sufferings are felt, but in the very deep and intimate part of the soul, where *this sudden flash of lightning reduces to dust everything it finds in this earthly nature of ours. . . .*
> [emphases added]

> I saw a person in this condition [Teresa herself, of course]; truly she thought she was dying, and this was not so surprising because certainly there is great danger of death.

There is no real danger of death, but try telling that to a psychic person to whom this has just happened. *Something* is definitely dying but what it is I don't know any more than Teresa did. Certainly the "old man" (Adam, the human personality) is dying and the "new man" (the Christ Self) is being born, but what exactly does that mean?

David Spangler speaking from within the Western esoteric tradition, says that the human, by a death and rebirth, is now becoming a "superman." As yet, we don't have any vocabulary except metaphor for explaining this event and others that occur at the higher levels of consciousness. St. Paul put the results of this death and rebirth this way, "When anyone is joined to Christ he is a new being; the old has gone, the new has come" (2 Cor. 5:17). Paul also said: "What does matter is being a new creation" (Gal. 6:15). That the advent of the Christ Self is the next step in human evolution on Earth, and that Jesus came to show us the path to it, I have no doubt.

Bernadette Roberts also gives a graphic description of this psyche-shattering event:

> The opening up of our deepest interior center may be likened to an *underground explosion, wherein all parts of being are sent flying out of control and scattered in every direction*. Prior to this experience, and by virtue of a strong will, we had fashioned our own unity according to what we knew of its parts, and thereafter held these parts together with the tight reins of self-control. In a word, we were masters of our own house. The entrance into the dark night, however, shatters this man-made unity. From here on, God takes over the reins of control and becomes master of the house.[59] [emphasis added]

This is how John of the Cross described the event:

---

[59]Bernadette Roberts, ibid., p. 49.

The two extremes, divine and human, which are joined here, produce the third kind of pain and affliction the soul suffers at this time. The divine extreme is the purgative contemplation, and the human extreme is the soul, the receiver of the contemplation. Since the divine extreme *strikes* in order to renew the soul and divinize it (by stripping it of the habitual affections and properties of the old self to which the soul is strongly united, attached, and conformed), *it so disentangles and dissolves the spiritual substance—absorbing it in a profound darkness—that the soul at the sight of its miseries, feels that it is melting away and being undone by a cruel spiritual death. It feels as if it were swallowed by a beast and digested in the dark belly, and it suffers an anguish comparable to Jonah's in the belly of the whale* [Jon. 2:1-3]. It is fitting that the soul be in this sepulcher of dark death in order that it attain the spiritual resurrection for which it hopes.[60] [emphases added]

For me this was the most traumatic event of my life. There is no describing the terror. I couldn't imagine what had hit me. In the Gospel Crucifixion narrative and in the Creed, this psyche-shattering spiritual event is represented by Jesus' death on the Cross and his descent into hell.

During this inner rendering, it felt, physically and psychically, like the contents of my right brain were onrushing into and mingling with those of my left brain. In a vision that I experienced during the psychic shattering, the image that came to me was of the earthquake that shook Jerusalem at the moment Jesus died and how the curtain of the Temple in Jerusalem was torn in two from top to bottom (Matt. 27:51). It was that type of horrendous, even cosmic, type of psychic rendering.

Putting the two images together, I wondered if the barrier between the left (male) and right (female) sides of the brain had "ripped" as the physical aspect of the advent of androgynous wholeness (Matt. 22:30, Gal. 3:28). Like Teresa I was shaken for days. Teresa says "the soul doesn't even have the strength to write."

---

[60]St. John of the Cross, ibid., chapter 6, pp. 403-404.

Torkom Saraydarian describes various "veils" which separate the different levels of consciousness in the person and cosmos. Saraydarian quotes Alice A. Bailey who writes in *Rays and the Initiations,* "They [the veils] lie between the subtle inner man, mental and astral, and his *physical brain* [emphasis in original]. They are that which prevents brain registration of the world of causes and the world of meaning." Saraydarian himself writes:

> The Hall of Choice is entered when the second veil is lifted or rent. This veil is called the *veil of distortion* and is related to glamors. After the glamors are entirely lifted up and cleaned, the Initiate enters into the Hall of Choice which leads him up to the Fourth Initiation . . . in which the Initiate will learn to stand on his own freedom between "the earth and heaven," renounce all that he has and all that he has been, and withdraw from the form life. This veil is called the *veil of distortion* because it presents a distorted picture of the reality beyond to the Initiate waiting in front of the veil. It is the body of glamors.
>
> We are told that it was the Christ who first rent this veil, ". . . from top to bottom" and let loose a great light. . . . This light has the nature of love; . . . It would seem that, after he rends this veil, the Initiate enters into . . . the Plane of Intuition, [also called] the Plane of Buddhi, or the Plane of Enlightenment.
>
> The second veil, referred to in the New Testament as the *veil of the temple,* is rent at the time of the Fourth Initiation. It is the symbol for a precious vesture which hides the Monad, the Father, and is called the Lotus, the Chalice, or the Temple of Solomon. When direct communication between the personality and the Monad [Father] is achieved, the Fire of the Monad [Father] rends and burns the veil, the Dweller in the Temple is released, and the unfolding human soul meets himself on the Buddhic plane."[61]

In Matthew and Luke's crucifixion narratives, the rending of this veil is symbolized by the vision I experienced; the

---

[61]Torkom Saraydarian, ibid., pp. 171-2.

rending of the veil of the Temple (Matt. 27:51, Luke 23:45). In Mark the rending is symbolized by the division of Jesus' clothes (Mark 15:24). John's narrative, however, stresses the psychological wholeness that results from this rending. In John this wholeness is symbolized by what was not torn to pieces—the seamless robe of Jesus as Christ (John 19:23-24).

Though she may be speaking about something else altogether, here is what Agnes Whistling Elk, a Native American spiritual master, says about the veil or seam: "Humans are not twins of themselves—you know, right and left. Both your sides are different and serve different purposes. There is a seam down the middle. A medicine man or woman can see the seam and break you right into two parts. It's easy. . . . When you are cracked in two, that's when a shaman can take you, take your spirit."[62]

The great twentieth century Hindu spiritual master Aurobindo Ghose[63] speaks of human consciousness as being made up of "two drops." One is our everyday personality consciousness; the other is the soul/psychic body consciousness that "transmigrates" from lifetime to lifetime until the soul is liberated. If Ghose is correct, it seems that those "two drops" are what merge at this point on the path, and the "veil" between them dissolves or is burnt.

---

[62]Agnes Whistling Elk, in *Medicine Woman*, by Lynn Andrews, Harper & Row, San Francisco, 1981, p. 163.
[63]Aurobindo Ghose (1872-1950) was born in India. He studied in England for fourteen years where he graduated from Cambridge, returning to India in 1893. For many years he led a secret revolutionary organization focused on Indian independence from England. He was eventually jailed by the British and, while in prison, experienced a religious conversion that changed his life. After prison he devoted himself to yoga and spiritual writing. He reinterpreted Hindu mysticism in the light of evolution, asserting that individual and social evolution is the result of higher and higher spiritual energies entering the individual and society. He also developed a new type of yoga called Integral Yoga. In 1926 he retired into seclusion and officially established a spiritual community (ashram). Among his written works are *The Life Divine*, *The Synthesis of Yoga*, and *Essays on the Gita*.

After a couple of weeks of being immobilized, I found the strength to pack my bags and go on vacation. I was still in terrible shape and hadn't a clue as to what would happen next. But God, as always, provided. An extremely gifted and spiritual psychic (whom I will call Deborah) received an "inner message" to drive forty miles to see me. When she arrived I was half scared to death. I had never consulted or even met a psychic. The idea had never crossed my mind. I had been a traditional Christian and, if anything, had the usual prejudices against such people. The irony, of course, was that I was extremely psychic myself, but I had never consciously put the "psychic" label on any of my experiences.

After she arrived, Deborah first tried to put me at ease by confirming what I already knew—that I had indeed broken through to what she called the "spiritual" (versus the "psychic") level, and that Jesus was *strongly* with me. I said I felt like I was dying, though I knew I wasn't. "Yes," she said with great compassion, "that's why I came. I sensed death. I didn't think you were going to die, but I knew I had to come."

After Deborah got me to relax, she said I was dealing with astral or emotional damages, and then began talking about past lives. I was horrified all over again. Here I was in the worst mental trouble of my life, feeling I was dying, fearing I was losing my mind, feeling terror-stricken with paranoia, and she was talking about past lives! This was something alien to my Christian path, and about which I'd never given a moment's thought. Seeing my resistance, Deborah said I could take what she said as symbolic if I wished. So I let her proceed.

She told me I was dealing with three neuroses (or "demons")—three masses of fear layered into the psyche, and a host of smaller ones. The two worst demons originated in past lives and the third lesser one in this current life. The dark forces were trying to use these negative energies of mine to do me in. I trembled when she told me that. But, due to my positive energies and my entrance into the light,

Jesus was standing guard over me, keeping the dark forces at bay, she added.

What the psychic called negative emotions and entities are the "demons" the Church normally deals with in exorcisms and that Jesus and his disciples knew how to cast out (Luke 9:1). They are never to be taken casually. Because emotional energy is always magnetic, emotions attract their like in others both positively and negatively. There is hell to be paid, literally, by any exorcist "attracted" to heal a person of such demons. The exorcist's own inner demons could be stirred up prematurely with insanity as a result. Due to this magnetism, the person's emotional damages may be linked to actual demons, the nonhuman negative emanations of Archangel Lucifer, or to the negativity of discarnate human souls. Only persons who have already cleared their own demons by having passed through the Dark Night of the Soul should ever attempt an exorcism on their own. Ideally, they should also be mental health professionals who know what they're doing.[64]

Deborah told me that the worst "demon" I had was a deeply ingrained fear of older men who had certain negative energies. This was a terror that had large portions of guilt and despair connected with it. This neurosis, she said, was because another of my soul's incarnations had been continually sexually molested by a religious superior he'd trusted when he was a "rather mystical" monk in Germany. The monk had ended up hating the priest/superior and wished him dead and, when the priest was struck by lightning and killed, the monk had then inserted layer after layer of guilt on top of the layers of terror, assuming that he had been responsible.

---

[64]It is not my purpose here to explore the very complex matter of partial or full possession, i.e., magnetic attachment to, a discarnate entity or entities. Suffice it to say that there are several types of such phenomena, each with its own complications. For purposes of this book, I'm concentrating on "normal" demons, repressed negative emotions of sufficient scope and intensity to cause neuroses and other emotional imbalances.

During the lifetime of the next incarnate personality created by my soul, these emotions drew an analogous situation to "me." That incarnation was a charismatic but minor American lawyer/politician. He was a Protestant who was betrayed and held up to public ridicule by an older politician he had trusted. This situation evoked all the buried feelings from the monk's life on top of those brought up by the current trauma. The old feelings were brought to light to be cleared, but instead of clearing the negative emotions, the politician fell into a terrible depression, despaired, and ended up taking his own life.

Here we may have one cause of suicidal depression, which contemporary psychiatry usually treats with mind-altering drugs. There is nothing wrong with countering the symptoms of such a life-threatening depression with drugs. Often this must be done immediately to forestall disaster. But much more has to be done for a complete healing to take place. Past life traumas such as this may also be the explanation for so many "unexplainable" major depressions, those in which the despair is out of proportion to anything that's happened in the person's current life. One person loses a job and recovers a week later, but another sinks into a suicidal depression. Why? For the second person, the job loss may have evoked emotional trauma accumulated from similar experiences in prior lifetimes.[65]

As Deborah described this "worst" of my emotional demons, I was shaken because she was putting accurate labels on many of the elements of my inner pain. I said, "I can relate to what you're saying because I spent some years studying for the ministry, and then, the last ten years, I've been an attorney/politician doing public policy." (What I didn't say was how central the issue she'd been describing had been for me, i.e., problems with abusive superiors, during both my ministerial studies and public service). Deborah

---

[65]For a fuller description of this subject, see Modi, Shakuntala, *Remarkable Healings*, Hampton Roads, Charlottesville, 1997.

said, "That's what you've been doing; You've successfully worked out these issues, and now you've been called to another level."

The second worst neurosis, she continued, involved a deep fear of older women with certain negative energies. This fear came, for the most part, from a life as a minor artist/monk in Italy during the Renaissance. At that time the artist/monk had a powerful, half-crazy mother (whom he loved) who was insanely jealous of his creativity and spirituality, and who constantly "tried to push him over to the dark side," the psychic said.

The third neurosis centered about the heart, and consisted of deep feelings of abandonment and betrayal. This neurosis came primarily from the totally frustrated four-year love affair earlier in my current life. The pain of that frustrated affair had been so deep because, she said, the other person and I had been either married, or gay lovers, or fellow monks or spiritual initiates in at least a dozen other lifetimes.

On top of the three principal neuroses were many "mini-demons." To name just a couple: the emotional trauma from having been hit by a car as a child; and the intense and prolonged fear I had absorbed while in the womb from my mother (all during the pregnancy she had been chronically worried and fearful for my father, who was fighting in World War II).

Finally, Deborah told me that, in the realm of consciousness I had gotten to, I had rendered myself wide open to every negativity on the face of the Earth. She concluded that I was going to need a lot more help than she could give me at one sitting and referred me to a Jewish mystic who had had mystical encounters with Jesus, and who also happened to be a psychiatrist in New York City.

Imagine for a second being hit full force—overnight—with the brunt of all this pain. There is no way to convey how horrible it is. St. Teresa says, regarding the pain's intensity, "With the presence of this spiritual pain, I don't believe that physical pain would be felt, little or much, even if the body were cut in pieces."[66] That is also why, as John of the Cross says, "But if it is to be truly efficacious, it will last for some years, no matter how intense it may be."[67]

As with the Night of Senses, however, the person who arrives here always has tremendous inner ego-strength and great awareness. The person *always knows* what is happening, in the sense that they at least know that it is God's doing (or the spiritual light's way of healing and purifying them). They are always given enough insight to make it through although, like John, Teresa and Bernadette, they may have no idea of the pain's source.

Unlike lower-level depressions, the person cannot continue repressing, denying, avoiding, or otherwise refusing to deal with these fears. Nor can one at this level continue projecting or displacing the positive or negative aspects of these neuroses onto other people, the "God in the sky," or "the devil." Once the contents of the unconscious have been exploded outward there is no way of undoing that explosion. Wracked with paranoia, the person will usually try to continue old habits, but it's too late for that. The neuroses are now exposed to the tremendous healing power of the spiritual light of the soul. If one trusts and "hangs in there," there no way the darkness can survive this light.

There was one "demon" that neither I nor the psychic found in the depths of my unconscious, or in what John of the Cross and Jesus called the belly of Jonah's whale. I discovered no pathology or "unnaturalness" about my same-sexual orientation or of that orientation in general. Nor did I find the slightest negative spiritual consequences of my same-sexual activity. In fact, the psychic said Jesus wanted me to know that those same-sexual experiences had been "necessary" for my breakthrough into the spiritual level.

More than a year before, when I discovered I was in the Dark Night of the Soul, I realized I was on what the

---

[65]St. Teresa of Avila, ibid., p. 423.
[67]St. John of the Cross, ibid., chapter 7, p. 408.

mythologist Joseph Campbell called the "hero's journey" to the depths of the psyche. I put on my most rigorous and detached scientific attitude, and promised God that I would keep an absolutely open mind on the subject of same-sexual expression. If, in the depths of my psyche, I found something "wrong" or pathological with it, I would accept the traditional Christian view against such activity.

But I found nothing of the kind. In fact, I found striking evidence to the contrary. For example, were it not for the psychic healing generated by such activity (such as accepting and loving my dark side), and were it not for the great spiritual power generated by the sexual activity itself, I would probably never have broken through into the causal realm. Regarding the morality of same-sexual expression, I now consider the case closed.

As I'm sure the Zen masters would agree, it takes *enormous* psychic power to make this breakthrough into Christ Consciousness, analogous to the great amount of rocket fuel needed to lift the space shuttles into orbit. That is because the person's consciousness is moving contrary to the inertial forces intent on keeping consciousness "weighed down" into spacetime. Perhaps that is what Jesus was alluding to when he said, "The Kingdom of heaven is taken by violence and violent men take it by storm" (Matt. 11:12).

Many spiritual traditions, especially the ancient shamanic and mystery traditions and Hindu tantra, deliberately make use of sexuality to heal psychic wounds and build the psychic power necessary to make breakthroughs into higher levels of consciousness. This was the purpose of the ancient temple sexual healers to whom some scholars believe Jesus was referring when he spoke of those who were eunuchs for the sake of the Kingdom (Matt. 19:12). Agnes Whistling Elk explained to apprentice Lynn Andrews at one point, "I could have sex with Red Dog [a black magician], and for me that act would be a gathering of power."[68]

---

[68]Andrews, ibid. p. 163.

Alan Watts also wrote favorably about the use of sex for the gathering and renewal of spiritual power.

As it turned out, the psychic's help was all I needed. Since I'd had the same issues to deal with during the Dark Night of Senses (naturally, since these now were the "roots" of the same problems) I knew how to cope. I knew about neuroses and how to "own" neurotic projections, and I knew that all I had to do was to relax and wait for the light to heal me.

I had the realization that Jesus was crucified upon a Cross (double-edge against double-edge) and between two thieves, one good and one bad, to symbolize two important things. The two thieves represent the shadow or dark side of the self, our divided inner house (Luke 23:32, 39-43). The good thief represents the denied truth that the dark side contains; like Jesus, one must now own this truth and bring it now ("this day") with you into paradise (wholeness). The bad thief, the "lie" of the neurosis, must be left behind. The Cross symbolizes how tricky this is. Both our conscious side and our unconscious dark side contain truth and lies. This is symbolized by the double-edge against double-edge. The truths must be embraced and the lies abandoned for one to be resurrected into wholeness.

After the session with the psychic, I decided it was time to shut down sexually and psychically. First, neither activity was any longer needed. Second, I had learned how the inner negativities could magnetically draw negative things, people, and even negative spirits from non-physical planes of existence. I wanted no more of this. Third, I was worn out.[69] Fourth, AIDS was by then becoming a menace.

I reopened John and Teresa's books and, sure enough, there was my experience in black and white, especially in Teresa. As always on the spiritual path, we can read the words all we want, but we will only understand them when we experience the

---

[69]Underhill notes on this point: "Psychologically considered, the Dark Night is an example of the operation of the law of reaction from stress. It is a period of fatigue and lassitude following a period of sustained mystical activity." Ibid., p. 382.

reality ourselves. Knowing I wouldn't be able to work anytime soon, I put my house on the market. My old life was over.

Six months later I saw the "Promised Land." Bernadette too spent six months before she saw the new world that now opens before our eyes, the level of the eighth or causal level of consciousness that Christians have traditionally called the "Unitive Way."

As my own experience shows, Jesus will intervene directly to bring a soul to the Christ Consciousness if intervention is what it takes. If we take the trouble and find the courage to seek within as he asked us to, we will find it (Matt. 7:7-8). If we reach the Dark Night of the Soul, Jesus and the our spiritual guides put us under intense 24-hour surveillance. There is no way, as John of the Cross put it, they intend to lose us to the "Devil."

If you're lucky, you may not find the degree of emotional damage I did. Some meditation techniques may ease the pain and make it easier, but it would be a mistake to count on an easy go of it. We are all a lot more fear-filled than we realize. Most adults are in heavy denial about the emotional damage of their childhoods and usually we have no idea of the emotional damage incurred by our soul's other incarnations, let alone what will be our apportioned share in the work of redeeming the planet's collective unconscious negativity.

The Dark Night of the Soul, the Crucifixion Initiation, or the Baptism of Fire and Spirit, may never be easy. Jesus showed us that on the Cross. Perhaps the principal reason Jesus chose to die that way was to existentially and symbolically manifest this inner passage, to encourage us to go through this narrow gate, and to help us shoulder the burden of this Cross. If we want to come fully into Love, this is the narrow gate of which Jesus spoke and which very few humans, including Christians, have found (Matt. 7:13-14). If we truly love him, we have no choice, when we have finally developed enough spiritually to be called, but to leave behind all that is of this world, our space-time personality and its goals, and to follow (Matt. 19:21).

The intensity of suffering in the Dark Night applies to persons whose souls are making the breakthrough into Christ Consciousness for the first time. Those who are born with the

Christ Consciousness usually have a much easier passage when they recapitulate this transition (see chapter 21). The American born spiritual master Franklin Jones (now known as Adi Da), underwent such a recapitulation (which he calls "the death of Narcissus") at age twenty-seven while studying for the Lutheran ministry in Philadelphia in the spring of 1967. He writes:

I was in the bathroom when this episode began. . . . As I looked at my face in the mirror, it appeared gray, disturbed and deathlike. The saliva in my mouth stopped flowing and I was overcome by a rising anxiety that became an awesome and overwhelming fear of death.

I was fixed in the certainty that I was soon to go mad and die. . . . All day I stretched on the floor in the living room, revolving in this same overwhelming fear of death.

Finally, on the third day after this process began . . . I lay on the floor, totally disarmed, unable to make a gesture that could prevent the rising fear. And thus it grew in me, but, for the first time, I allowed it to happen. I could not prevent it. The fear and the death arose and became an overwhelming experience. And I observed the crisis of that fear in a moment of conscious, voluntary death. I allowed the death to happen. And I "saw" it happen. It was not that an organic death occurred, but even organic death ceased to be a "concern." There was a spontaneous, utter release of identification with the body, the mind, the emotions of the separate person, and the self-contracting (or reactive and separative) act that is the "ego"(or the presumed person). . . . The body and the mind and the egoic personality had died (or been utterly released as a concern and an identity), but I remained as essential and unqualified Awareness (and purely That, but also Freely Aware of the physical body and its natural environment). [70]

---

[70]Adi Da, in *The Knee of Listening*, The Dawn Horse Press, Middleton, CA, 1972, 1995, pp. 196-199 in 1972 edition. Later in *The Knee of Listening* Adi Da cites the "death experience" of the great twentieth century Hindu sage Ramana Maharshi (1879-1950) which took place when Ramana Maharshi was twelve years old in 1891. That experience, a classic recapitulation, is described by Maharshi himself in B.V. Narasimha Swami, *Self-Realization: Life and Teachings of Sri Ramana Maharshi*. (Sixth edition, Tiruvannamalai, India, Sri Ramanaasramam, 1962, pp. 20-22.)

Chapter 15

RESURRECTION FROM THE DARK NIGHT

I was gradually resurrected from the Dark Night. The spiritual revelations and realizations I received as a result of the Night were similar to those of Teresa, John, and Bernadette Roberts, showing the essential structural similarities. Foremost was the direct revelation of the meaning of the Holy Trinity: Father, Son, and Holy Spirit. With the completion of the Dark Night, the Holy Trinity is clearly seen as a living cosmological reality in which we, as Christ, participate. There is also the realization of one's own Christhood and one's consequent immortality and sinlessness. The Dark Night ended when I experienced a of Baptism of Fire and the Holy Spirit analogous to that which the Apostles experienced at Pentecost.

After I put my house on the market I waited to emerge from the "belly of the whale." Wracked by darkness and paranoia, I found it very difficult to relax and let go. Often, in writing in my journal, I found myself explosively angry. I spent hours releasing that anger by writing. Underneath depression there is always anger; under the anger, there is always fear; and under the fear there is always hurt. All along the spiritual path, these feelings, layer after layer of them, must be encountered, felt, and released.

There are three ways to effect this release: (1) By spiritual healing practices, particularly meditation and psychic healing (including the laying on of hands, Reiki, yoga, psychotherapy, etc.), and even simple practices like a walk on the beach, getting a massage, or listening to soothing music. For Christians, a practice of inner transforming identification with Jesus in the reception of Holy Communion is an extremely powerful healing practice. (2) By physical disease, e.g., cancer, as the negativity flows out of the astral body to be "worked out" in the physical. (3) By violence, e.g., war, or the now commonplace occurrence whereby a formerly "mousy" person explodes in rage and kills ten people and himself. All three techniques are effective in clearing repressed emotions, but it is obvious which of the three is preferable.

The release of negative emotions must be done in a safe way so that no one gets hurt. It is too late to avoid having these negative feelings; they are already congealed as energy inside the self and are blocking the light. So, however unpleasant they may be, or however contrary to one's self-image of "goodness," we must allow ourselves to *feel* them (which is all they ever wanted in the first place) so that they can be let go of. There will be no resurrection from the Dark Night until we allow this process to complete itself.

As I went through this catharsis and healing, I couldn't hold a job, my house didn't sell, the mortgage payments ate into my savings and my retirement money, and my car died on the road. This loss of career, income, home, and car is typical of the Dark Night of the Soul as the sea of negativity, now at the conscious level, brings external consequences.

These trials may also be necessary as a test of faith and because we have to get the message that all "ego" or "worldly" goals, fueled by fear and geared to our acceptance by others, must be abandoned. In my case much of my "image" and many of my ego goals were fueled by fear. Most of us are always trying to prove ourselves worthy and admirable to others and to the "Sky God." We often read about even titans of industry or successful national politicians whose main goal is "to be loved," or to "make their parents proud."

What always accompanies these ego goals is their opposite, a fear of rejection, "failure," and "not measuring up." From the perspective of the soul, which exists in an environment of unconditional and nonjudgmental love, all these ego goals are worry about nothing. Worse, they are spiritually harmful, because as the primary cause of "stress" and aggression, they are detrimental to our physical health.

Today it is common knowledge that "driven," aggressive Type A personalities are at high risk of heart attack. What is not common knowledge is that, from the soul's point of view, virtually all adults in our society are Type A. Daily we create a society in our own image in which "heart" values are continually sacrificed to destructive competition and other forms of spiritual aggression such as wars on everything from terrorism to drunk driving to cancer to drugs. Everyone running for office is "fighting" for this and "fighting" against that. Our society pays a heavy toll for this pervasive, fear-fueled aggression.

This aggression is counterproductive because, if we fight something, we give power to it and strengthen it. Every action produces an equal and opposite reaction. That is why Jesus taught non-aggression towards enemies. Jesus did not teach "turning the other cheek" because he was a "softie" or wanted people to be "doormats." He taught non-aggression towards one's enemies because he knew the spiritual law and its consequences: put out aggression, you get aggression back.

Only a society as spiritually uneducated as ours would launch a "war on drugs." War only make matters worse. Gandhi, the great apostle of non-violence and non-aggression, never protested *against* anything; rather, he led campaigns *for* Indian self-determination (e.g., the march to the sea for salt and the home spinning wheel effort). The same was true of Rev. Dr. Martin Luther King, Jr., and it is also why the Dalai Lama refuses, and Mother Teresa refused, to sign "protest" petitions of any kind. These spiritually enlightened people understood the dangers and adverse consequences of fear-driven aggression.

Teresa also had to let go of her ego goals. She had to let go of the religious community in which she had spent most of her adult life, and start over again on her own. John of the Cross was twice thrown into jail by religious authorities. From now on, as Jesus said to his Father in Gethsemane, our life must be characterized by the adage, "not my will but yours be done" (Matt. 26:39, 42, 44). From now on, trust and obedience to the inner voice of the Father, regardless of external advice or consequences, is essential.

Regarding this part of the path, the early twentieth century American Protestant mystic Joseph S. Benner, in his little book *The Impersonal Life* has God saying the following:

> You, My Beloved, who have consecrated yourself to Me, and are bending every effort to find union with Me, but instead have found apparently that every prop of the World's support has been withdrawn or is being withdrawn, and that you are without money and without friends, and know not where to turn for human help.
>
> Learn, My Blessed One, that you are very, very close now, and that if you will only continue to abide in Me, letting my Word abide in you and guide you, resting and trusting absolutely in My Promise, I will very soon bring you to a Joy, a Fulfillment, a Peace, that human words and human minds cannot possibly picture.
>
> For you have obeyed My Commands, and have *trusted* Me, and have sought first My Kingdom and My Righteousness, and therefore will I add all other things unto you, even those the World has denied you.[71]

In the Dark Night we learn the truth of what Jesus spoke when he said, "Take no thought for your life, what

---

[71]Joseph S. Benner, *The Impersonal Life*, 1916, 1941, 1969, 1983, De Vorss & Co., Marina del Rey, pp. 233-234.

you shall eat or what you shall drink; nor yet for your body, what you shall put on" (Matt. 6:25) and "Which of you by taking thought can add one inch to his stature?" (Matt. 6:27) and "Take, therefore, no thought for tomorrow, for tomorrow will take care of itself" (Matt. 12:34).[72] In the Dark Night we learn *radical trust* in the God within ourselves. Having learned this lesson, Teresa afterwards founded convents with no guaranteed source of income. Mother Teresa easily operated her worldwide charities without soliciting funds.

After the Dark Night, radical trust becomes second nature. We understand *experientially* not only what faith means,[73] but that the only sensible way to operate in this world is by means of such radical faith and trust. The universe we formerly saw as full of threats of every sort is now seen as a non-threatening place, one full of gifts, abundance, and blessings.

For me, as for Bernadette, the worst of the Night lasted six months (the exact period the psychic had predicted). In the Gospel this passage is represented by Jesus' "three days" in the tomb. One day I felt the heavy darkness (which I likened to being buried immobile under thousands of heavy blankets) beginning to ease. A few days later I suddenly could "see."

I saw what Bernadette calls "the painful revelation of our deepest union with God." This union with God is the essential revelation. We see that being "made in the image and likeness of God" (Gen. 1:26-27) is not poetry, nor does it refer to humans as some pale imitation of God. It is

---

[72]Ibid., pp. 235-237.

[73]Many Christians think faith is adherence to a particular Christian belief system or to a set of doctrines, dogmas, moral norms, and practices. A person, therefore, who does not so agree or practice is said to have "lost" his or her faith. None of this has anything whatever to do with the faith described here, and as taught by Jesus in the Sermon on the Mount. Jesus was talking about faith as complete psychological trust in God, life in general, and God's universe.

literally true. We see that our own selves and all humans are made of "God-stuff," that we are, like Jesus, God Incarnate, begotten of God and made of the same substance and essence as God. We see that this has always been so but, up until now, we have been too blind to see it. I felt like the man in the Gospel whom Jesus said had been born blind so that later, after Jesus healed him, God could be glorified (John 9:1-3).

For me the revelation took the form of the reversal of the way I'd always regarded God and the spiritual path. Up until then I'd been pursuing the "God within" (Luke 17:21). But it was only now that I realized that I'd been picturing this inner God as a sort of invisible extra appendix, a God within but one definitely separate. Now I saw that the opposite was a fuller and better expression of the truth: *God isn't so much within us as we are within God*. We are actually cells in God's body, God's Incarnate, or Created, or Only-Begotten Body, the Christ (1 Cor. 12:12-27). I saw that what St. Paul said to the Athenians is true, that we live and move and have our beings *in* God (Acts 17:28). Anyone who reaches Christ Consciousness becomes more like an organ in the Body of Christ rather than just a cell. Like Jesus, we become the vine itself rather than a mere branch (John 15:5). Having died to identification with the personality, we are now capable, like the vine, of bearing "much fruit" (John 15:6-8).

I realized that what some Christians call the "Mystical Body of Christ" wasn't an exercise in fanciful poetry but was a *cosmological* description of the *actual* physical (and non-physical) universe. It is the way things really are, the way they operate. As Jesus had promised, I saw a whole new world, and I saw that this world, all of Creation visible and invisible, is nothing less than the Christ, God's "Only-Begotten Son," God's Word Made Manifest or Flesh (Gen. 1, John 1:1-3).

St. Teresa says this is an "intellectual" rather than an "imaginative" vision. She means an intellectual "realization" in contrast to what we usually call a "vision" or a "waking dream." She writes:

> Our good God now desires to *remove the scales from the soul's eyes* and let it see and understand. . . . The Most Blessed Trinity, all three Persons, through an intellectual vision, is revealed to it . . . and these Persons are distinct, and through an admirable knowledge the soul understands as a most profound truth *that all three Persons are one substance and one power and one knowledge and one God alone. It knows in such a way that what we hold by faith it understands, we can say, through sight. . . ."*[74] [emphases added]

John of the Cross set out his realization in several places in his writings. He wrote in his prologue to *The Living Flame of Love:*

> Submitting to the judgment and better opinion of our Holy Mother the Roman Catholic Church, by whose rule no one errs, finding my support in Sacred Scripture, and knowing the reader understands that everything I say is as far from the reality as is a painting from the living object represented, *I will venture to declare what I know.*
>
> There is no reason to marvel at God's granting such sublime and strange gifts to souls he decides to favor. If we consider that he is God and that he bestows them as God, with infinite love and goodness, it does not seem unreasonable. For he [Jesus] declared that the Father, the Son, and the Holy Spirit would take up their abode in those who love him *by making them live the life of God and dwell in the Father, the Son, and the Holy Spirit* [John 14:23 . . .[75] [emphases added]

For the Christian, and for the first time as Teresa says, there is a clear understanding of the "mystery" of the Trinity. One can now understand the Trinity because, in and

---

[74]St. Teresa of Avila, *The Interior Castle,* Mansion Seven, chapter 1, ibid., p. 430.

[75]St. John of the Cross, *The Living Flame of Love,* ibid., p. 646.

by the Dark Night, one's consciousness has finally been *experientially* "baptized in the name of the Father, and of the Son, and of the Holy Spirit," as Jesus commanded (Matt. 28:19).

John of the Cross points out that this substantial union with God has always been the case for everyone, the only difference now being the *conscious realization* of one's substantial union.[76] St. Catherine of Genoa states the same thing a little differently and more boldly. She wrote, "My being is God, not by simple participation, but by a true transformation of my being."[77] Mystics of the Eastern (Orthodox) Church speak of *theosis* or deification, though the word "deification" makes it sound like we "become" God, which is not correct; what happens is that we consciously realize the divinity that has always been ours.

Bernadette Roberts writes that, at this point in the path, she was "tempted" to declare that she was God but resisted the "temptation." Why did she hold back? The first reason is that, when most of us think of God, we mean God as strictly transcendent, and no one is equal to God in that sense, not even Jesus, as Jesus himself often said (John 5:19, 30, Luke 10:22). A second reason is that we don't want

---

[76]St. John of the Cross, *The Dark Night,* book 2, chapter 23, section 11, ibid., p. 453.

See also *The Ascent of Mt. Carmel,* chapter 5, where John writes: "This union between God and creatures always exists. By it He conserves their being so that if the union would end they would cease to exist. Consequently, in discussing union with God, we are not discussing the substantial union which is always existing, but the union and transformation of the soul in God. This transformation is supernatural, the other natural."

Commenting on this passage, Wilber correctly states that John is not talking about any "supernatural" intervention by God in nature. John is stating a view that "the natural union of Spirit with all things becomes a conscious realization in some, and that conscious realization is called supernatural." (In *Sex, Ecology, Spirituality,* p. 299)

[77]Quoted in Goswami, *The Self-Aware Universe,* G.P. Putnam's Sons, New York, 1993, p. 52.

people to think we're crazy. After all, there are lots of psychotics whose consciousness has somehow opened up to the fact of their divinity but who don't understand that divinity is *everyone's* nature. Third, there is always a reluctance by the Christian to classify oneself as in any sense "equal" to Jesus.

Despite these reasons for reluctance, all the great Christian mystics speak the essential truth that is realized upon coming into Christ Consciousness: we are indeed God, or, to put it more modestly, we could say we realize that "only God is and we are not" as in "I live, now not I, but the Christ (God Manifest) lives in and through me," (Gal. 2:20).

Many things follow automatically from this new trinitarian understanding, this new vision of reality. First, one now sees oneself (and everyone else), not as the historic personality Jesus of Nazareth, but as members of the Eternal Christ and joint heirs *with* Jesus of the Kingdom (Rom. 8:17). In all one's dealings with others, from now on, one is always aware that one is dealing with God's Son, and that, whatever one does to others, one does to God's Son (Matt. 25:35-40); in fact, not only to God's Son but to oneself (since we too are one in substance with that Son). One sees that in this world there are no "others," there is only Christ. One sees that this has always been the case but up until now, we had been blind to this truth. With St. Paul we can now declare that we have come "to that oneness in our faith and in our knowledge of the Son of God" as to become "a mature person, reaching to the very height of Christ's full stature" (Eph. 4:13).

Second, we see that, since humans are made of eternal "God-stuff," there is no death (1 Cor. 15:54). Our mortal self is now clothed with immortality exactly as St. Paul says (1 Cor. 15:54). We no longer have to *believe* in life after death. We see not only that we will never die but that we have never been born. With Jesus we can say, "Before Abraham was, I AM" (John 8:58). We are now totally identified with our eternal soul, our true Christ Self. Living in the Christ Consciousness we know we will never die (John 11:26). All fear of death is therefore lost. As St. Paul said, "Death has lost its sting" (1 Cor. 15:55). Teresa writes, "It [the soul or person] has no more fear of death than it would of a gentle rapture."[78]

Third, as St. Paul says, sin is conquered. Since we now see that humans are made of "God-stuff," and have always been divine, we see that *sin does not exist.* God, after all, cannot commit sin. Nor can God's only-begotten Son, the Christ we all are. All humans, therefore, are, and have always been, sinless. To say, as we Christians do, that Jesus was conceived and born "without sin" is simply another way of saying he was conceived and born with the Christ Consciousness. The same is true for Mary.

Regarding the person's *realization* of his or her sinlessness, John of the Cross writes:

> The soul thereby becomes divine, God through participation, insofar as is possible in this life. *And thus I think that this state never occurs without the soul's being confirmed in grace,* for the faith of both is confirmed when God's faith in the soul is here confirmed. [79] [emphasis added]

We will see that John was mistaken about this being the highest level of consciousness realizable in this life, and that he was also mistaken in thinking the person, at this stage, had attained the perfection of the Father (Matt. 5:48) that Jesus wanted for us. There is still remaining what Bernadette Roberts calls "subtle self-serving." But John's point that "sin" no longer exists as far as the person is concerned, is correct. By definition, there can be no "sin" in someone united to God, confirmed by God's grace, and

---

[78]St. Teresa of Avila, ibid., chapter 3, p. 440.
[79]St. John of the Cross, *The Spiritual Canticle,* Stanza 22, ibid., pp. 560-561.

otherwise participating in God's own divinity. It is just as 1 John 3:9 states, "Whoever is a child of God does not sin, because God's very nature is in him; and because God is his Father, he cannot sin."

From this point on, when faced with our own or others' negativity, the Christed person sees not sin but ignorance, that is, lack of awareness. We see that all the negativity people bring onto themselves and others results from a lack of awareness. Whenever we encounter negativity, with respect to both self and others, we join with Jesus on the Cross in saying, "Father, forgive them, for they know not what they do" (Luke 23:34). It is because this realization comes at exactly this point on the path that Jesus' saying is ascribed by Luke as having been spoken on the Cross. John of the Cross too, from this point on, begins to talk less about sin and more about ignorance, by which he also means a lack of awareness. John writes, for example:

> God is the light and the object of the soul. . . . When it is in sin or occupies its appetites with other things, then it is blind; even though God's light may shine upon it, because it is blind it does not see its obscureness, which is its ignorance. Before God illumined it by means of this transformation, it was in obscurity and ignorant of so many of God's goods, as the Wise Man says he was before wisdom enlightened him: *He shed light on my ignorance* [Eccles.[80] 51:26]. [81]

It also follows from this new vision of reality that no soul, each made of God-stuff, will ever be eternally lost. In the end, though some souls may indeed wander in darkness for thousands of years, God *cannot* fail Himself/Herself. It is impossible. In the end, every soul will be saved even if it takes a million years of painful negative learning to eventually bring that soul to God.

---

[80]In the Catholic Bible, Ecclesiastes goes to chapter 51 (i.e., it is not divided)

[81]St. John of the Cross, *The Living Flame of Love*, stanza 3, ibid., p. 702.

Moses was not allowed to see the Face of God because the process of evolution had not yet completed God's face (Ex. 33:20). *We* are God's face. That is why Jesus, speaking as the Christ for all of us, said, "He who sees me (the Christ) sees the Father" (John 14:9). Does one honestly believe, though the process itself (Holy Spirit) is infinite, that God will not eventually see His own reflection, His Son, His face, "completed" in each and every one of God's creations? Jesus himself, speaking as the universal Christ, explained that, "He who sent me wants me to do this: that *I should not lose any of those he has given me*, but I should raise them *all* to life on the last day" (John 6:39). The Christ, the firstborn of all creation, was sent to all humans and all humans have their life from him and have been given to him. Do we think the Christ will fail the Father's mission? Of course not. In the end, none will be lost, just as Jesus said.

A still further realization is related to God's omniscience or all-knowingness. Union with God brings the clear realization that *there is no question that cannot be answered* by going within. All the answers to any questions humans are capable of asking are contained within the depths of the self. The hard part, as any contemporary scientific researcher will tell us, is to ask the right questions. The second qualification is the law of *kairos* or "sacred timing." God, our own deep withinness, does not reveal things until the appropriate time, that is, until we learn enough to ask the right question. Apples had been falling off trees for eons before Isaac Newton asked why, and people were just as intelligent, but *kairos* determined that the revelation of gravity would occur only when the human race was ready to ask the right question. *Kairos* is why so many things are discovered by several different people at about the same time, two classic examples being the fact of evolution and the existence of the human immunodeficiency virus (HIV). Non-Euclidean geometry was discovered, independently, by four different mathematicians at the same time!

A third qualification, with respect to omniscience, is that the person, as Bernadette Roberts says she discovered to the disappointment of her ego, doesn't become any smarter in terms of either IQ or spacetime knowledge and information. Even if the person becomes an open channel for revelation, like the disciples of Jesus who wrote the New Testament, or like Teresa in writing her *Interior Castle,* the revelation comes through that person's previously learned thought-forms, vocabulary, cultural assumptions, and personal interests. Human limitations, though divinized, remain. One sees, therefore, that all humans are teachers for each other, and that all of us, no matter what our level of God-realization, have much to learn from each other. No one is superfluous. We each play our parts, and from God's point of view, seeing only the perfection of the Son, we always play them perfectly.

Still another realization relates to God's omnipotence or all-powerfulness. As Bernadette Roberts put it, one realizes that "God and I together are an unbeatable team" (cf. Rom. 8:31). There are no obstacles of any kind that cannot be overcome through faith in the power of the God within whom we now clearly see we live and move and have our being (Acts 17:28).

For me, the gaining of these new realizations made the Dark Night well worth the price I had paid, but they did not end the pain. Another six months passed. During all this time I "just happened" to be dealing with an older man who had been a religious official. Naturally, given the severity of my main neurosis, my anger and fear were projected onto this older man. The man, however, wrote me a kind and supportive letter that caused me to see that he was a friend, not an enemy. I was able then to "see" the projection clearly and withdraw it.

As soon as I withdrew the projection, letting go of the fear I had for that older man and replacing it with affection, two things happened. First, my house immediately sold (three offers in a week after 15 months on the market), and second, I experienced a profound physical healing as the emotional poison left my system. Both physical drainage systems were affected. The upper drainage system, located in the head, discharged its poisons with the result that several teeth became infected, even one that had already had a root canal. The lower system, in the torso, had an even bigger release, causing a large abscess in the groin.

Remembering that I'd had a smaller abscess during the Night of Senses, I asked the doctor what caused abscesses. I got the same answer as years before, "We don't know what causes them." But I felt I knew. My intuition (the causal level of consciousness is also called the level of "intuition" or pure "knowingness") told me that I was blessed that these poisons had been discharged. Otherwise they probably would have caused a serious illness such as cancer. I also knew, particularly since I had been born with these damages, that the physical healing had occurred even at the cellular and genetic levels, the body itself being reconfigured and transformed. Medical science, of course, is still not able to verify healings of this type but, who knows, it may be able to do so in the not too distant future.

After I sold my house, I moved near the ocean in another state. I walked the beach for hours on end. My solar plexus (the seat of emotions) was now in constant pain. Though I could ill afford it and had no medical insurance (I lived on a credit card that had been sent to me unsolicited), I went to a hospital and had the gastro-intestinal series and other tests done. The doctors found nothing. So, I confirmed my own knowingness that the pain was psychic, not physical. After another couple months I was able to withdraw the projection regarding older women. The stomach pain then disappeared.

At that point my heart center began to throb with psychic pain as the third neurosis (from the frustrated love affair) emerged into awareness for healing. That lasted for four months or so. Then one elbow began to throb. It had been broken when I was hit by a car as a child, and the emotional trauma of that event was stored there. After six weeks or so that pain also ceased.

In Bernadette Roberts' case, the major psychic pain was in her third eye, the point between the eyebrows that is the seat of psychic sight. But, though the pain lasted for many years, she herself never discovered the cause.

After these healings, I was again well enough to work, but only at a simple, non-intellectual job. I was guided to choose a job that involved working with the body, both for physical exercise and psychic grounding, a job that also kept me outdoors where I could allow the energies of nature to help in the healing.

Finally, two years and two months after the shattering of the old psyche, God brought me fully into the new causal level of consciousness. Because Teresa had said that the Night would end "usually by means of a great rapture, or with some vision," and because my own Christian path so closely paralleled hers and John's, I thought it might end in what both called "spiritual marriage" with Jesus (a vision of the Christ in which vows or rings are exchanged between Christ and the mystic). But, for me, the ending was to take a different form.

I visited Deborah three more times, once every ten months or so. She continued to help me and filled me in on some other past lives, including one as an Anglican priest in England, one as a Russian Orthodox priest in Russia, one as an initiate at the time of King Arthur and the Round Table, and several more as a Catholic monk. What she said made me realize how long and difficult the path to the Kingdom can be, and gave me an increased tolerance and respect for other paths to God.

Because of my experience with the psychic, and because I'd had a lot of time on my hands while unemployed, I'd begun to read extensively about the Buddhist, Hindu, Native American, and Western Christian esoteric spiritual traditions. I also became acquainted with some of the finer elements of the new age movement. A friend of mine invited me to a new age workshop run by several channelers of Vywamus, a very advanced spiritual being. Even after more than two years of healing and grounding, however, I was still feeling shaky and was wary and nervous about this new experience. For one thing, as a traditional Christian, I'd had no experience up until then with "new age" anything. But I need not have worried.

During the workshop, Vywamus addressed me for the first time through one of the channelers. Vywamus, with enormous compassion and gentleness, and the type of pleasant humor one exhibits when handing a person a surprise birthday gift, matter-of-factly declared, "I see you are surrounded by fire right now." Immediately, and to my amazement (as if Vywamus' words had actually brought it forth), I saw that a fiery wind of some sort had completely surrounded me. I was on fire from head to foot. Flames were everywhere. I felt such intense spiritual heat that it was like being consumed. I remember even waving one hand like a fan in an effort to cool myself down. I also saw all sorts of "black stuff" in my aura being burnt up and transmuted by the raging spiritual blaze.

After a few minutes the fire and its heat subsided. I slowly came back to my normal self. Vywamus then said, "Now go outside and get grounded." This experience, which I afterwards realized had been the "Baptism by Fire and the Spirit" spoken of in the Scriptures (Matt. 3:11, Acts 1:5 and 2:1-4), ended the Dark Night of the Soul. More healing remained to be done, but the pain was gone, and all my shakiness had been replaced by the deep, restful peace that surpasses the world's understanding that Jesus had promised (John 14:27, Philip. 4:7).

The American anthropologist Carlos Castaneda's experience of final entrance into the fullness of the soul level was also an encounter with spiritual fire. He writes:

> But one day, while I was in Los Angeles, I woke up in the early morning hours with an unbearable pressure in my head. It was not a headache; rather it was a very

intense weight in my ears. I felt it also on my eyelids and the roof of my mouth. *I knew I was feverish, but the heat was only in my head.* I made a feeble attempt to sit up. The thought crossed my mind that I was having a stroke. My first reaction was to call for help, but somehow I calmed down and tried to let go of my fear. After a while the pressure in my head began to diminish but it also began to shift to my throat. I gasped for air, gagging and coughing for some time; then the pressure moved slowly to my chest, then to my stomach, then to my groin, to my legs, and to my feet before it finally left my body. . . . *The two areas where the pain became excruciating were my knees and my feet, especially my right foot, which remained hot for thirty-five minutes after all the pain and pressure had vanished.* . . . La Gorda, upon hearing my report, said that this time for certain I had lost my human form, that I had dropped all my shields, or most of them. She was right.[82] [emphases added]

Bernadette Roberts' experience was less dramatic, hardly noticeable except for a change in awareness itself. She explains that, because her experience was one of a gradual acclimating process, she was not able to discern at exactly what point full union with God was realized. But she says that the full intuitive recognition that one has come into the unitive state is imperative as the key indication that union has taken place. She discovered that, by bringing her into the unitive state, God satisfied the whole person and exceeded all boundaries in doing so.

The experiences of Castaneda and myself were dramatic. And those who are familiar with the lives of Teresa and John know that their experiences of "spiritual marriage" were also rather dramatic. So it is perhaps best that I've ended the accounts of entrance into Christ Consciousness with the "ordinary" account of Bernadette Roberts.

---

[82]Carlos Castaneda in *The Eagle's Gift*, Pocket Books, NY, 1981, pp. 111-112.

There is a tendency for those who have set themselves seriously on the spiritual path to make a big deal over the dramatic experiences of the mystics. So I repeat what Teresa and John and all the others have said: it is the change in consciousness or awareness that counts, not the dramatics. In fact, to the extent the spiritual energies cause disturbances in the body, emotions, and mind, they are doing so because they meet resistance (though resistance is not to be judged). The body, emotions, and mind must be gradually raised (and in a way that, to be safe, constantly requires grounding) to the vibrational level of the new energies, another strong reason for following a scientific meditation technique. Once the person becomes fully accustomed to the vibrations at the new level, there is no longer commotion but peace—at least until the next level's vibrations begin coming into awareness.

I exempt from the term dramatics, however, genuine spiritual seeing, something John of the Cross, though he used it masterfully himself, was probably wary of doing because of the threat of the Inquisition. People who can genuinely see beyond the realm of spacetime have traditionally been, in all religions, the guides for other humans on the spiritual path.[83]

---

[83]Anecdotal evidence from many cultures and time periods suggests that the guides or "seers" have been disproportionately same-sexual in orientation. Some try to account for this by suggesting it has something to do with the pineal gland. Others have posited as the reason the natural union in one person of male and female energies (symbolic of the androgynous consciousness of the Kingdom of Heaven where "there is no male or female," Matt. 22:30, Gal. 3:28). Even today, despite centuries of persecution, the institutional Christian church would almost collapse overnight if the hundreds of thousands of lesbians and gay men who serve it went on strike, from the Cardinal bureaucrats in the Vatican to black Baptist choir members in rural Mississippi. If this natural talent for "seeing" is indeed true with respect to lesbians and gay men (and future researchers will verify or discount it sooner or later), then mythic Christianity will be seen to have paid still another very heavy spiritual price for its misguided judgments.

Before ending this chapter I also want to note that, in the last twelve years, I have been present at three other transforming spiritual events similar to the one that happened to me. In each case I was at a Christian new age channeling session and sat next to a woman whose consciousness was raised during the event from the psychic level of consciousness into the subtle level. In none of the three cases did the channeler, or I, or the woman recipient of the grace, know beforehand what was going to transpire.

In each case it seemed a normal channeling event, the channeler relaying spiritual teachings from Spirit. But behind the scenes, I could see that the spirits were working hard, deftly managing, using, and blending the energies of those present ("Where two or three are gathered in my name, I am in their midst," Matt. 18:20). In each session there were interruptions, seeming asides, questions, instructions to chant this or that, etc. Finally (and I say "finally" because I can remember growing restless and fidgety on at least one of those occasions) something happened.

All of a sudden, a wind entered the room, analogous to a gust prior to the downpour of a thunderstorm. It was not a random wind, but a purposeful wind, full of electrical or fiery charge. In each case, the wind "hit" the woman recipient. Usually, this was after first "going through" others of us who were there; it was like electricity being "stepped down" by a series of transformers. In each case the woman was "swept upwards." One woman was brought into the presence of her guardian angel. Two burst into tears of joy. One woman was "proclaimed" a "Daughter of God" by a loud spirit voice. One was lifted up off the inner "mountain" she had laboriously climbed. As I said, all three of these events occurred in Christian new age settings. Though I assume it may happen occasionally, I have never experienced such a visitation by Spirit in a mainstream Christian church.

This type of spiritual event, however, did occur regularly in the early Church, as spiritual power and new awareness was transferred to those who had passed their initiations and were now ready for transformation to a new level of consciousness. The Acts of the Apostles speak of such occurrences (see Acts 2:2-3). In addition, this is exactly the type of spiritual event described by John the Baptist in John 1:31-34. In that Gospel passage John the Baptist (after saying he did not at first recognize who Jesus was) states, "I *saw* the Spirit (Wind) come down like a dove from heaven and stay on him. I still did not know him, but God, who sent me to baptize with water, said to me, 'You will *see* the Spirit (Wind) come down and stay on a man; he is the one who baptizes with the Holy Spirit.' I have *seen* it, and I tell you he is the Son of God."

And in John 3:8 Jesus himself testifies, "The wind blows where it wishes; you *hear* the sound it makes but you do not know where it comes from or where it is going. It is the same way with everyone who is born of the Spirit (Wind)." The "wind," of course, as Jesus testifies, is the Holy Spirit. The events are seen and heard and felt with the psychic or subtle senses, not the physical senses. But they are of such power, effectiveness, and spiritual splendor that they are never forgotten by those who experience them. Nor is the consciousness of the person ever again returned to the pre-event level.

After I experienced the Baptism by Fire and the Holy Spirit, I continued my healing while working at the minimum wage, manual labor job. Then one day my phone rang. I was offered three different highly paid and responsible positions in my field of public policy. I had been off my career path for four years at this point, something all the advocates of worldly wisdom advise people never to let happen. Nor had I solicited any of these new jobs. The offers just came from friends who cared about me. I took the one that interested me most, as a counsel to one of the Congressional committees in Washington, D.C.

It was proved to me what Jesus had said, "Seek first the Kingdom of Heaven and all else will be added" (Matt. 6:33). Jesus, of course, knew how this world *really* works.

Jesus knew that *everyone*, free will notwithstanding and whether they know it or not, is nothing less than an instrument and expression of God, and that God *always* takes care of those who obey God's will (Matt. 7:21).

PART IV
THE CONSCIOUSNESS OF A HUMAN AS A REALIZED DIVINITY

Chapter 16

CHRIST CONSCIOUSNESS—

THE CAUSAL LEVEL

Christ Consciousness is the Christian term for causal consciousness. At this level the Christian is identified with his or her true Christ Self, which is seen as in a spiritual union with God the Creator. At this level one can truthfully say, "I live, now not I, but Christ lives in me," as St. Paul said. The person with Christ Consciousness sees all other human beings as the Christ and treats them accordingly. This is the level of true Christian love, which is spiritual love identical to what the Buddhist masters call true compassion. The person with Christ Consciousness is free from neurotic projections and emotional addictions, and is able to live solely in the present, curiously detached from everyday struggles and anxieties. One is able to commune silently with God, now seen as the Great Void or Mother Creator within, from which all creation and creativity arises.

We come now to the eighth level of human consciousness: causal consciousness. It is the first level of consciousness of the human, not as a human personality, but as a realized divinity. It is consciousness at the level of the soul, i.e., individualized Spirit. For Christians it is the level of Christ Consciousness, the level of true Christian love, and has traditionally been called the Unitive Way or union with God. To Buddhists this is the level of the bodhisattva, the being with the Buddha consciousness of true compassion. To students of the human aura, it is the level at which the crown chakra opens dramatically with the result that the head is now encircled with a halo.[84] The heart center also fully opens and we become vessels of tremendous love and compassion. This level is also called that of pure intuition or knowingness.

The reason the word causal is used is because this is the level of *causes*, the archetypal principles or ideal patterns by and from which the lower planes of existence (astral and physical) are built. The spiritual master Plato called these archetypal principles the Ideal Forms.[85] These principles are the "cause" of all the other lesser forms that spring from them. This is the level of the Logos, the Eternal Word of God (John 1:1-3) through whom, as the firstborn of creation (Col. 1:15-20), all else of creation comes.

---

[84]The crown chakra is the wheel of vibrant energy and light located just above the top of the head. Jesus and the saints are usually depicted with halos of golden-white light about their heads. This symbolizes the openness of their crown chakras, that is, their wholeness or sanctity. Anyone who has such an open crown chakra is by definition a saint because the crown chakra only opens fully as one realizes the Christ Consciousness. The existence of this pictorial tradition within Christianity shows that, at one time at least, the existence and significance of the chakras was known and understood.

[85]In Platonist philosophy these "ideal forms" are eternal and immutable and the rest of creation (the lesser forms) are pale imitations, and have no effect on the former. This is a static, nonhistorical, nonevolutionary understanding of this level. In light of evolution, these understandings now need to be modified. Our experience on the physical plane, by means of a continual biofeedback type of mechanism, does influence the ideal forms themselves. Though the ideal form is there at the level of the Logos (John 1: 1-3), we self-evolve or self-create our own uniquely individuated expressions of God by our choices and experiences over lifetimes.

Ordinarily this level is characterized by a great peace at our center or core. The "inner house" is no longer divided against itself but has been reorganized into a well-functioning whole. There can still be, and usually are, emotional disturbances on our outer layers, as Teresa, John, and Bernadette all admit. But the disturbances grow less and less the farther one travels into the causal realm as the great light in our core gradually transmutes these remaining negativities and integrates them around its center of wholeness. The remaining negativity tells us that we are not yet perfect. We have not yet reached, as Jesus instructed us to do, the state of perfection of the Father (Matt. 5:48). We, as "baby" divinities, still have to learn how to live this new divinized life, how to operate at this new level of energy vibration and awareness.

We must also learn to develop our intuitional senses, the equivalent at this level of the physical senses at the physical level, the psychic senses at the psychic level, and the subtle senses at the subtle level. These intuitional abilities, strictly speaking, are not "senses," for the soul has no "senses." We must learn to "translate" pure intuitions into understandable forms such as ideas, words, and images.

In prayer we sink easily into what St. Dionysios called the "Darkness" or "Void," the Father/Mother Source of All That Is, the great well of divine creativity from which God's Word and all creation continually arises (cf. Gen. 1:2). As Bernadette says, we learn to find refuge in that center whenever trials arise, getting better and better at "sinking down and sinking into" this Dark Void that we now see as our own center. Some Buddhists call the void *shunyata*, meaning "emptiness."

The need to practice this sinking down and into the void is critical because the healing begun during the Dark Night continues nonstop for all the years we live at the causal level. But, as Teresa says, "Even though there is much tumult . . . no one enters the center dwelling place and makes the soul leave . . . the suffering is not such as to disturb it and take away its peace. The passions are now conquered and have a fear of entering the center because they would go away from there more subdued."[86] These are the years in which our true Christ Self gradually brings us into the presence of the Father. These are the years during which the still higher energies of the nondual, Monadic level, the Kingdom of Jesus' Father, gradually come into our awareness.

With respect to my own path, I realized that "God as Mother" was a more accurate description of the creator void/darkness than the traditional image of the creator as "God the Father" for this reason: we traditionally think of God the Father as creating *ex nihilo*—out of nothing. In this traditional imagery God and creation are seen as separate, a "male" manufacturing type of imagery.

This, however, is not the case. God's Son (and through the Son all else of creation) is *begotten, not made,* just as the Creed says. God actually *gives birth* to the Christ and, through the Christ, the Firstborn, to the rest of creation. God begets truth from truth, light from light, beauty from beauty, true God from true God. God has never created *ex nihilo,* but gave (and continues to give) birth out of the Womb of Her Infinitely Creative Self. Agnes Whistling Elk says it beautifully:

> Remember, everything must be born of woman [the Void, the Darkness, the Great Womb]. It is a power the world has forgotten. Men [and separatist, rationalist "male" thinking like creation *ex nihilo*] are interlopers. Woman is the flowering tree . . . the center of the universe, of creation . . .
>
> Long ago, the sacred grandparents said that there was no day and no sun. The Great Spirit was the only. The Great Spirit was the center. The Great Spirit was the source [God as Mother] without end. . . . The Great Spirit hid and divided up into niece and nephew [female and male, the Christ, Jesus and Mary]. Together they sang the

---

[86]St. Teresa of Avila, *The Interior Castle*, Mansion Seven, chapter 2, ibid., p. 437.

creation song. Everything vibrates with this voice [Holy Spirit, AUM, the Great Amen]—the universe, the galaxies, the sun, and the earth. Light and darkness and all things are but a song of the Great Spirit. The Great Spirit is sleeping [immanent] in all the named and nameless things.[87]

The Kogi tribe of Columbia, South America, express this same truth as follows:

> In the beginning there was blackness
> Only the sea . . .
> The sea was the Mother.
> The Mother was not people, she was not anything . . .
> She was when she was, darkly.
> She was memory and potential.
> She was *aluna* [mind, consciousness].[88]

Emotionally, we will notice at the causal level a gradual unfoldment of great inner warmth for everybody and everything. Other people notice it too. We may be astonished to see that, no matter what the circumstances, we can't help but express this great emotional warmth. It comes through in speech, in manner, in humor, in gesture. There is no effort involved. It just is. This warmth is true Christian love, true Buddhist compassion. St. Paul describes this spiritualized love in the following familiar passage:

> Love is patient and kind; love is not jealous, or conceited, or proud; love is not ill-mannered, or selfish, or irritable; love does not keep a record of wrongs; love is not happy with evil, but is happy with the truth. Love never gives up: its faith, hope, and patience never fail.
> Love is eternal. . . .
> Meanwhile these three remain: faith, hope, and love; and the greatest of these is love. [I Cor. 13:4-8, 13]

---

[87]Lynn V. Andrews, *Medicine Woman*, Harper & Row, San Francisco, 1981, p. 96.
[88]Alan Ereira, in *The Elder Brothers*, Alfred A. Knopf, New York, 1992, p. 115.

Here is how Chogyam Trungpa describes compassion:

> The fundamental characteristic of true compassion is pure fearless openness without territorial limitations. There is no need to be loving and kind to one's neighbors, no need to speak pleasantly to people and put on a pretty smile. This little game does not apply. In fact it is embarrassing. Real openness exists on a much larger scale, a revolutionarily large and open scale, a universal scale. Compassion means for you to be as adult as you are, while still maintaining a childlike quality. In the Buddhist teaching the symbol for compassion . . . is one moon shining in the sky while its image is reflected in one hundred bowls of water. The moon does not demand, "If you open to me I will do you a favor and shine on you." The moon just shines.[89]

Another sublime description of Christian love comes from the pen of St. Isaac the Syrian:

> What is a charitable heart? It is a heart that is burning with charity for the whole of creation, for men, for the birds, for the beasts, for the demons—for all creatures. He who has such a heart cannot see or call to mind a creature without his eyes becoming filled with tears by reason of the immense compassion that seizes his heart, a heart that is softened and can no longer bear to see or learn from others of any suffering, even the smallest pain, being inflicted upon a creature. This is why such a man never ceases to pray also for the animals, for the enemies of Truth, and for those who do him evil, that they may be preserved and purified. He will pray even for the reptiles, moved by the infinite pity that reigns in the hearts of those who are becoming united to God.[90]

Finally, the late Mother Teresa wrote:

---

[89]Chogyam Trungpa, *Cutting Through Spiritual Materialism,* Shambhala, Boulder & London, 1973, p. 213.
[90]St. Isaac the Syrian, in *Teachings of the Christian Mystics,* edited by Andrew Harvey, Shambhala, Boston, 1998.

To me, God and compassion are one and the same.
Compassion is the joy of sharing. . . . It is only pride and
selfishness and coldness that keep us from having compassion. . . .
One's religion has nothing to do with compassion.
It's our love for God that is the main thing. . . . We must
love one another as God loves each of us. To be able to
love we need a clean heart . . . it is our love for God that
is the main thing because we have all been created for the
sole purpose to love and be loved.[91]

At the level of the emotions, we find ourselves
detached. St. Teresa says, "There is a great detachment from
everything and a desire to be either alone or occupied in
something that will benefit some soul."[92] Bernadette was
astonished when she saw herself remaining utterly at peace
while the woman she worked for went into a tirade and fired
her from her job.

In my own case, I noticed it first at the movies. I found
that, no matter how sad the movie, or how scary, or how tragic
or violent or heartrending, it didn't affect me as it had before.
I stayed at peace, observing, interested, and aware, but generally undisturbed. True, I felt great compassion for people
whose sufferings might be depicted, but the portrayals could
not move me from my own deep inner peace. At first, to be
honest, I didn't care for this change. I wanted to feel scared or
heart-broken or angry as I once had, but I no longer could.

Carlos Castaneda writes that, after he "lost the human
form" he had a similar experience:

I found myself in a most unfamiliar state. I felt
detached, unbiased. It did not matter what la Gorda had
done to me. It was not that I had forgiven her for this
reproachable behavior with me; it was as if there had

---

[91]Mother Teresa, Compassion in Action, in *For the Love of God*, ed.
Benjamin Shield, Ph.D. and Richard Carlson, Ph.D., 1990, 1997, New
World Library, Novato, California, pp. 179-81.
[92]St. Teresa of Avila, *The Interior Castle*, Mansion Seven, chapter 3, ibid.,
p. 440.

never been any betrayal. There was no overt or covert rancor left in me, for la Gorda or anyone else. What I felt was not a willed indifference, or negligence to act; nor was it alienation or even the desire to be alone. It was rather an alien feeling of aloofness, a capacity of immersing myself in the moment and having no thoughts whatever about anything else. People's actions no longer affected me, for I had no more expectations of any kind. A strange peace had become the ruling force in my life. I felt I had somehow adopted one of the concepts of a warrior's life—detachment. La Gorda said I had done more than adopt it; I had actually embodied it.[93]

At this point on my path I realized that all these familiar negative feelings had been addictions (the contemporary word for what Christian spirituality has traditionally called attachments and what many Buddhists call desires).[94] I realized that, once our own magnetic inner emotional negativity is substantially gone, i.e., we have grown beyond attachments, outside negative vibrations cease to have any effect because there is no longer a negative magnet inside us that they can attract.

Although great art, both comedy and tragedy, are healing to the degree they cathart inner negativity, this is not the case with most movies, popular entertainment, the tabloid press, or the evening news. The latter often feed our addictions to negative emotions like fear, anger, jealousy,

---

[93]Castaneda, ibid., pp. 112-113.
[94]Obviously a person cannot live without desires, nor is there anything wrong with desires per se. Nor would a Buddhist master be so simple-minded as to try to eradicate desires in the normal sense of the word as many Westerners have interpreted Buddhism to espouse. When the Buddhist master talks about eradicating desires he means attachments, those sticky (magnetic) emotional addictions that are based in fear, the type of attachment that is called blind because it fails to see the emotionally unbalanced projections (both positive and negative) that are always present in such addictions. When the Buddhist says that at the causal level the person becomes free of karma or desires, she is speaking of freedom from such addictive emotional programming.

revenge, and guilt. It is an endless exploitation because, like all addictions, they are impossible to satisfy. We can never get enough. At the causal level of consciousness, we find ourselves radically free of this endless horror, this never ending stress on the nervous system. We find ourselves peacefully looking at all of life with the same detachment we now have for a movie. The Hindu spiritual master Paramahansa Yogananda puts it this way:

> The sages of India since ancient times have spoken of the universe as a materialization of the thought of God. It is easy to say, of course, that this universe is a dream. But the verisimilitude of 'life' in our everyday experiences makes it nearly impossible for us to believe that the world is nothing more than a cosmic dream. It is necessary that we first develop mind power in order to be able to realize that the universe is actually made out of the thought of God and that, like a dream, it is structurally evanescent . . .
> *The root-cause of sorrow is in viewing the passing show with emotional involvement* . . . no matter what difficulties come, ever affirm, 'It is all a dream. It will soon pass.' Then no trouble can be a great trial to you. No happenings of this earth can in any way torture you. [emphasis added][95]

Another great benefit from this lack of attachment (lack of magnetic negativity) is that, generally, we can no longer engage others' egos. We don't get into fights or arguments with anyone over anything, not because we are trying to avoid fights and arguments, but because we now have very little "ego" and so are no longer capable of magnetically engaging the egos of others. Generally, everyone leaves us alone because we are absolutely unthreatening to anyone anymore. (I say generally because there are some people who are so negative that they feel very threatened by the light.) For the most part, everyone likes us because we

---

[95]Paramahansa Yogananda, *Man's Eternal Quest*, Self-Realization Fellowship, Los Angeles, 1975, 1982, p. 237

evoke the very best feelings in them and never trigger their negativity with our own.

None of this means we become emotional zombies. On the contrary, we are now free to feel the richness of the emotions of our present situation. Our emotions once more have the spontaneity of a child's (Matt. 18:2). Jesus wept when Lazarus died (John 11:35) and blazed scorching anger when he routed the moneychangers and vendors from the Temple (Matt. 21:12-13). But none of this was a result of past negative emotional programming. These were powerful emotions, exactly suited to the situation. Unlike the child, however, we are now never swept up in, or controlled by, emotion. We are so detached that, if the situation warrants, we can will one emotion to cease and immediately switch to another.

Free from neurotic projections, we can also see people and situations far more accurately, and speak and act accordingly. We can, as Castaneda says, "live in the present," appreciating the newness of each person and experience, rather than, as before, seeing everything through the same monotonous emotional conditioning. Both the Tibetan master Trungpa and Castaneda's Yaqui master don Juan describe this new perception by saying that there is now a "space" between whatever happens and our reaction to it. We are no longer emotionally programmed to react in a knee-jerk fashion. We can now use that space to *choose* how to react, or to not react at all. The farther we travel into the causal level, and the more skillful we become at using this spacious new way of seeing, the more interesting every person and experience becomes. We experience people and situations deeply, seeing each person and experience as sublimely unique and as having much greater mystery and beauty than we ever before appreciated.

Still another feature of the causal level, as alluded to by Teresa above, is an increasing appreciation of, and desire for, silence. Silence seems to become more wonderful than speech because it seems to have more depth. Often there is nothing we now like better than to be alone for a whole day or days at a time (cf. Mark 6:46).

It may seem (even to ourselves) that we are doing nothing during these times of silence. But that is not so. In the silence we are communing *without thought* at a deep level with the void that is the source of all creativity. Some Christians have called this the contemplative gaze. When we are drawn out of silence by the press of everyday affairs, however, we are often amazed at the new creative thoughts, impulses and actions that flow out of us, often things we never considered before. This is because the essence of God is perpetual creativity, and we are now finally taking our places as powerfully co-creative children of God.

Still another thing that happens at the causal level is that we become more active in spiritual work even while sleeping. The Communion of Saints, happy to have a new worker, presses us into service day and night in their great work. We may be more "out of body" at night, for example, helping people who have just died get to the light.

Generally, after someone dies, they remain in a realm near to the physical plane for a few days or weeks. This allows them to comfort those left behind, to guide others to tidy up unfinished projects, and even to satisfy their curiosity over such things as who shows up at the funeral. Sometimes, however, the person gets stuck in this in-between realm and fails to move on into the light. These cases may occur when there is an extremely strong emotional attachment to someone (e.g., a new spouse) or something (e.g., their home, alcohol, an unfinished project) and/or where the death was sudden, unexpected, and/or violent (in which case the person may not even admit to themselves that they no longer have a physical body).

These souls, of course, are the ghosts of haunting fame. They may be stuck for hundreds of years unless someone can induce them into the light. Teresa recounts that, during prayer, she helped to free many of these souls from what she (I believe mistakenly) thought was "purgatory." My reading of Teresa is that she helped free these souls from this in-between realm, not from what is ordinarily considered "purgatory."

All of this is not to say there are no challenges at this level. The detachment from the cares of this world, and the love of communing with God in silence, can get out of hand, and become immoderate and unbalanced. We now see everyone and everything as God-stuff, as part of the Christ, as the Word or Dream of God (as in the Buddhist *shunyata* or "emptiness of form"). Because we know with absolute certainty that God is running this world down to the finest detail, there can be a temptation not to care about the world anymore. There can be a temptation to forget that, here in spacetime, forms are important. Giving in to this temptation, by an overindulgence in the enjoyment of formlessness, can be not only a neglect of our new co-creatorship responsibilities, but a grave hindrance to realizing the next level of consciousness, the nondual. It is always a mistake to get attached to anything, including silence and emptiness. Chogyam Trungpa stressed that it is not enough to realize that form is emptiness; we must go on to the next level where we'll finally see that emptiness is form.

The Christian practice of returning to the world after realizing our union with God to work in selfless service for others becomes important if we are to get grounded enough to get to the next level. There is nothing like having an organization to run, bills to pay, or children to raise to keep us planted firmly on the earth. Bernadette, for example, left the convent, married, and raised four children, while Teresa and John were endlessly busy setting up their reformed religious community.

There can also be a temptation, in the other direction, to be so anxious to bring Christ to the world that we neglect the necessary communing with the inner creative void. As always, moderation and balance, coupled with continued effort forward, are the keys.

For those prone to detach themselves from this world and the distinctions of form, the initiatory tests for the next level, the nondual, will often be about learning to see that, though other people are indeed the Christ, they are also often deceitful, jealous, angry, fearful, and even treacherous. We must learn to see these negative energy forms clearly and cope with them appropriately. There is no room for a pollyannaish "everything is rosy" approach to life. As Trungpa says, you have to learn that, despite your wonderful vision of the world, things are indeed as bad as they seem.

Like the other levels of consciousness described previously, the causal level usually lasts many years. It seems to have taken St. Paul of the Cross, an eighteenth century Italian mystic, about forty years to go from spiritual marriage in his twenties to nonduality in his seventies. It took Bernadette about twenty years. Along the way she left our guides John of the Cross and Teresa of Avila behind. John and Teresa never realized the nondual level, at least as far as we can tell from what they wrote. Bernadette was puzzled to see herself beyond her mentor John and does a lot of soul-searching about why God brought her, but did not bring John, to nonduality (which she calls "no-self"). She overlooks the obvious. Neither John nor Teresa, in all probability, lived long enough. Teresa died ten years after she entered the causal level and John died at age 49, not many years after he realized that stage.

The spiritual path to the nondual vision of the Kingdom of Heaven is long and arduous. This is all the more reason for Christians to start early and work hard. For those who are serious about following the path Jesus laid out, Jesus advised no turning back once we put shoulder to the plow (Luke 9:62).

Chapter 17

NONDUAL CONSCIOUSNESS—ASCENSION INTO THE KINGDOM OF HEAVEN

At long last we consider the Kingdom of Heaven, the ultimate goal of the Christian spiritual path, and of all the great spiritual paths. Meister Eckhart and Bernadette Roberts are cited as the principal examples of Christian mystics with nondual consciousness, while Chogyam Trungpa is a recent Buddhist example and Paramahansa Yogananda a Hindu example. Nondual consciousness marks the end of all division between "creature" and "creator." It was the level from which Jesus spoke when he said that "The Father and I are one."

In Christian New Testament mythology, the entrance into the nondual level of the Kingdom of Heaven is symbolized by the Ascension of Jesus, body and soul, into Heaven. With the nondual consciousness of the Kingdom of Heaven on Earth, the person comes into what past Christian mystics have referred to as the "beatific vision." This is the end of the human spiritual path, that is, the end point of the evolution of human consciousness on Earth. Were all humans to realize the nondual consciousness of the Kingdom, this beautiful blue-green globe would indeed be Heaven on Earth.

We come now finally to the Kingdom of Heaven that Jesus preached, the nondual vision of *this world*, a vision so complete and wondrous that there are no words that can adequately describe its magnificence. It is a vision that, by definition, is beyond the dualities of human language and the linear, dualistic, chopped-up consciousness through which almost all humans now see the world. If the causal level of consciousness was characterized by peace, the non-dual level is characterized by joy or bliss. Hindus call this state of bliss *ananda*, the goal in consciousness of all Hindu monks (swamis). The Christian tradition has called it the "beatific vision of God" while on Earth. The vision of the Kingdom of Heaven is the level of consciousness of the human as fully realized divinity.

There are two senses in which the nondual level can be spoken of as the second level of divinity, or the ninth, final, or highest level of human consciousness. First, we must, in terms of consciousness development, go through the first eight levels in order to arrive here. Second, *as experienced* in the body and emotions, and *as experienced* by the mind in terms of depth of spiritual clarity, it is a level of energy vibration higher in frequency than those of the preceding eight. I say "as experienced" by our human faculties because, in itself, this level is vibrationless. It is the same from eternity to eternity; it is timeless and spaceless God prior to, and transcendent to, any vibration or manifestation. To say this level is vibrationless does not mean it is a vacuum. That's a physical concept. It's completely full, the fullness of pure potentiality, and that "dark" vibrationless fullness somehow gives birth to all vibrations without itself being affected or changed in the least.

There are also two senses in which it is not proper to call this final level a "level" at all. First, we don't get to this level of realization unless we first relinquish all polarities, including higher and lower, as a way of seeing or talking about reality, or definitively explaining anything, including the levels of consciousness of the spiritual path. In fact, as Wilber says, we have to "fall off" the path to get here. In other words, we finally have to stop seeing the spiritual life as a path at all. We have to once and for all simply surrender to what is and what has been all along: our divine identity now consciously realized and "seen."

The ninth or final level, in this sense, is not a level at all, but the divine ground of being that *underlies* all the levels. This same type of surrender, letting go of striving, and acceptance of what is, is necessary before the breakthrough into *any* new level of awareness, but this particular letting go is the final, most thorough, and most decisive letting go of all (Luke 9:24, John 12:24-26).

The second sense in which this is not a level as the others before is that this "level" of the Father is not so much a level above that of the Christ Consciousness (as if the Father were "above" the Son), but rather it is the fulfillment of the Christ Consciousness (John 10:30, 38). When the Gospel Crucifixion narrative has Jesus saying, "It is finished" (John 19:30) when he dies, it means just that. Once the human personality, in the Dark Night, is crucified upon the Cross of its inner contradictions by being plunged into the belly of Jonah's whale, baptized into Jesus' baptism, or subjected to the descent into hell (whatever image you prefer), the work is essentially done. It is indeed finished. The human as consciously identified with his or her space-time personality dies, and we are "resurrected" as a Christ (John 1:12-13). It is then Christ who unerringly takes us to the Father (John 14:6). That is why I said the healing initiated in the Dark Night continues non-stop throughout the causal level. The light of the Christ Consciousness is now always shining upon us and is forever healing and enlightening us (John 9:5). For the Christian, the causal level can be understood as the "forty days" between Easter and the Ascension. The "forty days" can be likened to the period between our resurrection into Christ Consciousness and our ascension into nonduality.

The great thirteenth century Christian mystic, Meister Eckhart, called the entrance into the nondual level of consciousness the great "breakthrough," a word he coined in German. I am calling this breakthrough what the New Testament calls it: the Ascension of the Christ (the Christed being), body and soul, into the Kingdom of the Father, the

Kingdom of Heaven *here on Earth* (Mark 16:19). After this breakthrough, the Christian can say with St. Paul, "And God has raised us up to Himself and has seated us with Him in heaven through Jesus the Christ" (Eph. 2:6). And again, "We are now citizens of Heaven" (Philip. 3:20).

Bernadette Roberts writes:

> I do not regard the resurrection as the final step; to see and know is not enough. Greater than this is the ascension, or final dissolution into the fullness of God. With the dissolution of his human form—seemingly into thin air—Christ suddenly becomes everywhere: the God within and without, as well as all form in which the manifested and unmanifested have fruition and become One. Thus, even the seeing of the Trinitarian aspects of God is not the final step. The final step is where there is no Trinity at all, or when all aspects of God are seen as One and all that Is.[96]

Bernadette Roberts calls the nondual level "no-self" because she could no longer find herself when she looked inside, and because she didn't know what else to call it. Her term, however, is unfortunate because "no-self" makes it sound like the self gets annihilated, which is not the case.[97] But it is one way of talking about this level. There are other ways but none are without logical problems. That is because the vision of the Kingdom of Heaven, being nondual, cannot, by definition, be expressed in dualistic human language. It can only be *experienced.*

---

[96]Bernadette Roberts in *The Experience of No-Self,* Shambhala, Boston, 1982, 1984, p. 132.

[97]The school of "no-self" is a branch of Buddhist theory that the Buddhist mystic/philosopher Nagarjuna logically demolished many centuries ago. Nagarjuna, who lived about 200 A.D., founded the Madhyamika (Middle Path) school of Mahayana Buddhism. His great contribution to philosophy was to logically demolish not only the "no-self" school but all the possible logical ways of talking about nonduality. He stressed always shunyata (emptiness) as a way of showing the relativity and inadequacy of all conceptualizations.

Chogyam Trungpa calls the nondual level that of "tantra" or "luminosity" while other Buddhists call it "nirvana." The Hindu Paramahansa Yogananda calls it "cosmic consciousness" (not to be confused with the cosmic consciousness of "nature mysticism" back in the psychic level). The Roman spiritual master Plotinus called it simply "the One."

In his book, *Sex, Ecology, Spirituality,* Ken Wilber begins his description of the nondual level by quoting Sri Ramana Maharshi, whom he calls India's greatest modern sage. Sri Ramana Maharshi writes:

> The world is illusory;
> Brahman [God] alone is real;
> Brahman is the world.

The first two statements, says Wilber, "represent pure causal level awareness, or unmanifest absorption in pure or formless Spirit; line three represents the ultimate or nondual completion (the union of the Formless with the entire world of Form). The Godhead *completely transcends* all worlds and thus *completely includes* all worlds."[98]

In Christianity, though there have been others (e.g., St. Gregory of Nyssa, St. Maximos the Confessor, and the Celt John Scotus Erigena), there is perhaps no greater spokesperson for the nondual level of consciousness than Meister Eckhart. Eckhart calls the nondual level that of *Deitas* or Godhead, the level, so to speak, above what we normally think of as God. It is the level of Jesus' Father, to which, as Jesus said, no one comes except by means of the Christ Consciousness, i.e., "through me" (John 14:6). What Eckhart's *Deitas* and Jesus' "Father" definitely are not is the Creator God whose existence had been "proved" by philosophers such as Eckhart's predecessor in the chair of theology at the University of Paris, St. Thomas Aquinas, using human dualistic or dialectical reasoning.

When Eckhart says, "I pray God to rid me of God," it is precisely Aquinas' reasoned-to Creator God that he wants to transcend. In fact, the secret to entering the nondual level is to

---

[98]Ken Wilber in *Sex, Ecology, Spirituality,* p. 302.

transcend all the archetypal forms of the causal level, that is, to cease seeing the world in this way rather than that way, or in any way at all that can be conceptualized and described in linear language (cf. Luke 17:21). Bernadette calls this process the letting go of all judgments (John 8:15). Trungpa says we must see the world *directly*, that is, without our normal, filtering, abstracting, conceptual glasses.

Eckhart advises:

> Empty yourself of *everything*. That is to say, empty yourself of your ego and empty yourself of all things and of all that you are in yourself and consider yourself as what you are in God. God is a being beyond being and a nothingness beyond being. Therefore, be still and do not flinch from this emptiness.[99]

Eckhart describes the nondual vision that comes from this radical emptying out:

> In the breakthrough, where I stand free of my own will and the will of God and of all his works and of God himself, there I am above all creatures and am neither God nor creature . . . I discover that God and I are one . . . I am an immovable cause that moves all things . . . there I had no God and was cause of myself. . . . There I stood, free of God and of all things. But when I took leave from this state and received my created being, then I had a God [Creator].[100]

At the nondual level of human consciousness all dualism disappears. That means the separation in our consciousness between subject and object dissolves entirely. The seer becomes the seen as well as the eye. The difference between the logical opposites "creator" and "creature" disappears, and the difference between the individualized Spirit (the soul) and universal Spirit (God), still present at the causal level, now dissolves. Christ and the Father are now seen as

---

[99]Matthew Fox, *Breakthrough: Meister Eckhart's Creation Spirituality in New Translation*, Image Books, Garden City, NY, 1980, pp. 104, 178, 242.
[100]Ibid., pp. 218, 217, 215.

one without a two, not (as at the causal level) as created Christ Consciousness in a "unitive marriage" with the Father/Mother Creator. The Christ, and any person who has followed Jesus as Christ to this level, is now no longer in an I-Thou relationship to God, but in what Wilber calls an I-I oneness, a pure subjectivity without an object.

A contemporary English nun, whom I know only as Petra, gives her account of the entrance into the nondual level and her experience of this I-I oneness:

> It was my 'hermit day' and I had an extraordinary sense of peace, as though nothing could ever touch me again. This peace had been growing for some weeks, but, being occupied with the community and other things, I hadn't stopped to taste it. This day, completely free from everything, it flooded into my consciousness and wrapped me round. I was in the garden, and for a moment I seemed to be looking within and I saw that *I* was not there. There was no 'I'. I can't say more than that. *I* had gone. It wasn't that I saw or felt God, but it was as if I were in a vast and lonely plain far removed from everything. For a few weeks, I lived to some extent outside myself, by which I mean only a very small part of me seemed in contact with what was going on around me. . . . This was bewildering joy.

Her friend and guide, another nun called Claire, responded:

> This is really what joy means, isn't it? Nothing but God—and God apparently not there . . . so that the whole soul is gift, is surrender, is that 'lived nothingness' we spoke of . . . your experience is of *what you are,* that is, an emptiness God has filled.[101]

---

[101]Correspondence between Petra and Claire, as quoted in *Guidelines for Mystical Prayer,* Ruth Burrows, Dimension Books, Denville, N. J., 1980, pp. 123-24. This book, which is written by Ruth Burrows, a fellow nun, is useful to the extent it describes the experiences of these three women. But its usefulness as a guide is minimal because, like most traditional Christian maps, it divides the entire spiritual path into merely three parts. Burrows also makes no distinction between the subtle, causal, and nondual levels, and, probably because of that, to some degree misinterprets the experience of St. John of the Cross and St. Teresa of Avila.

The reason why we can now no longer see God, either within or outside ourselves, is because God is no longer an object, either an intellectual object or a projected emotional object. Nor can we see our own self as an object. We are now totally identified with God so that, when we look out upon this world, God is the one looking out (cf. John 14:10). When we look within, it is into the voidness of the uncreated Father from whom there is no separation. There are no objects of consciousness to be found either within or without. We are now within the Father and the Father is within us (John 10:38). God and we, the I-I, are looking out upon the world together in such a completely identified way that there is a oneness without a twoness (duality). And any other person who encounters us is directly encountering God in human form ("he who sees me sees the Father," John 14:9).

I want to emphasize again that the individuated soul (the Christ Self) is not annihilated. Those Buddhists and other believers who take the "no-self" theory literally (or any Christian who understands Jesus' "losing of self" as literal, Matt. 10:39) are mistaken. The individuated soul is *transcended*, which means that it is both preserved and negated (just as, at the first level of consciousness, the body is preserved, i.e., remains in existence, but negated when the child ceases to identify the self with it). Here at the ninth level of consciousness, the seat of our identity once again shifts—for the last time. We now see our identity, our I, not as the individuated Christ Self, but as limitless spirit, as consciousness itself. The individuated Christ Self remains in existence. Very much so. For one thing, it would be impossible to operate in spacetime, or even in the invisible parts of creation, without it. For another, the creation of the Christ Self, the completely individuated divinized soul, is the entire purpose of material creation. It is the end point (omega) of human development in spacetime. It would make no sense for the Christ Self, the product of eons of spiritual labor, to then be annihilated.

Bernadette Roberts explains:

When the unitive life falls away [as we enter the nondual level], however, we do not suddenly become God; God does not suddenly disappear. All that happens is that we finally take our rightful place with Christ in the Trinity as part and parcel of God—God manifest. The ultimate realization of no-self is not its identity with Father or Holy Spirit—the omniscient unmanifested Father or the omnipotent manifesting Spirit—rather, it is the realization of our true nature, our true identity as the manifest aspect of the Trinity—Christ. In this breakthrough, we also realize the Oneness of Christ, Father and Spirit, three distinct, non-interchangeable aspects of the Godhead. There are no such things as greater or lesser aspects of God; the three act as one, and to finally see how this works is what no-self is all about.[102]

On entering the nondual level, one of the things that Bernadette discovered was that, echoing the words of Eckhart quoted earlier, there is now no difference between God's will and our own will. Our human will is now seen as one with the will of God. So we can give up all the constant fretting over what God's will might be, and whether or not we are truly following God's will. Because the will of the Father and Son (God's and our own) are now the same, we have a tremendous unification of life-force power in ourselves, a laser-like unification with intense energy and focus. This is so much so that, as with Jesus, it gradually becomes more and more the case that what we "decree" God decrees. When we forgive, God forgives (Luke 7:48). If we curse a fig tree, it may die (Matt. 21:19). When we say, "you are healed," or "your sins are forgiven," that is the case (though the faith or repentance of the one being healed or forgiven is equally important (Luke 7:9, 50).

Like all powers and realizations, this one too keeps developing and deepening ever afterwards. Like all realizations,

---

[102]Bernadette Roberts in *The Path to No-Self*, Shambhala, Boston, 1985, p.195.

the truth revealed here has always been the case for all humans, though the house-divided-against-itself status of most human consciousness (Luke 11:17) prevents people not only from seeing this, but also from being able to use this unified power.

Because of this laser-like focusing of the life-force, the person lives afterwards in what many mystics have called the "Eternal Now." We live totally in the present. Those of us who are unable to let go of our addictions, on the other hand, are forever living in the past, incorrectly seeing and interpreting present events and people through the foggy lenses of prior emotional and belief-system conditioning. At the same time (the opposite pole of this inner imbalance) we might be forever trying to live in the future, always saying, "Things will be different and better after . . . (insert: graduation, marriage, a new job, children, a new partner, my children's graduation, my children's marriages, retirement, 'after I get to the after-death heaven')." The problem for those of us addicted to the past or the future, is that life—the present moment—more or less passes us by. Only now, at the nondual level, is this problem solved once for all. Only now can we really *live*, bearing much fruit, as Jesus said, in the process. Petra comments:

> Looking back I see that nearly all my life and with growing intensity I have suffered from profound anxiety. The anxiety was rooted in my relation to God. Not that I feared his 'wrath' or anything like that, it was just a fear of existence, a fear of the Other. Anxiety as to how I stood to him; only he mattered, was I loving him? *Time, terrible time was passing away . . . was I near to God? . . . time was ambiguous and threatening, threatening on all levels. [Now] I possess him. Time has no meaning.* [emphasis added]

Petra's friend Ruth Burrows writes of her:

> Petra is aware, more at some times than at others, that all save a tiny portion of herself is absorbed elsewhere. She

is not aware of what she is absorbed in, what she is knowing or loving. . . . She is content just to be; life passes by,
passes over her; she feels, reacts, can be hurt, cast down,
groan under the pressure of life, but in another sense be
'away,' almost with a sense of nonbeing which can frighten
at times. Below the level of superficial questionings and
doubts is an assurance, an inability to worry or be anxious; no temptation 'to do something about it' by way of
rousing the attention, applying the mind, making an
effort . . . there is only sufficient attention and room for
what she has to do in her daily round.[103]

For Petra the terrible anxiety that many of us feel due
to the relentlessness of time's passage is no more. Once we
live in the eternal all such anxiety ceases. We can now focus
completely on the creative task at hand, taking immense joy
in the exercise of our divine creativity, but completely
detached from future outcomes and expectations. Like a
child, we become carefree in a way most adult humans can
only fantasize about (Matt. 18:3). We now live in a dimension free of time, in eternity.

Many Christians try to "live in the present," or "live in
the presence of God" as a spiritual practice, but, no matter
how hard we concentrate on so living, the practice doesn't
succeed. This practice is impossible *until* our consciousness
comes into the nondual level. In this, as in everything along
the spiritual path, consciousness unfolds naturally, by law,
from one step to another. We cannot jump steps.
Paradoxically, once our consciousness enters the nondual
level, we cannot help but live in the present; it is impossible
to live otherwise.

There is also another sense in which our consciousness
has now become like that of a child. We have perhaps heard
people say (perhaps we have said it ourselves) that, no matter how old our bodies may look in the mirror, there is a
part of us that feels exactly the same as when we were little.

---

[103]Burrows, ibid., pp. 137-139.

That part of ourselves seems (and actually is) timeless. It also seems (and actually is) spaceless, because it hasn't changed in the slightest, even though we may now live in California whereas, as a child, we lived in Illinois. This timeless-spaceless withinness of ours (which is the identical timeless-spaceless withinness that is within everyone else) is none other than God. At the nondual level of God-consciousness we actually come to operate on the everyday level *from* this consciousness, *from* this timeless spacelessness. We no longer have to go within to feel it. We *are* it. Always. Consciously. In that sense, we have once again become a child, operating from the same wondrous spaceless "place" and timeless "time" we first felt inside ourselves when we were very young (Matt. 18:3).

At the nondual level, all the polar opposites disappear for they are now all seen as complements that forever make wholes. This includes the polarities of negative and positive; at this level they are seen as making a one. Any judgment, therefore, that what people see as positive is better than what people judge as negative must also be left behind. The world is now perceived *directly* with no concepts, judgments, reasonings, or other intellectualizations getting in the way. It is the final letting go. This is the final loss of self that Jesus preached (Luke 9:24, John 12:24-26).

When Jesus said that the devil (*diabolus* in Latin) is a liar and the Father of Lies (John 8:44), he was talking about the rational dualistic vision by which almost all humans see this world, the intellectual seeing that chops up the world, separates us from each other, and separates us from God. The words "devil," "diabolus," "demon," and "duality" are all based on the root word "two" or, in Greek, *duo*. In Genesis the devil, the Father of Lies, is pictured as a fork-tongued (dual tongued) snake. In nondual consciousness, the Devil, or duality, is now finally and completely vanquished.

When Genesis has God saying that he would forever put enmity between the offspring of Eve (woman) and the offspring of the lying, forked-tongue serpent (the Devil) (Gen. 3:15), one of the meanings is that the perpetual struggle we encounter between the demands of our inner life-force (the feminine) and the demands of our reason (the masculine, dualistic, and the origin of the lie of separation) will go on until the "woman" triumphs by giving birth to nondual awareness in Christ (see Revelation, chapter 12).

The nondual transcendence of identification with a self does not mean that we get absorbed or annihilated into God like a drop of water entering the ocean as Evelyn Underhill suggested it might be after reading the accounts of certain Muslim Sufi mystics, or as one might conclude after reading some of the literature of the Buddhist no-self school. There is no annihilation of the individuated soul. Rather, the soul is taken up into the Father so that the entire universe enters into the soul. The ocean enters the drop of water.

So completely are we raised up that, for example, we see the entirety of Creation as our own body. Because of this radical raising up the passage from the causal level to the nondual level is sometimes called the "Ascension Initiation," the last of the five major initiations of consciousness that Jesus acted out for us.[104]

By this Ascension we enter into the Kingdom of Heaven *in our bodies* while on earth. In fact, the *only* way to enter the Kingdom of Heaven is bodily. Those of us who do not reach the nondual level of consciousness in this life will generally have to keep returning to this planet or another physical planet until we do. Ascension into the nondual vision of the Kingdom of Heaven is the reason for the whole human enterprise God has created on this planet. *By means of our bodies* we somehow become gods (John 10:34-35), even lords over the angels as Eckhart and the Scriptures say (1 Cor. 6:3). By means of the polarities and dualities of

---

[104]Mary's "assumption, body and soul into heaven"' symbolizes the same inner spiritual passage as Jesus' Ascension, though expressed in a "feminine," hence passive, way.

spacetime, we somehow transcend spacetime forevermore. It is a project, this assembly line for the production of gods, that is well worth whatever price we pay for living on this planet, no matter how many lifetimes it may take.

The Hindu yogi calls the movement from causal to nondual awareness the movement from *nirvikalpa samadhi,* utter absorption while at prayer in formless cause, to *sahaj samadhi,* the state in which our God consciousness is so absolute that there is no need to pray at all (in order to "reach" God, that is). We now go about *as God* doing the busiest tasks and rendering service to all. Meister Eckhart explains:

> Therefore, *if all creatures are asleep in you,* you can perceive what God works in you . . . seize God in all things for God is in all things. . . . Love your neighbor as yourself. If you love one human being more than another, that is wrong. If you love your father and mother and yourself more than another human being, that is wrong. And if you love your own happiness more than another's, that is also wrong. . . . Love God in all things equally. *For God is equally near to all creatures.* And among all these creatures God does not love anyone more than any other. *God is all and is one.* All things become nothing but God.[105] [emphases added]

Note the radical type of love of which Eckhart writes. There are no judgments of any kind here, for God's love does not judge (John 8:15). To get to this level, therefore, all judgments, including moral judgments, must be surrendered. We must stop calling anyone "good" just as much as calling anyone "bad," because both are judgments. God is now seen as neither good nor bad. God is just God. As long as we hold onto any moral judging of anyone or anything, we will not enter the Kingdom of Heaven. That is because in judging others we automatically judge ourselves, just as Jesus said (Luke 6:37). Since anything we judge against even in

---

[105]Fox, *Breakthrough*, pp. 67-68, 138, 96, 191, 249.

the worst "sinner" is a part of ourselves that we are rejecting, we cannot afford to judge anyone or anything. As long as we judge we keep our consciousness locked in dualism.

Meister Eckhart ran into trouble with Church authorities for saying, as I have above, that "God is not good," a statement which the authorities thought in conflict with Jesus' statement that "only the Father is good" (Luke 18:19). This is precisely the kind of difficulty we can get into in trying to express in language the nondual level of consciousness, which by definition is beyond language. Eckhart, as he himself unsuccessfully tried to explain, was not denying to God the Father *as Creator* the traditional positive attributes of good, true, or beautiful. But he was trying to say that here at the nondual level he was not talking about the Creator God but was talking about the Godhead about which nothing can be either attributed or denied in dualistic language. Jesus appears to contradict himself at times, and for the same reason. When Jesus said "only the Father is good," Jesus was talking about his relationship, as Son, to the Father as Creator, that is, he was expressing the truth at the level of the Christ Consciousness. But when Jesus seems to contradict himself by saying "the Father and I are one," he is expressing the truth as seen at the nondual level of consciousness wherein the Son and Father are one without a two.

Ultimately, when seen from the nondual level of consciousness, the terms "goodness," "beauty," and "truth" (as well as their definitional opposites "evil," "ugliness," and "falsehood") are seen as inadequate, one-sided distortions when applied to either God *or* Creation. The ultimate goodness, beauty and truth is not propositional. It is simply "what is," just as God and we are "Who Are."

In making these statements I am not denying (any more than Eckhart did) the legitimacy of law, ethics, aesthetics, or logic on the physical plane, provided one keeps in mind these rational disciplines are dualistic (and therefore inherently imperfectible) and recognizes (as indeed the Church always has) the supremacy of conscience or inner wisdom over all.

In making the transition to nondual consciousness, Bernadette and Petra say they lost all conventional sense of beauty. To them a pile of trash became as beautiful as a painting by a master artist. Why? It is all just God. It is all just what is. Some saints at this level were accustomed to kissing lepers and other persons shunned as disgusting or ugly by most people. To persons at this level, a leper is as beautiful as a movie star. They see the person as the light of Christ. The Buddhist Trungpa makes the same point, saying we see everywhere the "isness" of things, the *waterness* of water and the *garbage-heapness* of a garbage heap. No subjects, no objects, only *this*.

The Zen master Daisetz Teitaro Suzuki, who is often credited with introducing Zen Buddhism to the West,[106] saw kinship with Eckhart in the latter's emphasis on the suchness of things. St. Paul of the Cross, at this stage, used to admonish the flowers not to make so much noise as they forever screamed to him, "God, God, God."

Wilber says:

> It is the radical end to all egocentrism, all geocentrism, all biocentrism, all sociocentrism, all theocentrism, because it is the radical end of all centrisms, period. . . . The All is I-I. I-I is Emptiness. Emptiness is freely manifesting. Freely manifesting is self-liberating.

Zen, of course, would put it all much more simply, and point directly to just *this*.

> Still pond
> A frog jumps in
> Plop![107]

---

[106]Daisetz Teitaro Suzuki (1870-1966) was educated at Tokyo University and in the United States. He taught at universities in Japan, the United States and Europe. His works include *Essays in Zen Buddhism, An Introduction to Zen Buddhism,* and *Mysticism: Christian and Buddhist.*
[107]Wilber, ibid., p. 310.

This is the end of the line, the place where Jesus said he and the Father were one (John 10:30), the place in consciousness he told us to strive for in which we are perfect as the Father is perfect (Matt. 5:48). This is the Kingdom of Heaven on Earth. The person who enters into nondual awareness knows this is the completion of the human journey on this Earth. Bernadette Roberts, representing the Christian tradition, Ramana Maharshi, representing the Hindu, and Chogyam Trungpa, representing the Buddhist, all say the same thing: the final goal of human spirituality has been realized. Jews, Muslims, and others who reach this place will agree. Eventually, God only knows when, everyone who lives on this planet may live in this Kingdom of Heaven on Earth. The Lord's Prayer, the one prayer that Jesus instructed us to pray daily, will then finally be answered (Matt. 6:10) because the Kingdom of Heaven will have come on Earth.[108]

It is not necessary that we become theologians or intellectuals to come into nonduality. On this point, something that Bernadette experienced is instructive. When she came into nonduality, by the spiritual principle of like attracting like, she met an elderly woman who, being at her level, understood her. The elderly woman's only surprise was that Bernadette was still a relatively young woman. This was a surprise because the older woman thought that the transition to nondual consciousness was a normal part of the aging process! She had not seen it as mystical or supernatural or

---

[108]I realize that there are some schools of thought, Theosophy for example, that would say that this is not the end of the line, even for consciousness evolution here on Earth. Theosophy talks about as many as seven subsequent initiations. But, because I have not experienced further levels (so that anything I would say would be pure speculation), and because I believe that nine levels are sufficient for the purposes of this book, I have chosen to end the path here. You may ask, "what could be beyond 'union with God' or 'identity with God'?" But, as always on the spiritual path, we should not get trapped or limited by words. They are only metaphoric stand-ins for reality, not reality itself. Since there is no end to God, there probably is no end to the spiritual path.

even religious. This elderly woman was one of thousands of souls who arrive in these realms with no particular expertise in mysticism or religion. So, to any readers discouraged by all the theology, take heart, it is not necessary to know spiritual jargon to get into heaven. All that is essential is to surrender to the action of God's grace within the self.

A person with nondual consciousness is a liberated soul (John 8:32). On dying, he or she will enter the after-death Heaven to which all believers aspire. But it matters not, for one is already in Heaven, and knows it. "For this is eternal life, to know you, Father, and to understand the Christ whom you send forth" (John 17:3).

BOOK TWO

INTRODUCTION TO BOOK TWO

The first half of this book was concerned with describing the path to the inner Kingdom of Heaven that Jesus preached. The second half of the book will explore some related questions and issues of concern to Christians.

Part 5 will explore four major obstacles that the Christian may encounter as he or she attempts to follow Jesus into the Kingdom. All four obstacles are "conceptual," that is, they are four common ways of thinking about Jesus and about what he taught that present a distorted understanding of Jesus and his teaching and, therefore, are an obstacle on the path to the Kingdom. I hope these chapters will serve as a clarification of some of these points so that none of these four conceptual obstacles will hinder us in realizing the Kingdom for ourselves.

Chapter 18 examines the historical overemphasis on Jesus' divinity at the expense of his humanity, which has created a huge chasm between Jesus and most Christians. Chapter 19 explains Jesus' teachings about good and evil, and examines whether or not following moral law is the way to the Kingdom. Chapter 20 explores the various theological understandings of the Cross of Jesus and shows how a distorted view of what Jesus did for us on the Cross can be an obstacle to our own realization of the Kingdom. Chapter 21 looks at why the Christian saints have often seemed so far up on a pedestal that many of us, despairing that we could ever be like them, have not made the effort to become saints ourselves.

Part 6 is entitled "Further Reaches of the Kingdom of Heaven." It discusses other ways in which heaven is understood by Christians. Chapter 22 discusses the after-death heaven and life after death. In doing so it draws on the words of Jesus, my own mystical experience, the *Tibetan Book of the Dead,* and the teachings of don Juan Matus, the teacher of Carlos Castaneda. It stresses, as Jesus did, the fact that, upon death, very few Christians will have evolved sufficiently enough to enter the realm where Jesus himself dwells.

Chapter 23 discusses the Christian belief in the resurrection of the physical body and the eventual establishment of the Kingdom of Heaven on Earth. That Kingdom, prayed for daily in the prayer that Jesus taught us to say, will come when all the inhabitants of this planet see and operate with the Christ Consciousness.

In the afterword I discuss where we go from here, both as individuals and as Church.

PART V
SPECIAL PROBLEMS FACING THE CHRISTIAN ON THE PATH TO THE KINGDOM OF HEAVEN

Chapter 18

THE PROBLEM OF JESUS' LAST NAME

The problem of Jesus' last name is a misunderstanding most Christians have about who Jesus was. Even Pope John Paul II's book of private reflections, Crossing the Threshold of Hope, *contains this metaphysical misunderstanding. There is a metaphysical distinction between Jesus of Nazareth, the historical human personality, and the Christ as God's "Only-Begotten Son" (Nicene Creed), the Second Person of the Holy Trinity.*

Ordinarily, when we speak of Jesus, we talk as though Christ were Jesus' last name. We say, "as Jesus said to the woman at the well," or we might say, "as Christ said to the woman at the well," or again, "as Jesus Christ said to the woman at the well." This ordinary usage is convenient but it can create a serious problem in understanding not only who Jesus was but also who we ourselves are.

Most Christians, of course, know that Christ was not the last name of Jesus of Nazareth but a title given to Jesus by the early Christians, meaning the "anointed one" or Messiah. Nevertheless, even though we know the origin and meaning of the title Christ, we still ordinarily use the word Christ as if this were Jesus' last name in the same way that

Smith is used as a last name for persons whose ancestors were blacksmiths. Understanding the origin of the last name doesn't alter the usage in either case.

What exactly is the problem? The problem comes when we try, in light of this familiar usage, to interpret the words of the Nicene Creed: "I believe in Jesus Christ, the Only-Begotten Son of God." What we usually end up *mistakenly* thinking is that the Creed means Jesus of Nazareth is God's Only-Begotten Son. That is, we mistakenly think that Jesus, and Jesus alone, was God's Son, and that all other humans are therefore less than Jesus. That is *not* what the Creed means. To think so is a serious metaphysical error. And this error is so grave that, unless corrected, it can actually prevent us from taking our place with Jesus in the Christ Consciousness, and later in the Kingdom of the Father.

It is the Christ who is God's Only-Begotten Son, not Jesus. True, Jesus of Nazareth knew he was the Christ; that is, that he had the Christ Consciousness (and the higher nondual consciousness of oneness with the Father). He knew that, *as Christ,* he had been directly begotten by God from all eternity. But Jesus knew and preached that the same was also true *for us.* We too, according to Jesus, are to become Christ by putting on the mind of Christ, that is, the *awareness* that we too are directly begotten by God. One of the reasons Jesus called himself the Son of Man was that he wanted us to realize that our reality and destiny are the same as his.

Most Christians make this theological mistake of thinking that Jesus of Nazareth, rather than the Christ, was God's only-begotten Son. I made it myself, and it caused me a great deal of confusion when my consciousness was trying to realize Christ Consciousness. Even Pope John Paul II makes this exact mistake in his book of private reflections, *Crossing the Threshold of Hope.* The Pope asks why Jesus, "this Jew condemned to death in an obscure province," isn't considered by Christians to be in the same category as Socrates, Buddha, or Muhammad. He answers himself by saying that: *"Christ is absolutely original and absolutely unique* . . . . He is the one mediator between God and humanity . . . Christ is unique!"[109]

The Pope starts out by talking about the historical personality Jesus of Nazareth, a Jew from an obscure province who was condemned to death. So far, so good. Then, when he talks about the Second Person of the Trinity, the one and only, original and unique mediator between God the Father and humanity (and the rest of creation), he uses the word Christ. No problem here either. But then he combines Jesus and Christ, just as if Christ were Jesus' last name, and begins comparing Jesus Christ to the historical personalities Socrates, Buddha and Muhammad. Naturally, Socrates, Buddha and Muhammad come out second-best.

With all due respect, the Pope's analysis is faulty. In comparing the divinity of Jesus to the humanity of Socrates, Buddha and Muhammad, he is comparing apples to oranges and seeing not only Socrates, Buddha and Muhammad, but Jesus himself, in a one-sided (though opposite-sided) fashion. I don't know about Socrates, but both Buddha and Muhammad, like Jesus, had *at least* the Christ Consciousness, although they called it something else. Both, in fact, had nondual consciousness, the level *above* Christ Consciousness. Both Buddha and Muhammad, therefore, are, like Jesus, what the Western Christian esoteric tradition calls ascended masters (as, for example, is the Jewish prophet Elijah, who was "taken up to heaven in a fiery chariot and whirlwind" (2 Kings 2:11). Jesus, however, was born with the Christ Consciousness, while Buddha and Muhammed were not.

Jesus himself, according to the Scriptures, was careful to make the distinction between a great human being understood only *as* a human personality and *any* human being understood *as* a divinely Christed being. That is the distinction Jesus was making when he said that John the Baptist,

---

[109]John Paul II, *Crossing the Threshold of Hope*, Alfred A. Knopf, New York, 1994, pp. 42-43.

understood as a human personality, was the greatest man ever born of woman, but that the least person in the Kingdom of Heaven, i.e., with the Christ Consciousness, was greater than John (Matt. 11:11).

The same confusion surrounds the mythic doctrine of the Virgin Birth. The Scriptures are clear that, *in accordance with the flesh,* Jesus of Nazareth was born of Mary, that his father was Joseph (John 1:45), that his brothers were James, Joseph, Simon, and Jude (Matt. 13:55), and that he had sisters as well (Matt. 13:56). But, as Jesus himself stated to Nicodemus, there is another way to be born—*in accordance with the Spirit* (John 3:3-7). In accordance with the Spirit, Jesus, *as the Christ,* was born directly (virginally) *from* the Father, *through* the Holy Spirit, and *out of* Mary (the Nicene Creed). The same is true of anyone who consciously realizes the Christ Consciousness as John's Gospel clearly states, "Some, however, did receive him and believe in him; so he gave them the right to become God's children. They did not become God's children by natural means, by being born as the children of a human father; God himself was their Father" (John 1:12-13).

Mary, the new Eve, in the doctrine of the Virgin Birth just described, and identically to the Buddha's mother Maya, stands for woman. Archetypally and psychospiritually, woman stands for the womb, the watery baptismal abyss, human emotional depths, the human unconscious, and the belly of Jonah's whale. As Mother (and again identically to Eve and Maya) Mary represents matter (mother is *mater* in Greek and Latin and has an equivalent meaning in many other languages). She therefore represents the dualism of *maya,* the physical world, understood as separate and apart from God.

The Christed being is always "born again" directly (virginally) from the Father, and or through the Holy Spirit, out of this "Mary" (womb, matter, unconscious, *maya,* emotional depths) in the baptism of the Dark Night of the Soul. That is why, spiritually, Mary is the Mother of God not only in Jesus' case but in the case of every person who is reborn into the Christ Consciousness. This is the point the Gospel of John is making in having Jesus, on the Cross itself, say to Mary, "Woman, behold your son," and then to John, "Here is your mother" (John 19:26-27).

I agree with the Pope that Jesus of Nazareth is unique. But his status as Christ is not what makes Jesus unique. *Anyone* who reaches the level of the causal, at which one understands the Trinity as a living cosmological reality in which that person (and all humanity and creation) participates, is a Christed being (John 1:12, Gal. 3:26). Mary was a Christed being from the moment of her conception. All of the Apostles were Christed beings after they were finally baptized by the Holy Spirit (Acts 1:5) at Pentecost (Acts 2:1-4). So too were the other non-Apostle authors of the New Testament.

St. Paul and St. Teresa of Avila, invoking for herself the words of Paul, said, "For me to live is Christ" (Philip. 1:21). Paul also said, "I live, now not I, but Christ lives in me (Gal. 2:20)." Neither Paul nor Teresa said "Jesus" lives in me. Nor did they say "Jesus Christ" lives in me. They said Christ lives in me. The Christ, by definition, transcends any human personality identification, including that of the historical personality Jesus of Nazareth. When the Christian passes through the Dark Night of the Soul and enters the first level of divine identity, the causal, all of this becomes crystal clear. Before that time, however, the meaning of Christ will normally seem murky to anyone without Christ Consciousness (that is, anyone who wrongly thinks his or her human personality is the "real me").

By putting Jesus on an unreachable pedestal so that others such as Buddha and Muhammad can't get near him (that is, by understanding Jesus *only* as divine and the others *only* as human), we also prevent *ourselves* from getting near Jesus. We set up a major obstacle to our realization of Christ Consciousness and our own entrance into the Kingdom. According to Wilber, even St. Augustine couldn't get himself past this incorrectly understood uniqueness of Jesus.

This type of reasoning has also driven an unnecessary wedge between Christians and Muslims. One reason Islam has traditionally insisted upon the oneness of Allah has been in reaction to the type of Christian trinitarian theology that *seems* to elevate a human being, Jesus of Nazareth, into a second God, fully co-equal with Allah. Muslims are very careful not to do that with Muhammad, and can be deeply offended when Christians call Islam Muhammadism. When Christians treat Jesus as though Christ were Jesus' last name, the Muslim criticism is right on the mark. While it is true that the whole of God was incarnate as Jesus of Nazareth (as the whole of God is also present in the Holy Communion and, for that matter, in every grain of sand), and while the nondual consciousness of Jesus of Nazareth was perfectly aware of his oneness with God, Jesus never claimed to be equal to God as transcendent, nor even to be the complete expression of the Christ, God's Son.

When the passage of the Pope's book cited above was recently brought to the attention of the Vietnamese Buddhist spiritual master Thich Nhat Hanh, he reportedly said, "It appears the Pope does not understand the Trinity." Sadly, the Vietnamese master is correct. Nor, from what I can see, does the leadership of any other Christian denomination, none of them having first put on the "Mind which was in Christ Jesus" as we were instructed to do (Matt. 6:33, Philip 2:5).

Paramahansa Yogananda also addressed this problem of Jesus' last name, one he called the problem of Jesusism versus Christianity. He wrote:

> I am glad that Christianity was not called "Jesusism," because Christianity is a much broader word. There is a difference of meaning between *Jesus* and *Christ*. Jesus is the name of a little human body [personality] in which the vast Christ Consciousness was born. Although the Christ Consciousness manifested in the body of Jesus, it cannot be limited to one human form. It would be a metaphysical error to say that the omnipresent Christ

Consciousness is circumscribed by the body of any one human being.[110]

Let us set aside the comments of Buddhist and Hindu spiritual masters, however, and look at what the Scriptures and Jesus himself say. Directly contrary to the idea that Jesus was uniquely the Christ, St. Paul states flatly in his first letter to the Corinthians:

> Christ is like a single body, which has many parts; it is still one body even though it is made up of different parts. In the same way, all of us, Jews and Gentiles, slaves and free men, have been baptized into the one body by the same Spirit, and we have all been given the one Spirit to drink. . . . All of you, then, are Christ's body, and each one is a part of it" [1 Cor. 12:12-13,27].

You couldn't get much clearer than that. Note too that Paul is talking about baptism by the Holy Spirit, the baptism by spiritual "fire" (energy), not baptism by water.

Jesus, quoting the psalmist, asked us, "Do you not know that you are gods?" (John 10:34-35; Ps. 82:6). What sense would Jesus' question make if we too could not claim our own divine heritage? How, for instance, can we be "joint heirs with Jesus of the Kingdom" (Rom. 8:17) if we are not divine by "participation" (to use John of the Cross' word) in the same divine Christhood in which Jesus participated? What is the use of being "baptized with Jesus into his death" (Rom. 6:3) if we cannot fully share, as the "friends" he called us at the Last Supper (John 15:15), in the full glory of his Resurrection, which, for us, is the realization of our Christhood (Rom. 8:17)?

Jesus also said, "Whoever believes in me will do the works I do, and even greater ones" (John 14:12). How can we expect to be able to do such things, and even greater things, if we are not ourselves divine in the same sense that he, the carpenter of Nazareth, realized he was? And again,

---

[110]Paramahansa Yogananda, ibid., p. 297.

Jesus prayed to the Father that we may be one *just as* the Father and he were one (John 17:11), and that we might live in God *just as* Jesus lived in the Father and the Father in him (John 17:21). Was Jesus praying in vain? Was he mistaken in what he was asking? Of course not. Jesus knew exactly what he was saying and what he was praying for. From these, and from a host of other Scriptures throughout the New Testament, it is abundantly clear not only that we are every bit as divine as Jesus was, but that our entire Christian spiritual quest consists of *consciously claiming* our divinity just as Jesus did.

Meister Eckhart, having realized the nondual vision of the Kingdom of Heaven, exulted:

> Everything good that all the saints have possessed, and Mary the mother of God, and Christ in his humanity [i.e., Jesus], all that is my own in this human nature. Now you could ask me: 'Since in this nature I have everything that Christ according to his humanity [Jesus] can attain, how is it that we exult and honor Christ [in his humanity, i.e., Jesus] as our Lord and our God?'
>
> That is because he became a messenger from God to us and brought us our blessedness. The blessedness that he brought us was our own. [111]

The "good news" of the Gospel is that we, none of us, are mere human beings. We are now, and have always been, divine. All of the doctrinal statements of the early Christian Councils, in which the Church's understanding of Jesus as the Christ was hammered out, are statements about *us*. They tell us who *we* are. We are, here and now today, all the things the early Councils said Jesus was. All we need to do to be "saved" is to consciously realize who we have been all along. We need to realize our divinity, own it, take up the responsibility of it, and live it.

---

[111]Meister Eckhart, in *Meister Eckhart, The Essential Sermons, Commentaries, Treatises, and Defense,* translated by Edmund Colledge, O.S.A. and Bernard McGinn, Paulist Press, 1981, p. 182.

There is another reason why many Christians prefer to keep Jesus, seen only as *divine*, up on a pedestal, why they'd almost prefer to forget that the carpenter from Nazareth was a human being like ourselves. Many Christians like the idea that Jesus did all the work of salvation for them (he being *divine* after all, and they *only* human). They find solace in the theory of "vicarious redemption," that, by his sufferings and death, Jesus somehow made up for and appeased God for all of our sins. Such Christians often place heavy emphasis on the "Lamb who was slain for us" (Rev. 5:12), even in the hymns that are sung every Sunday in church.

But, while it is true that Jesus, by his suffering, took upon himself and transmuted a great deal of our negativity (just as does any Christian, to a lesser extent, who takes the Crucifixion Initiation), Jesus did not do everything. Nor can Jesus do what is ours to do (Col. 1:24). God for our own ultimate good would not allow it. It is our responsibility to grow up into our own divinity, paying whatever price we need to in the process. Neither Jesus, nor anyone else, can do the work of individuating our own souls into Christ Conscious wholeness for us. When we all become conscious Christs then, and only then, will all the world's sin be forgiven (1 John 2:2).

The overemphasis on Jesus' divinity has resulted in centuries of enormous practical harm to Christians in their search for God. Countless Christians have not taken to the spiritual path because they've felt either that the *divine* Jesus did everything for them, or because, since they saw themselves as *merely* human, and Jesus *only* as divine, they thought the path impossible.

This thinking has resulted in a huge chasm between the human and the divine, and between the ordinary Christian and Jesus. What this thinking does is to actually nullify in one swift stroke the essential "good news" of the New Testament, that we are divine and free from sin and death. It throws us back upon salvation by the law, by doing good and avoiding evil, which is no route to salvation at all but a recipe for continued slavery to duality.

Who was Jesus of Nazareth? Where did he come from? This question has puzzled Christians for the last two thousand years. To say Jesus was the Son of God does not help much to answer the question because we too are sons and daughters of God in the same sense. To say that he was divine, and shared the substance and nature of God, is another way of saying the same thing. To say he was the Christ, the only-begotten of God, also does not help, for we too are members of the Christ.

To say Jesus was the Messiah of the Jews does distinguish him as unique. But it is the Christ Consciousness, not Jesus as a human personality or even as an individual soul, that is the Messiah, the liberator, and the redeemer from all sin (1 John 2:2). To say that Jesus was conceived and born with the Christ Consciousness, that is, without sin, distinguishes Jesus from the vast majority of us humans (and from the Buddha and Muhammad), but not from other *avatars*, the Hindu word for liberated souls who are allowed or requested by God to reincarnate here on Earth to help the rest of us. Nor would it distinguish him from Mary, who was also conceived and born without sin.

Some Christians believe that Jesus is distinguishable from the avatars in that he never had a past life on this planet nor has he ever incarnated since. Jesus of Nazareth, they believe, was the one time only incarnation of the *fullness* of the Christ, the Second Person of the Trinity, on Earth. The personal view of Pope John Paul II, cited above, seems to be the same. I suppose this may be a possibility, for "with God all things are possible"(Matt. 19:26), but there are problems with this understanding. First, there is Paramahansa Yogananda's objection that the vastness of the Christ Consciousness couldn't possibly be contained in, or expressed by, one human personality. Second, how could we, as St. Paul says, "fill up what was lacking in Jesus Christ"(Col. 1:24) if, as the fullness of Christ, he lacked nothing? Or how could we, as Jesus promised, "do greater things than" Jesus (John 14:12) if, as the fullness of Christ, Jesus by definition could never be surpassed?

Finally, this understanding edges in the direction of the view that Jesus, though he had a human body, did not have a human soul. The early Church councils repeatedly rejected one form or another of this view; for example, the view that Jesus had a human body and human emotions but not a human mind, the view that Jesus had a divine will but not a human will, and the view that Jesus had a divine nature but not a human one. The councils insisted that Jesus was fully human as well as fully divine. (cf. Heb. 2:17 "This means he had to become like his brothers *in every way.*")

So, if Jesus had a human soul, and not only that but a perfectly developed human soul, with perfected emotions, fully developed intelligence, psychic powers, will, etc., how did Jesus get such a soul? Did the Christ, wholly apart from the normal, divinely ordained human evolutionary process bypass this in Jesus' case and create, all at once, a perfect human vehicle? It may be possible but I don't think it at all likely. What would be the point? It would make Jesus, not like us in every way (Heb. 2:17), but a human anomaly. He would certainly be unique, but this uniqueness would estrange him from the rest of us and from human history and evolution. He would hardly be the "new Adam" (1 Cor. 15:22, 45) if he had no connection to the first Adam (except for his body) and no connection to human consciousness evolution. How could he be understood as the Lord of History if his birth was some kind of special, miraculous divine interventionism into our history?

At least one Western esoteric tradition suggests that the individual soul that incarnated as Jesus was the first consciousness evolved entirely on this planet that had been able to realize the Christ Consciousness. That tradition suggests that prior souls who had realized the causal level of consciousness (Krishna, Buddha, Lao-Tse, and Plato) originated elsewhere. Because of this colossal achievement, God commissioned Jesus to enact with his life, from birth to Ascension, the entire map of human consciousness evolution, the Way, the Truth, and the Light. In other words, Jesus was the "new Adam" (1 Cor. 15:45) the founder of a new race of Christed beings. That seems a more grounded and realistic possibility.

I have tried to set out in this book, in as contemporary a way as possible, the path to the Kingdom of Heaven, the Way Jesus showed to us by his life, particularly by his Death and Resurrection. But the Kingdom of Heaven is only the end of the earthly journey into God, not the entire journey. There is, in fact, no end at all to the journey just as there is no end to God. And I suspect that, however far we journey into God, Jesus, whoever he may really be, will always be there lighting the road ahead.

Chapter 19

THE PROBLEM OF GOOD AND EVIL

One of the realizations we receive when we put on the mind of Christ is that sin does not exist. Once we find out who we really are (namely, God), sin, just as St. Paul preached, is no more. Just as was the case with the Pharisees of Jesus' time, the vast majority of Christians today believe that the way to the Kingdom of Heaven is to do good and avoid evil. This is a spiritual mistake. This misunderstanding is precisely the wide road of following the law that Jesus warned us was a dead end. Citing the Scriptures, particularly Genesis' account of the "Fall" and the letters of St. Paul, we see that seeking psychological wholeness is the way to the Kingdom, the way within that Jesus pointed out.

The problem of good and evil, or the problem of sin, presents a second major obstacle to the Christian trying to follow Jesus' path into the Kingdom. Most of us have been taught that the way to Jesus' Kingdom is to spend our lives trying to do good and avoid evil. (At a church service I recently attended, the congregation was led to pray, "Lord, teach us right from wrong and so lead us into the Kingdom.") In society and politics we have been taught to foster goodness and defeat evil. Unfortunately, as far as entrance into the Kingdom is concerned, all this is a red herring. Most of us spend our whole lives following this red herring, the wide path of adherence to the law, and thereby miss the narrow path within that Jesus said was the only one leading to the Kingdom (Matt. 7:13-14).

The Pharisees, the popular Jewish teachers of Jesus' time, taught that adherence to the law of Moses, the moral, ritual, and purity laws of the Jewish religion, was the way to the Kingdom of Heaven. Jesus disagreed, and he spent half his ministry arguing with the Pharisees on this point. Jesus did not urge people to disobey either the civil or religious laws. He told people to do as the Pharisees said (Matt. 23:3), and he advised rendering to Caesar what was Caesar's (Matt. 22:21). But he constantly emphasized that following the law was not the way to the Kingdom of his Father. Jesus said that the Kingdom was within ourselves. By his teachings and parables, and above all by his Cross and Resurrection, he tried to show us the way to this inner Kingdom, the psychological wholeness that we call Christ Consciousness.

Jesus stressed that all the laws are fulfilled if we come to the place in consciousness (the Christ Consciousness) where we will be at last *able to love* God and our neighbor as ourselves (Luke 10:27), and where we are *psychologically capable* of loving each other the way Jesus loved us (John 13:34). The extent of our ability to love, preached Jesus, is the sole yardstick by which God measures our spiritual progress (Matt 25:31-46). Jesus' Kingdom is not of this world, but the law is very much of this world, humanly manufactured, and humanly flawed. In the end, only love matters and, as Jesus said, only those who know how to love (i.e., have been born again into the Christ Consciousness) will enter the Kingdom (John 3:5).

Jesus taught us not to throw the first stone (John 8:7), to make the moral judgment of calling anyone a sinner. For Jesus, sin, in the moral sense of an offense against God, did not exist. Jesus knew that God never judges, just as the father of the prodigal son did not judge. And he knew that nothing we could ever think, say, do, or omit, could ever make God any happier or unhappier. God is never pleased or displeased. God, pure love, is above all that. Even as he was being killed by those he had come to help, Jesus refused to judge his killers as sinners. "Father, forgive them for they know not what they do," he prayed. He saw them as ignorant, but not sinful.

But "didn't Jesus talk about sin, telling the woman caught in adultery to sin no more" (John 8:11), and saying "He who is without sin, cast the first stone?" Here the problem is historical and translational. Jesus did not use the word sin in the moral theological sense. Jesus was a Jewish teacher speaking in Aramaic. The word Jesus used for sin did not mean what we mean by sin or intrinsically moral evil today. The Aramaic word means simply to err, to "miss the mark," "to make a mistake," that is, to act in ignorance of our true good. Jesus, as in the case of the woman caught in adultery, recognized such ignorance when he saw it. But, as the incident itself shows, he never passed moral judgement on such sinners, i.e., "mistaken ones." Similarly, when Jesus told us to pray, "Deliver us from evil" (Matt. 6:13), the word he actually used, in Aramaic, meant "error," "ignorance," or "illusion," not evil in the morally defined sense.

Later, because the first Christians found what Jesus taught about the law and morality hard to grasp, St. Paul, a former Pharisee and man of the law, spent much of his letters trying to explain that we are not saved by following the law but by putting on the mind that was in Christ Jesus, the Christ Consciousness. To give two examples, he wrote to the Romans, "No man is put right in God's sight by obeying the law" (Rom. 3:20). And to the Galatians, "If a man is put right with God through the law, it means Christ died for nothing!" (Gal. 2:21). St. Paul even went so far as to say that the only purpose of the law is to allow (and enable) people to label themselves and others as sinners. (Rom. 3:20).

St. James, who also had the Christ Consciousness and for whom, therefore, sin did not exist, preached what he called "the perfect law of liberty" (Jas. 1:25). And St. John wrote, "Whoever is a child of God does not sin, because

God's very nature is in him; and because God is his Father, he cannot sin (1 John 3:9)." Later St. Augustine said we should love God and then do whatever we want.

In chapter 15 I cited the testimony of St. John of the Cross, who, when he came into Christ Consciousness, realized that for him sin was no more. The contemporary Vietnamese spiritual master, Suma Ching Hai, whose background is both Roman Catholic and Buddhist, was recently asked if people are sinners. She replied that, "Yes, people are sinners, because they believe themselves to be so, just like you will see yourself as muddy if you imagine yourself to be playing in a mud pile. Once you are enlightened [i.e., find out who you really are], sin no longer has any relevance for you."

Similarly, the contemporary Greek Orthodox mystic Spyros Sathi (called *Daskalos* or "teacher") is reported by University of Maine sociologist Kyriacos C. Markides to have taught as follows: "Daskalos emphasized that there is no 'sin'. . . . There is only experience. All human souls will . . . grow spiritually until the attainment of *Theosis* or the realization that one is an integral part of God or the Absolute."[112]

We are here in this world to grow in awareness by means of individual and collective experience. We don't condemn children, saying they've committed a sin and offended God when they fall as they're learning to walk, or when they babble as they learn to speak, or when the first-grader makes his letters backwards. Wouldn't it be more Christlike to afford to adults, including ourselves, the same understanding and compassion as we learn the extremely difficult and complex soul lessons of the physical plane? And perhaps compassion and understanding are especially needed when either we or others have the courage (and it often takes a good deal of courage) to make individual experiential choices that are contrary to the law or the prevailing ethical consensus. Jesus himself never condemned anyone. He had compassion for others both in big things and small.

---

[112]Kyriacos C. Markides, in *Homage to the Sun, The Wisdom of the Magus of Strovolos*, Penguin Books, London, New York, 1987, p. 7.

St. Paul warned the first Christians not to become "slaves" to the law all over again (Gal: 5:1), but often we have done just that. Over the centuries the various Christian denominations have replaced the Law of Moses by a host of moral laws (shoulds and should-nots) and sectarian regulations. For today's Christians, sin gets its power from these Christian laws just as, in the Jewish religion of St. Paul's day, sin got its power from the Law of Moses (1 Cor. 15:56). What St. Paul wrote, however, applies to these Christian laws every bit as much as to the law of Moses. Christ, i.e., the putting on of Christ Consciousness, redeems us from Christian laws too (Gal. 3:13). When we come into the Christ Consciousness we realize that there is no such thing as sin.

Our spacetime world is made up of positive and negative polarities, but neither of these polarities are evil. There are matter and anti-matter, positive and negative electrical charges, health and disease, love and fear, pain and pleasure, up and down, in and out, hot and cold, black and white, and thousands of other polarities. Negative emotions, by definition, are negative. But, like all the other negative poles of creation, they also serve a purpose and have their own truth, or else God would have left them out of creation. Every physical substance has positive and negative components, as does every human choice. People often learn as much or more from negative experiences as from positive ones. *Both* positive and negative, natural polarities as they are, are *equally* necessary for the world of spacetime to function as the womb of awareness for the sentient beings who live here.

Lawrence Richardson writes, "In order for the physical universe to exist there must be polarity. There must be a positive and negative aspect to it. This creates vibration and the vibration allows the physical universe to exist. . . . There could be no dream of Divine Consciousness (life, with all that is involved in it) without it. Evil is a term that we use. From the viewpoint of infinity everything exists without any judgment about what it is."[113]

---

[113]Lawrence Richardson on his website: www.chrmysticaloutreach.com

God spells out this lesson clearly in Genesis: On the first day, God made light and its opposite, darkness (a polarity), and together these (day and night) formed "*one day*" (Gen. 1:1-5). On the second day, God divided the blue water above (the sky) from the blue waters below (the sea), also a polarity, and together they made *one firmament* (Gen. 1:6-8). On the third day, God divided the land from the sea (a polarity), and they made *one planetary surface* (Gen. 1:11-13). And it was good.

On the fourth day, God divided living from non-living things. This polarity was also called good and made a *whole*. Also on the fourth day, God created another polarity, the Sun to rule the day and Moon to rule the night; together they made a *oneness* that was found to be good (Gen. 1:14-19). On the fifth day, another two polarities were created, fish and fowl, and creeping and walking land animals. This was found good (Gen. 1:20-23). Finally, on the sixth day, God made a "human being to his own image." God made the human being *male and female* (the last polarity), the two poles of which, in the language of Gen. 1:27, form one whole (androgynous) image of God. And God found it all good.[114]

What you will notice is that every one of these polarities that God created had their goodness, not in their

---

[114]I am not alone in interpreting Genesis 1:27 in an androgynous sense. This interpretation was "given" to me by revelation but not to me alone. The great student of comparative religion, Mircea Eliade, writes, "Several rabbinical commentaries give us to understand that even Adam was sometimes thought of as androgynous. In this case, the 'birth' of Eve would have been simply the division of the primeval hermaphrodite into two beings, male and female. 'Adam and Eve were made back to back, attached at their shoulders; then God separated them with an axe, or cut them in two. Others have a different picture: the first man, Adam, was a man on his right side, a woman on his left; but God split him into two halves.' Bereshit Rabbah, I, 1, fol. 6, col. 2; etc.; for further texts, see A. Krappe, *The Birth of Eve, Occident and Orient,* Gaster Anniversary Volume, London, 1936, pp. 312-22." Mircea Eliade, *Patterns in Comparative Religion,* copyright Sheed & Ward, 1958, New American Library, 1963, p. 423 and accompanying footnote on same page.

separate poles, but in the fact that, taken and understood together, they made *wholes*. The entirety of spacetime, and of the dualistic spacetime language we have created to "name" and "describe" spacetime (per the instructions God gave to Adam and Eve, Gen. 2:19), is made of polarities. All of these *natural polarities,* including light and darkness and positive and negative, make unified wholes. You cannot have a wholeness without both positive and negative poles. It is this *wholeness* that God always deems "good."

But then a fly came into the ointment, a forked-tongued dualistic "snake" into the garden (Gen. 3:1-13). This snake was a liar and the Father of Lies (John 8:44). He induced Adam and Eve to use their dualistic reasoning minds to create still another polarity, this one an entirely *unnatural* one, one not found in Nature or anywhere else in the creation of totally good wholenesses (each made up of a positive and negative pole) that God had just finished making. Falling for the snake's seduction, Adam and Eve used their dualistic reasoning minds to create the wholly artificial, synthetic, and *false* polarity of good versus evil. This, as we all know, is the "original sin." The *original sin*—as described with great accuracy in the third chapter of Genesis—is believing that there is such a thing as sin in the first place! And from this original lie has come so much misery.

The contemporary Native American spiritual master Chokecherry Gall Eagle, who was raised in both the Catholic Christian and Native American traditions, was given the same spiritual realization concerning original sin after he prayed for understanding during four days of fasting. He writes:

> Adam and Eve were without shame and were told to be fruitful and multiply. Sex is certainly not a sin. Adam and Eve were diligently practicing being fruitful before they ate the fruit of the tree of knowledge. Rather, the tree reveals what is good and what is evil. It is knowledge of right and wrong. If everything was created by the Creator and only He existed, then creation came into

being as a manifestation of the Creator's intent. This is the Spirit in all things, the Creator within His creation. If everything is perceived as a manifestation of the Creator, and imbued with Spirit, there can be no perception of a right or wrong act because everything is within the movements of the Spirit in all things—Holy Spirit.

In other words, before eating the fruit, humankind could not perceive right from wrong because everything was within the Holy Spirit in all things, and therefore only good could [be] perceived. When people ate the Biblical fruit, and could therefore perceive right from wrong, they committed the Original sin of removing themselves from the flowing Holy Spirit in all things. They discovered isolation and ego, for they suddenly became embarrassed for the first time because they were naked.[115] [emphasis added]

From the creation of the concept of sin by the dualistic human mind came not only embarrassment, but separation from God (since God, by definition, cannot sin) and separation from the wonderful Garden of Eden and its wholeness. The Garden of Eden, of course, is the Kingdom of Heaven, but placed by the writer of Genesis into the past rather than, as in the New Testament and this book, into the future.[116] Once the human dualistic mind created the concept of sin, there also followed, as Genesis says: shame and

---

[115]Chokecherry Gall Eagle, in *Beyond the Lodge of the Sun,* Element Books, Rockport, MA, 1997, p.127.

[116]The author of Genesis, like the other ancients (Plato, the Neoplatonists, and the founders of Buddhism and Hinduism), had no understanding of history, particularly the modern understanding of history as progress or evolution. The author therefore placed the Kingdom of Heaven (here called the Garden of Eden) in the distant past and believed that the spiritual path consisted in restoring what had once been, and from which mankind had "fallen." There are similar past Golden Ages in Hinduism and other spiritual traditions. Nevertheless, the author of Genesis understood the Kingdom correctly—as the conscious rising above duality into androgynous, nondual wholeness. Nor am I "reading into" Genesis what is not there. Jesus "fulfilled" the Law, the Prophets, and the Scriptures (the three divisions of the Old Testament), that is, he "summed up" the truth that was already there.

guilt (Gen. 3:7), fear (Gen. 3:8), blame and fault (Gen. 3:12-13), sorrow and remorse (Gen. 3:16), toil and effort (Gen. 3:19), and the loss of the direct seeing of one's immortality (Gen. 3:19); in short, all the mental/emotional hells that the concept of "sin" brings with it. "What the law [of good and evil] does is make a man know that he has sinned" (Rom. 3:20). "The law [of good and evil] brings God's wrath; [previously] when there was no law, there was no disobeying of the law" (Rom. 4:15).

Adam and Eve, as the snake had promised, did create like gods. But they created a nightmare of mental imbalance (and consequent emotional and physical disease) because their unnatural creation had no wholeness. It was left for Christ, the new Adam (along with Mary, the new Eve), to demonstrate how to restore that wholeness (Gen. 3:15).

St. Paul's preaching emphasized the realization of freedom from the law and of sin that comes with Christ Consciousness. But he may not have fully realized the chasm that separated his own Christ Consciousness (with its unconditional lovingness and great awareness) from the consciousness of the average Christian convert. To his dismay, his preaching had just the sort of consequences a teacher of the law might expect: his converts in Corinth apparently went wild, coming drunk to Holy Communion, engaging in incest, and otherwise having a grandly irresponsible time for themselves. Paul reacted by taking them sternly to task, but, throughout his letters, he never changed the basic thrust of his teaching that the Christ Consciousness frees us from what he called the tyranny of the law (Gal. 3:10-13).

Even today, two thousand years after Jesus and the teaching of St. Paul, most of us, because of false-belief programming since early childhood ("Be a *good* little boy or girl"), are still heavily invested intellectually in our imagined goodness under the law. To the extent we have repressed our own emotions in order to appear good, we also have a heavy emotional investment in that goodness. These intellectual and emotional investments make it very difficult for us to get free of sin by eradicating from our consciousness the unnatural distinction between good and evil. They are the principal reason the Night of Senses and Night of Spirit (and earlier analogous spiritual passages and depressions) are often so confusing and painful. A lot of this pain, which all of us already carry deep within us, could be alleviated if the good news of the Gospel, including freedom from even the concept of sin, were preached rather than good and evil under the law (cf. Gal. 3:10, 13).

For the Christian, sin is finally overcome when each of us becomes psychologically whole. When, by the Dark Night of the Soul, we are baptized with Jesus into his death (Rom. 6:3), and afterwards resurrected into the wholeness of the Christ Consciousness (having learned to accept the truths contained in our own "dark sides"), we will see clearly enough, if we cannot see it now, that good and evil or sin in the moral sense is a false polarity created by the human dualistic mind, and that, for us, it is no more (Rom. 8:1).

This does not mean that a Christed being is so "morally perfect" that he or she always chooses good *as distinct* from evil in an ethically defined sense. Not at all. It means a Christed person, in realizing he or she is the immortal divine child of God is done thinking in terms of good and evil (or sin) in the first place. The rationally constructed polarity of good versus evil dissolves, and with it the entire legacy of the "Fall" of Genesis: shame, guilt, fear, blame, fault, sorrow, remorse, toil, and effort, and the blindness to one's divine immortality dissolves along with it. That is what St. Paul means when he writes, "But now God's way of putting men right with himself has been revealed, and it has nothing to do with the law" (Rom. 3:21). And Paul also wrote, "Should we continue to live in sin so that God's grace will increase? Certainly not! We have died to [the concept of] sin—how then can we go on living in it?" (Rom. 6:1-2).

It is also important to note that moral goodness also dissolves along with moral "evil." Goodness is replaced with humility, a simple acceptance of the human condition, positive and negative, as it is, and an acceptance that positive and negative polarities are both necessary in spacetime to produce wholeness. That is perhaps one reason why Jesus said, "Remember this! Unless you change and become like children, you will never enter the Kingdom of Heaven. The greatest in the Kingdom of Heaven is the one who *humbles himself* and becomes like this child" (Matt. 18:2-4). Children, of course, take life as it is. They know nothing of sin or good and evil until they are programmed into such by well-meaning but spiritually-mistaken adults.

This does not mean that a person with Christ Consciousness, like a criminal or defiant child, goes about disregarding moral, denominational, secular, or other laws or conventions. The person with Christ Consciousness, understanding that such laws and conventions are necessary for humans to live in community, will ordinarily comply. But like Jesus when he defended his disciples for breaking Jewish law by picking wheat on the Sabbath (Mark 2:23-27), and unlike the criminal or child whose defiance is actually a negative form of enslavement to the law, the person with Christ Consciousness retains a radical freedom to disregard any law or convention that is unjust, silly, arbitrary, contrary to conscience, or otherwise inappropriate to the situation at hand.

At the present time we have Mother Teresa, who now, after her death, will be subjected to the usual canonization process. Her life will be examined from start to finish to see if she was "good" (by the investigators' current standards of good and evil under the law) and to see if any hidden "evils" (breaches of those standards) can be uncovered. The FBI conducts the same sort of background check (though probably not anywhere near as thorough) on people who need top-secret clearance, often interviewing practically everyone the person has known since childhood.

In the case of Mother Teresa, none of this is necessary. In the first place, as don Juan Matus explained to Castaneda, any clairvoyant, developed enough to "see" spiritual energies, could tell you in five seconds if Mother Teresa was a saint (psychologically whole) by looking at her aura. And her peers, those who have the realization of the Christ Consciousness, can tell from her thinking and words (John 10:14-15). In the second place, and more fundamentally, the process itself shows just how far off track much of the Church remains in understanding Jesus on the question of good and evil. Jesus told us not to judge, but much of the Church continues to heed him not.

A person with Christ Consciousness no longer judges. He or she no longer thinks in terms of good and evil. And, looking back, he or she often sees that the use of these judgmental categories was an exercise in egotism. That is because the use of the term good automatically creates, by the law of polarity, an opposite evil. If I considered myself good because I attended church, then those who didn't, by definition, were evil. If I thought I was good because I was monogamous, or gave money to the poor, or obeyed the tax laws, then those who weren't or didn't were automatically labeled as evil. Everyone uses goodness this way because it's the only way the unnatural polarity of good and evil can be used. There is not a drug lord or organized crime figure in this world who does not see himself as good and his enemies as the evil ones. After all, they may say, "I am supplying goods and services people want, and only the evil puritans and moralistic busybodies hate me."

Hitler, as always, is the extreme example. He saw white, Gentile, heterosexual, non-Communist Aryans without disabilities as good. He happened to be one of them, of course, one of the "good guys." This is how it always works: the egotist labels as good whatever he or she happens to be or do or believe. Because these Aryans were seen as the only good humans, all other humans by definition were evil and could be justifiably wiped out. Hitler, by intending to rid the world of those he saw as "evil" humans and secure it for those he labeled "good," was as much the idea of "goodness" in action as he was the idea of "evil" in action. In the end, the distinction created by the fork-tongued snake in Genesis always results in justifying murder.

Does the non-existence of sin mean we can do anything we please? Two answers: Yes, we can do anything we please. And we have been doing just that since Adam and Eve, including murder, rape, war, cannibalism, and all manner of other horrors. Free will means precisely that: we can indeed do anything we please. We are divine sinless beings here to experience spacetime to the fullest and to grow in awareness thereby. We are free to experience whatever we like, positive or negative. That is why Jesus said in Revelation 3:15, "How I wish you were either hot or cold!" We are here to experience and to grow, not to take the safe path of being "good little boys and girls."

There is a second answer: Since God is all in all (1 Cor. 15:28) and everyone is divine and has God for their being (Acts 17:28), whatever we do to anyone else we do to God, to Christ, and to ourselves (Matt. 25:40). There is no other. Whatever we do to the supposed other, therefore, necessarily comes back to the self. As Jesus said, "He that lives by the sword shall die by the sword" (Matt. 26:52). That is why Jesus also warned that we should, "Do unto others what you wish to have done unto you" (Matt. 7:12). St. Paul admonishes that "A man will reap what he sows" (Gal. 6:7-8). The Old Testament set forth the same spiritual law, saying that an eye would be paid for an eye, and a tooth for a tooth (Lev. 24:20, Deut. 19:21). Buddhists and Hindus call this spiritual dynamic the law of karma (action and reaction).

Spiritual laws, though they may have different names in different religions, are universal. Christianity has no agreed-upon name for this particular spiritual law (except perhaps "justice"), but that doesn't mean God has suspended its operation with respect to Christians. We have the word of

Jesus himself that the law of karma applies, and its justice, if not always swift, is sure. Mercy can override the law of karma, and so can love, which is what St. Peter meant when he wrote that "love covers a multitude of sins" (1 Peter 4:8). But, though love and mercy can override justice, they do not negate it.

Spyros Sathi teaches that, "There is no 'sin' as such. . . . There is only experience. All human souls will eventually be redeemed through the law of karma."[117] And Gary Zukav says in his beautiful book *The Seat of the Soul*, "Karma is not a moral dynamic. Morality is a human creation. The Universe does not judge. The law of karma . . . serves humanity as an impersonal and Universal teacher of responsibility."[118]

The law of love, as Jesus pointed out to the Pharisees, can often be much tougher than whatever current moral codes people have devised for their societies. Jesus gave an example, the case of Jewish divorce as it was then legislated, where spiritual principle, he said, demanded more of men than the current religious law (Matt. 5:31-32). He made similar points with respect to the laws on adultery (Matt. 5:27) and murder (Matt. 5:21-24). In the United States it is generally legal to abort a fetus during the first two trimesters of pregnancy. But that in no way relieves those involved from any karma they may incur for terminating the life plans of another soul.

Even a society like our own, which is very moralistic and legalistic, and which manufactures laws by the thousands every year, cannot legislate everything. Under spiritual law, however, we are responsible for everything—everything we think, say, do, and fail to do (Matt. 12:36). We are gods (John 10:34-35). Our inner essence is pure love. To the extent we are at one with this inner essence of love, we will think, speak, and behave accordingly.

---

[117]Markides, ibid.
[118]Gary Zukav in *The Seat of the Soul,* Simon and Schuster, New York, 1989, 1990, p. 41.

"But," someone may say, "aren't law and ethics necessary?" Yes, of course they are necessary for people to live harmoniously in community here in spacetime and for the operation of any human institution, religious or secular. But "here in spacetime" are the key words. Laws and ethics are "of this world;" the Kingdom of Heaven, however, is not (John 18:36). Our entrance into the Kingdom depends only upon inner spiritual and psychological wholeness, and, as St. Paul said, that "has nothing to do with the law" (Rom. 3:21).

Some spiritual masters, like Moses, Muhammad, and Gandhi, instituted or promoted ethical reforms. St. Paul, as a practical organizer of churches and as a former man of the law (Pharisee), (Acts 26:5), and despite his preaching that, in Christ, sin was no more, gave plenty of ethical advice to the early churches. St. Peter did the same. Jesus, however, taught on a higher plane; he did not spend his time formulating or teaching a detailed ethical code for the Jewish culture of his time. He concentrated on the essential business of religion, increasing a person's inner level of awareness, the raising of a person's consciousness. He stressed always the purification of the "inner eye" so that people could eventually come to "see" the Kingdom in their midst (Matt. 6:22-23).

It has always been the Church's tradition that the contents of all the books of the New Testament, including the letters of Peter and Paul, are the "revealed word of God." This means that they were either written by persons with the Christ Consciousness or that they were channeled from the Christ Consciousness level of Spirit. In the case of Peter and Paul, the former is certainly the case, and the latter may be true on occasion. There is a distinction to be made, however, between the revelation of spiritual principles and the practical application of those principles to the everyday affairs of life in the context of the culture of the first century.

When St. Peter or St. Paul apply spiritual principles to such matters as the relationship of slaves to masters (1 Peter 2:8, Col. 3:22), or the relationship of wives to husbands (Col.

3:18), or to the type of headwear appropriately worn to Christian services (1 Cor. 11:7), or to the expression of same-sexuality (Romans 1:27), they are not giving the "word of God" as engraved in stone. Cultural and personal human limitations, assumptions, and even unexamined prejudices, necessarily condition their words. Christians today have the responsibility to apply the same spiritual principles, but in the context of our present world. We shirk our responsibility if we pass it off to Peter and Paul or any other Biblical writer.

For the Christian, the proper first principle of ethics is not "do good and avoid evil." Rather, the proper first principle is "Do unto others what you would have them do unto you" (Matt. 7:12) or "love your neighbor as yourself" (Luke 10:27). What is it that we would like done unto us? First and foremost, we want freedom, the ability to exercise our free will without interference so that we can experience the divinely created realm of spacetime to the fullest. Both ethics at the personal level, and politics at the social level, should have as their purpose the maximization of personal freedom but in the context of community and relationship. Exactly how these principles are expressed in a particular society will vary enormously, one key factor being the general level of consciousness in that society.

Keeping in mind that the spiritual laws of love and karma apply at all levels, people and societies at different levels of consciousness see the world differently. In general, the lower our consciousness (the closer to matter), the more we define what is ethically positive or negative by materialistic measurements, for example, in terms of physical behaviors, or in terms of obedience to defined rules and roles. The higher our level of awareness, the more we define what is ethically positive and negative in terms of such qualities as purity of intention and degree of love. Jesus did not condemn the prostitute who anointed his feet, because her heart was pure (Matt. 5:8) and because she had, perhaps even by means of her experience as a prostitute, learned to love much (Luke 7:47). On the other hand, he wasn't impressed by the worthies whom his society and religion honored as good because he knew their hearts were full of judgments, separatism, pride, and self-serving even in their prayers and almsgiving (e.g., Luke 18:9-14).

I am not espousing ethical relativism. As the last paragraph implies, the values of persons and societies at the higher levels of consciousness *generally* contain more awareness, caring, existential appropriateness, and tolerance or nonjudgmentalness, that is, the affording of maximum personal freedoms (in the context of community) to self and others. The values of contemporary liberal democracies are generally superior to those of medieval Christendom, just as the values of a rational-level humanitarian atheist or secular humanist are *generally* spiritually superior to those of the aggressive, mythic-level, Christian moral crusader. And the values of a Mother Teresa are head and shoulders over both.

Another mistake we have made (and Christians are not alone here) is to try to equate negativity with evil and positivity with good. In the first place, there is often no consensus, except by the arbitrary rule of law or custom, as to what pole is positive and what pole negative. To one person, eating broccoli, paying taxes, or practicing polygamy may be negative. Another person might think them positive. The same torrent of rain may be positive for the farmer and negative for the couple holding an outdoor wedding. And so it goes. Many Christians, including St. Paul as a creature of his society, once accepted slavery as a positive thing (or at least as an unexamined neutral "given"). Medieval Christianity and Islam saw lending money at interest as a major negative (Christianity, but not Islam, no longer sees it that way).

Two prime examples of this approach in the history of Christianity have been the equating of Eve (and therefore all women) with the negative (St. Augustine and St. Thomas Aquinas being the most influential proponents of this view), and the associating of Africans and others of dark skin color with the negative. Today some Christians are applying the same logic to persons of same-sexual expression. But equating negative poles with evil, and positive poles with goodness, simply does not work. Instead it tends to create, as in these examples, great personal and societal imbalance, injustice, suffering, persecution, tyranny, and even warfare. In the extreme it always ends up justifying murder.

Why did St. Augustine and St. Thomas (and Christianity in general following them) equate women with the negative and, by extension, persons of same-sexual orientation, particularly males? Putting aside St. Augustine's well-known personal and philosophical hangups regarding sexuality, I believe it was because, in terms of human consciousness development, the mental or rational level had not yet been clearly differentiated from the emotional/biological. Human *identity*, therefore, had not yet clearly transcended the emotional/biological. Women, mythologically, are associated with both the biological and the emotional, the lower part of human nature (in the judgment of those such as Augustine and Thomas). It was from women, therefore, the biological/emotional, that the rational mind (the "male") had to be freed in order for human identity to ascend to the rational level.

This shifting of human identity from identification with the biological/emotional to identification with the rational mind has been the principal spiritual task of the last two thousand years. As discussed in chapter 7, Augustine, Thomas, and many other Christians played important roles in helping human consciousness make this transition, a task substantially completed in the advanced countries only in the last couple hundred years. As Wilber says, it was only when reason was fully differentiated from the biological/emotional, and when human identity had transcended the biological/emotional, that womens' liberation began (with Mary Wollstonecraft in the early eighteenth century). That is because the purely rational worldview, stripped of mythic, biological, and emotional confusions, sees men and women as equals.

In the process of this transition to rational consciousness, however, Western society (as so often happens in individual consciousness development) was not content to differentiate reason from the body and emotions. It went much farther. It made a god of reason and judged reason (the male) superior. Society, including the Church, then used reason to suppress the biological, the emotional, the sexual, and the feminine. The result was a patriarchal system of oppression as well as the exploitation of Mother Earth by reason's technologies, civilian and military.

With respect to Christian spirituality, I believe it is no accident that the modern apparitions of Jesus' Mother Mary, beginning in the first half of the nineteenth century and increasing in number even today, have been roughly contemporaneous with the rise of womens' liberation. The apparitions are one indication that the spiritual balance between the male and female principles must now be restored. If humans as a whole are to progress beyond reason into the psychic and other higher levels of consciousness, the restoration of the feminine spiritual principle ("God as woman" in shorthand) is essential. Mary's appearances reflect the importance God places on such a rebalancing.

Finally, it is useful to point out that, during the astrological "Age of Pisces," (the last two thousand years) patriarchal, anti-sexual, anti-emotional, anti-Earth thinking has not been limited to the West. Eastern traditions, such as the Hindu, were also caught up in the planetary transition to rational consciousness. Paramahansa Yogananda, who died in Los Angeles in 1953, made the following astonishing assertion: "To hold man to earth life, Satan created sex." Satan no less! On the same page he interprets the fruit of Genesis to be sex, and a footnote explains that, "Man expresses more the aspect of reason, with feeling hidden; woman expresses more the aspect of feeling, with reason less predominant."[119]

In the end, no matter how hard we try, we will never have a perfect ethical or moral code. It is an impossibility in

---

[119]Yogananda, ibid., p.281

this world of polarities and choices. We can never be justified or saved by adherence to law, including moral law (Gal. 3:11). If we take law too seriously, we can be enslaved. Law is *inherently* dualistic: its very essence is to draw a distinction between the approved and disapproved. To seek salvation in the law, by doing good and avoiding evil, is to entrap oneself forever in dualism and to forfeit Jesus' Kingdom (Gal. 3).

Love is not and never will be an ethic (though one form of its expression may be charity or compassion). Love is a way of being. It is, precisely, a *particular* level of consciousness, one that transcends positive and negative, making of the two (duality) one wholeness (cf. Eph. 2:14-22). Love is the psychological wholeness of the Christ Consciousness. Love is the Christ, Christ is God, and God is Love. Wherever you find one—Christ, God, or Love (Son, Father or Spirit)—you find all three, and anyone with the Christ Consciousness is one in essence with all three.

God, our souls, and persons at the level of Christ and nondual Consciousness, whether incarnate or discarnate, have great compassion for us and for the painful situations we create for ourselves. They are, however, very detached, forever and serenely "above it all." They know we can learn love and awareness through both positive experiences and negative experiences; and all of us, to be honest, do it both ways. How we do it, positively or negatively, is up to us. In the end, all human experience on this wonderful planet, no matter how negative or painful, will be fully and completely redeemed. That's guaranteed.

Chapter 20

THE PROBLEM OF JESUS' CROSS

The problem of understanding Jesus' Cross can also be a significant obstacle for Christians seeking the Kingdom. To explain why, I examine four different theological "understandings" of Jesus' Cross. Each understanding is characteristic of the type of thinking that arose during a particular era of human history. I call each understanding of Jesus' Cross by the name of the historical two thousand year period which that type of thinking or understanding represents: The Age of Taurus the Bull, Aries the Lamb, Pisces the Fish, and Aquarius the Water Carrier. The later understandings are progressively more adequate, each representing a deeper and fuller understanding of what Jesus accomplished for us by his sacrificial death.

A third major obstacle facing Christians in our efforts to realize the Kingdom of Heaven is an inadequate understanding of the Cross of Jesus. St. Paul said that he preached only one thing: Christ Crucified (1 Cor. 1:23). I have been doing the same. Whether you or I as Christians realize the vision of the Kingdom of Heaven within ourselves may depend to some degree on *how* Jesus' Cross is understood.

In general, there are four understandings or "theologies" of the Cross of Jesus. I call them the Taurean, Arien, Piscine and Aquarian, each corresponding to a two thousand year period of history: The Age of Taurus the Bull (4000 B.C. to 2000 B.C.), Aries the Lamb (2000 B.C. to 1 B.C.), Pisces the Fish (1 A.D. to 2000 A.D.), and Aquarius the Water Carrier (2000 A.D. to 4000 A.D.). I am using these terms as *historical* labels, not *astrological*, labels, but it is important to note that astrology was widely practiced at the time of the early Church. Many of the authors of the Bible, and many in the early Church, made use of astrological symbolism. To give just two examples: Jesus himself was represented symbolically by the early Christians as a fish because, they believed, he (and his fishermen disciples) ushered in the Age of Pisces. The magi who "followed the star" to Bethlehem were astrologers who had been searching the heavens for a sign of Jesus' birth.

The first and oldest of the understandings of Jesus' Cross comes from the type of thinking that originated in the Age of Taurus the Bull (4000-2000 B.C.). That historical period, among the forebears of Judeo-Christianity, was an age of tribalism, polytheism, and magical consciousness. The magical consciousness of the average adult in the Age of Taurus roughly corresponds to the consciousness of a modern child of ages two to seven (see chapter 5 on magical consciousness).

In the Age of Taurus the gods were many, most of them personifying forces of nature. There were as many female goddesses as male gods, and often, because the principal occupation was agriculture, the principal deity was an Earth goddess or goddess of fertility. These gods and goddesses were understood magically, as arbitrary and threatening: they could bestow good weather one year and bad the next. The basic attitude of people towards them was awe and fear. The practice of human sacrifice to try to appease and control the gods was common. Often the sacrifice of a human victim, perhaps once a year, was seen as "enough" to keep the tribe in the good pleasure of the gods.

To please the gods nothing much was required of the person as an *individual* just as, from ages two to seven, nothing much is required of a child. In the Age of Taurus people weren't understood *as* individuals in our modern sense, but only as members of the tribe. The tribe acted on the individual's behalf and the sacrifice of the human victim was seen as sufficient to obtain the good of all.

Psychologically, the gods and goddesses represented the various biological and emotional forces of the human psyche, just as is the case in a child from ages two to seven. The fear and awe correspond to a child's view of its often-times arbitrary parents; and the principal goddess corresponds to a child's mother, the dominant figure in a young child's life. Often, in order to get its way, the young child's chief mode of relating to the parents is to "appease" them in whatever way it can, especially by "sacrificing" itself, that is, surrendering its narcissistic wishes.

When the Cross of Jesus is understood with magical consciousness, according to the type of thinking that prevailed in the Taurean age, Jesus is seen as the one victim appeasing an arbitrary and fearful God on behalf of us all. No responsibility is required of us as individuals for working towards our own salvation. To hold on to this understanding of God, and to this idea that Jesus somehow did everything for us so we need do little or nothing is to hold on to the thinking of a child rather than an adult (1 Cor. 13:11). Yet parts of every adult Christian's consciousness, the parts of us that were repressed prior to the age of seven, remain stuck at this level. Those parts of ourselves, *irresponsible* parts when seen from the viewpoint of the adult, *prefer* the idea that Jesus will do everything for us, serving as an appeasing buffer between us and this arbitrary God (a stand-in, generally, for those aspects of our parents that we feared as a small child).

Cosmically, the Age of Taurus ended four thousand years ago, two thousand years before Jesus. But most of us still have to deal to one extent or another with the repressed emotions and childish thinking that originated in that age and in the corresponding period of our own childhoods.

Our problem on the spiritual path is that, as long as we keep these fearful parts of ourselves repressed, and hold on to the magical, irresponsible thinking that automatically goes with these parts, we are prevented from entering the higher levels of consciousness, especially the final level, the Kingdom of Heaven. For most of us this is not some slight bump on the road; these repressed parts of ourselves are a serious spiritual problem, one we may have to work hard on for years.

Human consciousness moved a great step forward with the Age of Aries the Lamb, the age that lasted from 2000 B.C. until the time of Jesus. In the Age of the Lamb, tribes were replaced by empires (amalgamations of tribes), polytheism by monotheism, and magical consciousness by mythic consciousness. Human sacrifice was now abandoned because people began to have some sense of the worth of each person as an individual. Psychologically, the rise of monotheism corresponds to the inner rise of a child's mind or ego as the one unifying focal point and lord of the psyche. Thus, the Arien Age roughly corresponds to the mythic age of a contemporary child's consciousness, ages seven to adolescence.

The Bible tells of Abraham, who became the unifying Father of many nations or tribes (Gen. 17:4-5), and was a devotee of the one unifying God who replaced the many tribal gods. This one God was understood primarily as a "Sky God" who lived in the heavens and was separate and apart from humans. Abraham, the Bible says, intended to sacrifice Isaac, his only-begotten son, to appease this one God, but an angel of enlightenment appeared and told Abraham that human sacrifice was no longer necessary. A ram (the symbol of the Arien Age) replaced Isaac as the sacrificial offering, marking the end of human sacrifice as a religious practice (Gen. 22:1-18). Sacrifice continued, using animals, but it was now "symbolic," a relic of the prior age.

The sacrificing of animals also represented the sacrificing of the lower animal-like parts of human consciousness, particularly aggression and sexuality, so that the tribes could live together in a more or less civilized fashion. This also applied to the individual. Psychologically, the rise of the human ego, the mind, understood as male like its outside Sky-God counterpart, meant the subjugation (and often repression) of the body and emotions (the old female gods). At both the individual and societal levels, human self-consciousness (the I) was no longer identified with biology and emotions, but began to transcend these aspects of our natures and began identifying with the mind. This was the primary spiritual task to be accomplished in the Age of Aries.

Later, in the fullness of the Age of Aries, Moses introduced the concept of commandments and laws whereby the mythic believer could be assured he or she, *personally*, was doing right by God. No longer was the tribe the sole mediator between the person and God. The individual, now that the inner individual ego had begun to operate, was expected to actually do something himself to secure his own worth in God's eyes. This he could do by following the law and conforming to the gender and other roles of his society. I say *his* because the rise of the male ego and the male Sky-God also brought, at the level of society, the rise of patriarchy, Abraham again being the Bible's supreme example. The Bible's *Book of Leviticus,* which is full of roles and rules, comes from this early understanding of God and the responsibility of the human towards God.

The God of the Age of Aries, the God of the Law, was far less arbitrary than the Taurean God. He followed rules; his relationship with humans was seen as a contract or covenant. If you obeyed the rules, God would be pleased; if not, God would be displeased. This God, like all mythic level gods, was a God of law and order, a God of Commandments, a God of external roles, rituals and conventions. This mythic understanding of an outside Sky-God is the one that we all had as children during our own age of mythic consciousness.

Today, adult mythic-level Christians, as well as those parts of all of us that are stuck at ages 7-13, still hold on to a mythic Arien understanding of Jesus' Cross, imagining that Jesus, as a sacrificial lamb, fulfilled the law of justice of his stern legalistic Father by dying for our sins (Rev. 5:6-14). God is seen as a God of law, rules, conventional roles, and stern commands. Jesus is no longer a stand-in or go-between for us and God, as he was seen with magical consciousness. But Jesus, like the parents of pre-adolescent children, still gets to carry the primary load of responsibility for our salvation. All *we* have to do is to adhere to the law and to traditional roles and conventions.

For a Christian today to hold on to this Arien thinking is to think like a child instead of a responsible adult (1 Cor. 13:11). Arien thinking was beginning to become outdated even at the time of Jesus, two thousand years ago. The moneychangers whom Jesus chased from the temple were there because people needed to buy goats, lambs, and pigeons for sacrifice. One of the reasons Jesus chased them out was to put a symbolic end to the thinking of the Age of Aries (see Matt. 12:7 where Jesus says, "The Scripture states, 'I do not want animal sacrifices, but kindness'").

Now, another two thousand years have passed, and many Christians and denominations are *still* holding onto this Arien theology and words like "sheep," "flocks," and "pastoral." Jesus, of course, used Arien images to try to bridge the Arien Age, just then ending, and the Age of Pisces the Fish that he and his fishermen disciples inaugurated. But two thousand years later I believe it may be time to seriously consider wrapping it up.

Jesus inaugurated the Age of Pisces the Fish, and the early Christians used the sign of the fish to symbolize Jesus and themselves. The Piscine Age saw another huge step forward in the understanding of God and our relationship to God. Jesus preached an understanding of God as a Loving, rather than a Judging Father. He said that loving one's "neighbor," whom he defined and demonstrated to be *not* limited to people of the same culture (the good Samaritan), sex (Mary Magdalene), age (the little children), or religion (the Roman centurion) as ourselves, not only fulfilled the law, but transcended it. Taking advantage of the older sacrificial motifs while transcending them at the same time, Jesus gave the fullest expression and example of his new commandment, that we love one another as God loves us, by his sacrificial death on the Cross.

Jesus' preaching cost him his life. It brought down upon his head the wrathful judgment of the fear-filled devotees of the God of Law. Jesus threatened everything that gave the Pharisees and Sadducees their externally defined sense of self-worth: their adherence to law and socially-approved rules and roles. Worse than that, his teaching deprived them of their external power over the people, because they were the ones who, in the name of God, made up the laws that other people had to follow. Jesus, as St. Paul later preached across the Roman Empire, gave his life to bring us the "good news" of our freedom from the law, and our consequent freedom from sin and death.

The Piscine understanding of the Cross as the symbol of sacrificial love (and of God as love) was a big step forward for human consciousness. Although many Christians interpreted Jesus' Cross in light of the earlier Taurean and Arien understandings of God, Christianity in general has gradually understood the message that it is not enough to follow the law. To gain the Kingdom of Heaven also requires one to take on the responsibility, like Jesus on the Cross, of sacrificing oneself in loving service to others. The great external works and institutions of charity and social justice that are now the glory of Christianity arose from this understanding. For Christians, Jesus, by his sacrificial love, became the prime exemplar of the highest form of human altruism.

Psychologically, the Age of Pisces corresponds to the age of reason—not the concrete mental world of laws, rules, and roles of the prior age, but the full flowering of abstract reasoning that follows adolescence. The age that, in a real sense, culminated when the French philosopher and genius Descartes proclaimed, "I think, therefore I am." Speaking for the newly emerging rational-level culture in general, Descartes meant that his self-identity had now transcended the physical and emotional levels, and even the concrete mental level. The self was now squarely identified with the rational-level abstract mind. This triumph of the rational level of consciousness had been a long time coming. Along the way the Christian Church, despite its often recalcitrant magical and mythic adherents, labored hard, from the early Church Fathers to Thomas Aquinas, to Protestant Reformers like Martin Luther and John Calvin and counter-reformers like St. Ignatius Loyola, to bring the West into the rational age. With respect to the Church itself, all these efforts succeeded in producing a highly rationalized Christian theology.

Mainstream Christianity has by and large adhered to this rational-level theology (including a somewhat rationalized mythology) during its four-hundred-year war against the excesses and limitations of the Age of Reason (e.g., rationalism's myopic rejection of the spiritual realms). The proponents of reason, on the other hand, have often waged war on the Church, opposing the equally myopic cruelties, stupidities, intolerance, and tyrannies of mythic Christianity. That war is only now sputtering to a close.

Christianity and rationalism have been worthy opponents but it has been costly for both sides. Today there are millions, if not tens of millions, of rational-level nominal Christians who are deeply estranged from their churches, and who, as Mother Teresa often noted, are spiritually starving. On the other side of the equation, the protracted warfare has resulted in the leadership of large parts of the Church (Protestant, Catholic, and Orthodox) falling into the hands of intolerant, mythic-level Christian crusaders. These Church officials, in accordance with the worldview of the mythic level of consciousness, see the spiritual realm not as situated *above and beyond* rationality (in the transpersonal realms), but as located *below* rationality.

Even today they insist upon such things as a literal interpretation of the Christian myths, opposition to other spiritual paths, missionary proselytizing, a dominator hierarchy form of governance (with barely more than lip-service paid either to the action of the Holy Spirit in the Church membership, or to elementary rational-level standards of due process in handling theological disagreements), opposition to the mainstream scientific consensus in the case of evolution, adherence to all sorts of conventional (and often antiquated) rules and roles, particularly in the areas of gender and sexuality (sometimes based on a rudimentary science baptized as "natural law"), and aggressive moral/political crusades designed to impose their particular ethical views upon the rest of society.

In short, these Church officials are scarcely more spiritually aware than the Pharisees of Jesus' own time. The "cold war" against rationalism is now drawing to a close. But the Church leadership, and more particularly the Christian people, have paid a very heavy price for the decision (contrary to everything Jesus taught) to wage that war in the first place.

For the contemporary Christian who wants to personally realize the inner consciousness of the Kingdom of Heaven, however, there are limitations to even the Piscine understanding of Jesus' Cross. That understanding was a great deal more interior than the prior two understandings, but it was still externally oriented. Piscine thinking generally interpreted Jesus' message of sacrificial love only in terms of external charity. The inner meaning of the events of Jesus' life—their meaning in terms of the inner evolutionary development of human consciousness—seems to have been known by only a handful of people, such as those who wrote the Gospel narratives.

The Age of Aquarius will bring a much fuller understanding of Jesus' Cross in terms of the *inner* evolutionary development of human consciousness. Love will be understood not so much in terms of external good works, but rather in terms of what Christian love essentially is: a particular inner level of awareness, a particular level of human psychological development—the Christ Consciousness.

This book is one attempt to usher in this new awareness, to explain, for example, exactly what St. Paul meant when he said we had to be baptized into Christ's death (Rom. 6:3). Paul certainly wasn't talking about external baptism by water, but about the profound inner transformation this book has been attempting to describe. Many other Christians throughout the world, as scheduled by God, are now coming into this same understanding, so much so that I expect this new approach towards the Cross of Jesus will soon predominate.

The old Piscine understanding of Jesus' Cross also presents a second obstacle to the inner realization of the Kingdom. In the Piscine Age, Christian love has often been understood by putting a rationalized overlay atop the prior Taurean and Arien theologies of sacrifice. This rationalized interpretation of Christian love often *equated* love with suffering. As a result a cult of suffering arose within Christianity, a belief that, to put on the mind that was in Christ, we had to deliberately seek out suffering, which was often seen as a good in itself. Poverty too was often seen as a positive value to be cultivated; the poor were seen as somehow "worthier" in God's eyes.

During the Age of Pisces this mentality showed itself in thousands of ways, some extreme examples being the imposition by the Church of fasting, poverty, celibacy, and other ascetic practices, not as skillfully used aids to increasing inner awareness, but as external ascetic ends in themselves; or the practice among Catholic monks of beating themselves with whips; or the annual Good Friday ritual still held in the Philippines during which devotees have themselves nailed to crosses. Perhaps the cult of suffering, in the last eight hundred years, is best symbolized by the stigmata (the psychosomatic production of the five wounds of Jesus in one's own flesh) first by St. Francis, and then proliferating in the latter years of the Piscine era.

I do not use the term psychosomatic pejoratively. Everything that occurs in the body, after all, is psychosomatic. What I am pointing to is the belief system operating to produce such a phenomenon. That personal belief systems are at work here is shown, among other things, by the fact that the wounds have virtually always occurred in the palms of the hands, contrary to recent scholarship that indicates the Roman method of crucifixion was to drive the nails through the wrists. It is often what one *believes* to be true that ends up being true; to a large extent we create our world by means of our beliefs.

The result of this Piscine legacy is that even today most devout Christians feel guilty if they are financially secure, healthy, lead sexually satisfying lives, or are otherwise suffering-free. Somehow, Christians feel, they should always be sacrificing and suffering.

We have probably all heard preachers describe Jesus' sufferings in the most graphic and gruesome detail, the object often being to stir up our desire to suffer for God as he did. St. Teresa of Avila, even after she had realized the Christ Consciousness, was still prone to writing things like, "The second effect [of union with God] is that the soul has a great desire to suffer, but [she catches herself] not the kind of desire that disturbs it as previously."[120] Mother Teresa wrote, "*And I think it's very good when people suffer. To me, that's really like the kiss of Jesus. And a sign, also, that this person has come so close to Jesus, sharing his passion*"[121] [emphasis added]. I agree with Mother Teresa that we should see the suffering person (and our own suffering) as sharing in the Passion of Jesus; but even so, her first sentence shows the lingering legacy of the Piscine understanding of the Cross.

Nor am I entirely free from the remnants of this love-equals-suffering belief system. Raised as a traditional Piscine

---

[120]St. Teresa of Avila, ibid., Mansion Seven, chapter 3, page 439.
[121]Mother Teresa, ibid., p. 179.

Age Christian, I *expected* to suffer along with Jesus. My mentor along the spiritual path, John of the Cross, expected the same. So we did: in the Dark Night of the Senses and Dark Night of the Soul previously described, and in many more mundane ways.

Why is this *expectation* of suffering so harmful to the Christian working for inner realization of the Kingdom? First, to the degree deliberate ascetic suffering is spiritual athleticism or spiritual attention seeking, it is an exercise in ego, as John of the Cross points out, and has no place on the spiritual path. Second and more significantly, it is spiritual law that what we pray for, think is necessary, or expect, we create. If we seek and long for suffering, consciously or unconsciously, we'll get it—obstacles, persecution, disease, poverty, loneliness, whatever. We will manifest these negativities in our lives if we think or feel we deserve them; if we think we need them to be like Jesus; if we think these negativities somehow have a greater value in the eyes of God than their positive opposites; or if we think that nothing good can be accomplished or realized without struggle, that is, "no pain, no gain."

The negative manifestations these beliefs create are of no intrinsic help in realizing the Kingdom. More often than not they impede our progress. How, for example, can we expect to bring in, accustom ourselves to, and exercise the powerful energies of the higher levels of consciousness with a sick body? If we are always exhausted? With people putting obstacles in our way all the time? If we are in extreme pain? Or if we can't afford a nutritious diet, warm clothes, or a decent place to live? It isn't likely to happen.

The spiritual path is challenging enough without the misguided pursuit or expectation of suffering, based on a faulty external understanding of what it means to take up the Cross of Jesus. This error alone, like the others previously described, has cost countless Christians the realization of the Kingdom. The spiritual path, properly understood as the "sweet yoke" Jesus said it *can* be (Matt. 11:30), is one of ever greater health, energy, abundance, creativity, peace, and bliss. The Piscine cult of suffering has no place on it.

The fourth understanding of the Cross of Jesus is the Aquarian model I have tried to set forth in this book. It is an understanding that the Cross of Jesus, particularly as described in the Gospel Crucifixion/Resurrection narratives, is symbolic of the inner death and rebirth we must undergo in order to come into the Christ Consciousness and later the nondual vision of the Kingdom of Heaven. This theology of the Cross is more interior than any of the preceding understandings and, as such, it requires of us the greatest personal responsibility and effort. It also requires an acknowledgment that no one is going to save us but ourselves. Of course, God, Jesus, and the universe in general are there to assist us, and most of what we must do to save ourselves is simply to get our fears out of the way and allow God's grace to unfold within us.

The principal spiritual task of the Age of Aquarius is for Christians to begin taking up the work of their own salvation. We need to take up this task conscientiously and skillfully, and to help design a society and institutions that will foster rather than frustrate inner growth in consciousness. To accomplish this, the institutional Christian church and its forms will probably have to be significantly recast. A lot of work needs to be done to free Christianity from the inadequate understandings of Jesus, good and evil, and suffering described in this part. Christian practice and worship also need to be updated to incorporate more effective techniques for accelerating inner growth.

For example, it would be of immense profit for the Church and for Christians generally if the early Church practices of bringing in direct guidance from the world of Spirit were restored. It would also be helpful if the scientific meditation techniques of the East, especially those which minimize psychic pain and suffering, were taught systematically to Christians and incorporated into worship. Finally, it would also be of immense help if mainstream Christianity reintroduced spiritual healing techniques like the laying on of hands and trained its millions of congregants in the various arts of spiritual healing (to some extent this is already occurring).

Native Americans and others of the shamanic spiritual tradition also have valuable things to contribute. The shamanic tradition has a wealth of very powerful rituals and practices, such as those to retrieve parts of the soul that have been lost, that is, those damaged parts of the emotional body that have been split off from consciousness. I cited the late Carlos Castaneda earlier as an example of a person who realized the formless consciousness of the causal level. There is no record that he had to go through the Dark Night of the Soul. That is perhaps because the shamanic techniques his teacher don Juan used to heal him obviated his need to suffer such a Night.

New spiritual techniques will probably be discovered that can accelerate the growth of human consciousness without great pain. One promising new technique is hypnotic regression therapy. The American psychiatrist Shakuntala Modi, M.D., for example, reports success with this therapy in her book *Remarkable Healings.*[122] Dr. Modi has had years of experience with hundreds of patients. She reports that, even after just one or two sessions of this therapy, many patients have been healed of deep-seated emotional damages and even freed from partial possession by (magnetic emotional attachment to) negative spiritual entities such as discarnate humans and demons.

If all goes well, particularly if the Church with its millions of devout adherents is spiritually revitalized, the Age of Aquarius *will* see the Second Coming of Christ, a time when the whole of Earth's planetary culture will come to operate on an everyday basis with the Christ Consciousness of love, compassion, and never-ending creativity (Matt. 13:52), a time when the Kingdom of Heaven will at last come on Earth (2 Peter 3:13, Rev. 21:1).

---

[122]Shakuntala Modi, M.D., *Remarkable Healings,* Hampton Roads, Charlottesville, VA, 1997.

Chapter 21

THE PROBLEM OF GOD'S FAVORITES

*Reincarnation is an issue that has not been generally dis-
cussed by the Christian church since the early centuries of the
Christian era. Many Christians do not seriously dedicate
themselves to internal spiritual development because their
common sense tells them that, no matter how hard they might
try, they are never going to be another Mother Teresa or
Francis of Assisi, let alone an heir with Jesus to the Kingdom.
They instinctively realize that one short lifetime is not enough
and, since the Church has told them that's all they get, they
throw in the towel before they've half-begun, trusting that Jesus
will save them.*

*The failure of the Church to recognize the reality of rein-
carnation (and the evolution of souls), is a major obstacle
keeping Christians from the Kingdom. Citing my own experience, that of other Christian mystics, the New Testament, the
discussion of reincarnation in the early Church, and other
arguments, I will make the case that some form of reincarnation is a spiritual fact of life.*

A fourth major obstacle that prevents many Christians
from realizing the vision of the Kingdom of Heaven is the
traditional treatment and understanding of the Christian

saints. The problem is similar to the one described in chapter 18, the overemphasis on Jesus' divinity. The saints, like Jesus, have been traditionally put up on pedestals and understood as special, as God's favorites, and as somehow the recipients of extraordinary graces and blessings not available to the ordinary Christian. The average Christian has no expectations, and normally makes no effort, to become a saint, any more than he or she would try to become an Albert Einstein, Michelangelo, or Michael Jordan.

Part of the reason the saints have been treated this way is because, as with Jesus, it is safer for our egos to keep the saints up on pedestals. Ruth Burrows writes:

> Our cowardice and our pride are past masters of disposing of the saints. We don't burn them: we put them on a pedestal, which is the same thing as putting them on a shelf. They do not challenge us any more. They are no longer men and women just like ourselves, flesh, blood, nerves; somehow they are quite special, they have been given what we have not. They did not really spring from our common stock. This flower of holiness is not of our soil. Those far above us do not challenge us, it is the one close to us who does what we do not do, becomes what we do not become, this is whom we fear, this is the one we must dispose of. [123]

Burrows gives a graphic example, from the life of St. Thérèse of Lisieux, of this process of shelving the saints:

> She [Thérèse] grasped this so well. She deliberately and persistently rejected the attempts of her sisters to force her into the role of 'saintliness.' She knew God had made her holy but she refused to play the role of the saint. There was no admitting to fine sentiments she did not feel. . . . Encouraged to say a few edifying words to the doctor—words from the lips of a dying 'saint'—she refused; the doctor must think as he likes. One has only to read the unabridged version of *Novissima Verba* to see

---

[123]Ruth Burrows, ibid., p. 131.

how Thérèse was misunderstood. It is just not true to say her message in no way suffered through the editing and expurgating of her writings and sayings. We see a careful elimination of any word or deed that did not conform to the accepted standard of holiness.[124]

It is clear from Burrow's example that part of the process of shelving the saints involves the substitution of culturally defined goodness (see chapter 19) for holiness or psychological wholeness. It is an effective way of *distancing* the saint from the ordinary Christian with the result that the Christian believes there is no point in trying to become like the saint (now made into an inhuman caricature).

There is another more serious aspect to this problem that Burrows does not examine. It is not only for reasons of ego that the saints are put on pedestals. Every Christian's common sense recognizes that, in some way, the saints *are* special, as special in their own way as a Mozart or Picasso. Take St. Thérèse. Thérèse died at the end of the nineteenth century at the age of twenty-four. Yet, as Burrows admits, Thérèse "knew God had made her holy." How many Christians of age twenty-four, no matter how dedicated to the spiritual path, and no matter how sincere, prayerful and surrendered to the action of God's grace in their lives, have such a knowingness? Scarcely any, and usually no one that we know personally.

When I was eleven years old I decided that, since for a Christian the goal of life was to become a saint, this had to be my top priority. Taking heart from Thérèse and other saints who had died young, I reasoned, "If they could become holy by age twenty-four, then so can I." I spent practically every waking hour of the next thirteen years intensely pursuing this goal, attending church daily, praying for endless hours, and meditating up to three or four hours a day. By God's grace, I made great progress. I was in John of the Cross' Night of the Senses by age nineteen and

---

[124]Ibid., p. 130.

finished that Night by age twenty-five. But I did not realize my goal by age twenty-five any more than most sincere Christians do, no matter how long they may live.

Most Christians do not expect to be like Jesus. They mistakenly understand Jesus, though human, as *primarily* divine, and mistakenly think that divinity is somehow *better than* humanity; in reality, both are the same reality seen from different vantage points in consciousness. This is the seemingly unbridgeable chasm we discussed in chapter 18. We do feel closer to the saints, but only slightly so. We identify with the fact that most of the saints, like us, had to work hard at the spiritual path throughout their lives. We realize that the saints, like us, were usually unable to walk on water, create food out of thin air, or raise the dead.

But common sense tells us that the saints, like Jesus, did not start their spiritual paths at ground zero. The evidence (which, in many instances, has been thoroughly documented) indicates that the saints began the path with a big head start. We have seen examples of this phenomenon throughout the book.

Most of us, as creatures of our culture, are at the rational level of consciousness (see chapter 7). Many of us are still in mythic consciousness (see chapter 6). A few of us are at the level of vision-logic consciousness (see chapter 8). And a few serious spiritual seekers have realized psychic consciousness (see chapter 9). But, as we have seen, John of the Cross and Teresa of Avila begin their description of the spiritual path at psychic consciousness. Bernadette Roberts begins her path near the endpoint of subtle consciousness (see chapter 11), and Meister Eckhart speaks only of causal and nondual consciousness (see part 4). Each of these authors begins the path at a point usually well beyond the normal starting point for most of us.

The opposite phenomenon (that of people whose place on the path is far below that of average Christians) has also been noted and well documented. Child psychologist and popular novelist Jonathan Kellerman writes:

The notion that there exist individuals who are simply evil—bad people—and that such evil cannot be explained by any existing combination of nature and nurture is an assault upon a therapist's sensitivities [i.e., their genetics and/or environment belief system].

I knew such evil people existed. I had seen a mercifully small number of them, mostly adolescents, but some children. I remember one boy in particular, not yet twelve years old, but possessed of a cynical, hardened, cruelly grinning face that would have done a San Quentin lifer proud. He'd handed me his business card—a bright rectangle of shocking pink paper with his name on it, followed by the single word, *Enterprises.*

And an enterprising young man he had been. Buttressed by my assurances of confidentiality, he had told me proudly of the dozens of bicycles he had stolen, of the burglaries he had pulled off, of the teenage girls he had seduced. He was so proud of himself.

He had lost his parents in a plane crash at the age of four and had been brought up by a baffled grandmother who tried to assure everyone—and herself—that down deep he was a good boy. But he wasn't. He was a *bad* boy. When I asked him if he remembered his mother, he leered and told me she looked like a real piece of ass in the pictures he had seen. It wasn't defensive posturing. It was really him.[125]

Putting aside the judgmental words evil and bad, this fictionalized composite picture of a child psychopath is an accurate portrayal of the type of child (and future criminal adult) encountered on a daily basis by such professionals as psychologists, psychiatrists, clergy, criminologists, and law enforcement personnel. As Kellerman, by discounting both nature and nurture (genetics and environment), in effect admits, there may be no other rational explanation of the data than that these people were born with this negativity. He is correct. Children like this are *born* with great inner

---

[125]Kellerman, Jonathan, in *When The Bough Breaks,* Signet, NY, 1985, p. 90.

darkness and with all the cruelly manipulative behavior patterns that go with their already repressed negativity.

We have seen in this book that the traditional mapping of the Christian spiritual path into only three stages, the purgative, illuminative, and unitive ways, does not work. The map does not accurately describe the territory, especially once one gets a clear glimpse of the vastness of that territory. Nor does the traditional map give us any realistic picture of the great number of years it would take to start at ground zero and work one's way to nondual consciousness. That span of years, given how many years at each level it normally has taken even people as dedicated as the saints, far surpasses that of an ordinary human lifetime.

What all of this comes down to, of course, is that reincarnation *in some sense* is a spiritual fact of life, just as the majority of the world's believers assert. Similar to how apples were falling off trees long before Newton, the phenomenological data supporting reincarnation is already before everyone's eyes, both the positive data regarding the saints, and the negative data regarding the psychopaths; there is also plenty of data with respect to people in the middle. In addition, there is the inner spiritual experience of countless psychically gifted Christians, the overwhelming majority of whom are women, who have testified to the truth of reincarnation through the centuries. This evidence and much more is available to both science and the Church, if either would look into the matter seriously.

Besides the saints and psychopaths, there are also child prodigies of every sort, in mathematics, music, languages, chess, dance, sports, poetry, psychic abilities, and many other fields of human endeavor. These people too are building upon past accomplishments. There are also people who, for example, have a tremendous fear of water or fire or confined places, fears totally inexplicable in terms of their present lives. There are people with natural affinities for certain languages, climates, places, and activities that cannot be explained by either nature or nurture in the conventional sense.

Reincarnation also provides a reasonable answer to a number of questions that conventional Christian theology has been unable to satisfactorily resolve. For example, the question of justice that arises when the children of darkness seem to prosper while those of the light suffer; the question of salvation for the millions of persons who are afflicted with severe mental disabilities that would appear to make growth in consciousness almost impossible; and the question of salvation with respect to those children and young people who die before having had a chance to develop spiritually.[126]

Though most of our soul's other lifetimes are veiled from everyday awareness for good reason (imagine, for example, the confusion of a child if he or she remembered 100 different languages), sometimes there can be a bleed-through into present awareness, especially in the case of young children whose everyday consciousness in this life has only begun to develop.

The soul remembers everything about our past lives just as, for example, it remembers every dream we have ever had, every person we've ever met, and every meal we've ever eaten. But there is no way we could handle such an overload of information in our everyday lives. It is only at the psychic level of consciousness (see chapter 9) that one begins to have anything resembling regular access to the part of selves, including the soul, that survives death and that has access to this information and much more.

Here is an example of a bleed-through from a past life in the case of a small child. I was once sitting down to dinner with a thirty-month-old Christian boy and his parents. The child asked his father what we were having. The father answered, "pork." Suddenly the child looked utterly astonished, his eyes bugged out, his faced puffed up, and he

---

[126]The theory of "limbo," where unbaptized children, excluded from heaven, wait patiently for Jesus' "Second Coming" at the end of the world, is a theory that, for good reason, Christians have never found very palatable. I find it grotesque.

exclaimed loudly, "Pork! Pork! We are having pork! What are we doing eating pork!?" The bleed-through here was so astonishing and obvious that the adults had all they could do not to laugh. The father, grasping immediately where the child was "coming from," chuckled and said, "In this life you can eat pork." The boy's attention went elsewhere as the attention of two years old do, and the incident passed as suddenly as it had arisen.

Another type of bleed-through is the psychic phenomenon known as speaking in tongues. I know a person, a former Pentecostal minister, who often "falls into the Spirit" and "speaks in tongues," giving the Spirit's messages in another language—not incoherently, but in fluent Arabic. At the conscious level he knows only English and he never knew he was speaking Arabic until a man who knew that language heard him one day and translated the message. As St. Paul said in 1 Corinthians, this "gift" is of limited usefulness unless there is a translator.[127]

Though seldom noted, several verses of the New Testament appear to assume a belief in reincarnation. For example, the disciples asked Jesus, "Who has sinned, this man or his parents, that he should be born blind?"(John 9:1). Although Jesus used the disciples' question to make a different spiritual point about fault, blame, and judging, the disciples' question makes no sense at all if reincarnation or a belief in reincarnation is not assumed. Otherwise, how could the man's blindness from birth conceivably be his fault?

Even more on point is the discussion between Jesus and the disciples about whom people said Jesus was. Jesus asked his disciples, "Who do people say I am?"(Mark 8:27). "Some say

---

[127]I suspect the brain center (and the corresponding astral body light center) for listening to Spirit is connected to, or perhaps adjacent to, the brain center and light center with access to languages learned in other lives. So perhaps, in pressing one "button," people often mistakenly press the other at the same time. Something of that sort seems to be happening in this type of bleed-through.

you are John the Baptist," they answered. "Others say that you are Elijah, while others say that you are one of the prophets" (Mark 8:28). Again, the conversation makes no sense outside the context of reincarnation. Nor did Jesus, in this instance, bother to refute the peoples' educated reincarnational guesses.

Jesus knew of the prophecy that Elijah would be reborn as the preceder of the Messiah ("Behold I will send you Elijah the prophet, before the coming of the great and dreadful day of the Lord" (Mal. 4:5). To make clear that he was the Messiah, therefore, Jesus said of John the Baptist, "If you will receive it, this is Elijah, who is to come" (Matt. 11:14).[128] Jesus also identified John the Baptist as Elijah in Matt 17:10-13: "And the disciples asked him, saying, 'Why then do the scribes say that Elijah must come first?' But he answered them and said, 'Elijah indeed is to come and will restore all things. But I say to you that Elijah has come already, and they did not know him, but did to him whatever they wished. So also shall the Son of Man suffer at their hand.' Then the disciples understood that he had spoken of John the Baptist."

In Revelation 3:12 Jesus says, "Him who overcomes I will make a pillar in the temple of my God. Never again will he leave it." In other words, a person will not have to return to Earth if he or she finally "overcomes" the world. Until then, it would appear, such returns to Earth are necessary. Finally, we find this passage in the Epistle to the Ephesians, 1:4: "He chose us in him before the foundation of the world, that we should be holy and without blemish in his sight and love."

---

[128]The Church Father Origen was fully aware of the reincarnational implications of this passage. What troubled him, however, was not so much the idea of reincarnation but rather John the Baptist's conflicting statement that he was not Elijah (John 1:21). Origen, trying to reconcile the sayings of Jesus and John the Baptist, does his best in his Commentary on John 6:7 to interpret Jesus' saying in a non-reincarnational manner, saying Jesus meant only that the "spirit and power of Elijah" were upon John. That certainly is one possible interpretation. But a simpler explanation is that John meant, "I am now John, not Elijah."

There is also considerable evidence for a widespread belief in reincarnation in the early Church. Most of the Church Fathers were familiar with some form of the idea and held a variety of opinions on the matter. For example, they were virtually unanimous in condemning the then popular notion of transmigration, the idea that a person's soul might pass after death into a dog, cat, or other animal. They found this idea, correctly, "indecent" (St. John Chrysostom) and "nonsensical" (St. Basil the Great).

Though they used common sense rather than metaphysical principles to reject transmigration, there are two sound metaphysical principles they could have used. First, there is almost universal agreement among metaphysicians that most members of the animal kingdom participate in "group souls." They are not individualized spirits as are humans (though some of the higher animal forms such as certain mammals are on their way to individualization). Second, evolution always proceeds forward into greater and greater complexity, never backward. So no human soul ever regresses backward into one of the lower animals.

The Second Council of Constantinople (A.D. 553) effectively put an end to early Church discussions of reincarnation when it condemned several ideas attributed to the Church Father Origen. Ironically, however, and contrary to a belief that is apparently widespread in new age circles, the Council did not actually condemn reincarnation. The condemned ideas, which were based on the idea that matter itself is evil, stated that our souls, which before our births had been in conscious union with God, deliberately turned away from God and allowed the divine love in them to grow cold, turning towards evil and *thereby* becoming incarnate. Although these ideas could be read as merely an overly-literal understanding of the first half of Jesus' parable of the prodigal son (who consciously left his Father, God, and ended up among the pigs, Luke 15:11-16), the Council was correct in rejecting them, and for several reasons.

First, matter is not evil, and the process of creation (and incarnation) is not a falling away from God into evil. Rather

God, not believing the Godhead anything at all to be clung to, empties herself (*kenosis*) and begets first her eternal Only-Begotten Son, the Christ, the Divine Logos or Word, and then, through the Christ, the rest of creation, down to and including matter (cf. Philip. 2:6). This process of creation, whereby each stage descends from the level above, is usually called involution. All of creation, including matter, is begotten by God and is therefore divine. Matter, the lowest rung on the ladder, is merely the *least conscious* part of divinity.[129]

Second, our souls have not existed from all eternity (or before our present births) in *conscious* union with God. Rather, they have existed *without self-consciousness* from all eternity as Eternal Ideas in the Christ, that is, as *potentially conscious* participants in Christ (St. Jerome). And they existed before our own births as the permanent part of self previously described, as *not fully conscious* Christs. Our souls incarnate in order to develop self-conscious awareness. There would be no need for us to incarnate if we already had such awareness.

Third, creation is *not* cyclical, a never-ending series of involutions "downward" from God into matter, followed by evolutions "upward" from matter into God, as ancient thinkers like the Platonists, Buddhists, Hindus, and the Neoplatonists theorized. Such cyclicality would make God's exercise of creation non-evolutionary, and, in the last analysis, utterly meaningless. Creation would still be the dance and play of God—but it would be a monstrously cruel and pointless entertainment considering the immense suffering involved, that of all sentient beings including ourselves.

No, creation is "going somewhere." It has a purpose, and that purpose is the production of self-aware Christs. As St. Paul wrote, all of Creation groans as it labors in childbirth

---

[129]When I write that all of creation, including matter, is "divine" or "made of God-stuff," I mean that all of creation is conscious, or made of consciousness. Matter is consciousness with the least self-awareness of the fact that it is consciousness. The divinized human, particularly at the nondual level, is fully aware of Self as Consciousness Itself, that is, of the Self as "God."

to virginally bring forth Christed sons and daughters (Rom. 8:19-26), Christed beings who can thereafter *consciously* share in God's own divinity and co-creatorship. The immensity of this gift to us is so far beyond our wildest imaginings that the only appropriate response is endless thanksgiving.

During the process of evolution towards divinization, our souls function as archetypes, i.e., ideal patterns, eternal ideas in the Christ. They call us, lifetime after lifetime, to build (individuate) our Christ selves by means of our free choices in the physical plane. Our souls forever beckon to us—but it is we, through our choices in the course of many lifetimes, who have to build the house in which the Christ Consciousness can finally find a home and thereafter live.

Today the subject of reincarnation has been reintroduced into general American conversation by both the Buddhists and the Christian new agers, the latter citing not only the traditions of the East but the Native American/shamanistic and esoteric Christian traditions as well. As a result, one often hears Christians discussing whether or not they "believe" in reincarnation as if it were an arbitrary matter like a preference for vanilla or chocolate. Similarly, prior to Columbus, Christians probably could have been heard in the courts and streets of Europe discussing whether or not they "believed" the world was round or flat. In both of these cases, however, it matters not one whit what one "believes." In the final analysis, it is a question of fact.

When most people talk of reincarnation, they usually assume a long linear series of lifetimes through history. They forget that, outside of spacetime, where our souls already reside (Matt. 8:10), there is no time. Many Christian new agers, only partially understanding this point, conclude that all of our soul's incarnations, past, present, and future, are simultaneous.[130] What they forget is that the word *simultaneous* is

---

[130]Simultaneous is also a linear concept. We have no idea what realities in other dimensions are like. They may be completely "other" than our concepts of either past-present-future or simultaneity.

every bit as time-conditioned as linear past, present, and future. They also fail to appreciate the truth of spacetime as a legitimate, non-illusory, energy flow (probably a chosen subset of a larger multidimensional flow of probabilities). Both the linear and simultaneous models of reincarnation, however, are useful and, taken together, they hint at reincarnation's true multi-dimensional nature.

Reincarnation is merely a model, and perhaps a crude one, for a multi-dimensional reality that somehow impacts upon our spacetime lives. With respect to this multidimensionality, the spiritual entity Seth, as channeled by the late Jane Roberts, stated:

> Your idea of one soul, one self, forms a significance and a selectivity that blinds you to these other realities that are as much "here and now" as the present self. The units of consciousness that compose your physical being alone *are* aware of those *greater* significances, to which your limited ideas make you opaque . . . . *Reincarnation simply represents probabilities in a time context*—portions of the self that are materialized in historical contexts. All kinds of time—backward and forward—emerge from the basic unpredictable [inherently free] nature of consciousness.[131]

But model though it may be, reincarnation provides a rational explanation for all sorts of phenomena that are inexplicable without it, some of which I have touched upon in this chapter. Reincarnation also serves to connect our lives to those of the saints in an eminently meaningful way. For Christians it promises that, if we are not at the level of a Mother Teresa in our present life, we can be soon enough if we truly dedicate ourselves to the spiritual path. In this way, we too can be one of "God's favorites."

Many Christians will have trouble accepting reincarnation as true. It was a hard struggle for me to accept the idea,

---

[131]Jane Roberts, in *The "Unknown" Reality,* Prentice-Hall, Englewood Cliffs, NJ, 1977, pp. 78-9.

so I understand. An acceptance of reincarnation is not necessary for salvation. So, take it or leave it as you see fit. But there is no point in omitting from this book a spiritual reality I now believe deeply affects us all, whether we realize it or not. I can also testify that my path would have been far less confusing, particularly as my consciousness traversed the transpersonal astral realms, had I known something about reincarnational realities beforehand.

PART VI
FURTHER REACHES OF THE
KINGDOM OF HEAVEN

Chapter 22

THE KINGDOM OF HEAVEN AFTER DEATH

In discussing life after death, I draw on the words of Jesus, my mystical experience, the Tibetan Book of the Dead, and the words of don Juan Matus, the teacher of Carlos Castaneda. Upon death, very few Christians will have evolved sufficiently enough to enter the realm where Jesus himself dwells.

Although Jesus focused his ministry on the inner realization of the Kingdom of Heaven on Earth, and on showing us the way to that inner Kingdom, he never denied the reality of a heaven *after* death.

He taught three basic things about the after-death heaven. First, such a non-spacetime heaven exists (e.g., Matt. 6:20); second, the after-death heaven contains "many mansions" (John 14:2); and third, the after-death mansion to which he himself was to return is also promised to those of his disciples who successfully followed him on the path to love (John 14:2). Jesus also admitted that there were some things about the after-death world that even he did not know; for example, who the Father would eventually allow to "sit at his right side" in that Kingdom (Matt. 20:23).

Based upon my spiritual experience, I can join with Jesus (and the mystics of all the world's religions) in confirming the three truths Jesus set out. I know, with absolute certainty, that what Jesus taught is true.

It has been the custom for the past century for spiritual writers to argue with those who deny, or are agnostic to, the reality of life after death, usually based upon the latter's adherence to one or another branch of the philosophy of materialism. I will not follow that custom. I am as appreciative as anyone of the amazing accomplishments of science, including medical science, in the material sphere. But, like all spiritual teachers, I reject the *philosophy* of materialism, which holds that only matter exists, and the *ideology* of materialism, which holds that only sciences which are measuring extensions of the physical senses are legitimate.

Even though much of our scientific, medical, and university establishment still clings to materialism, the time for argument is over. At a certain point, as Jesus said, the dead must be allowed to bury their dead (Luke 9:60). Materialism as a philosophy, if not intellectually dead, is today hard-pressed to defend itself in a world in which even physicists find matter equatable to energy and energy at the finest level scarcely distinguishable from thought. That much of today's intellectual establishment refuses to recognize materialism's demise is not the problem of the Christian or other religious believer. It is the problem of the materialist. I see no reason why believers should expend more time or energy debating the issue.

What happens after death? There have been a great number of books published in recent years about the near-death experience (NDE). There are now thousands of documented cases of people who have come close to death (through an auto accident, drowning, heart attack, etc.) and who have reported their experience upon recovery. The stories are remarkably uniform. Virtually everyone reports going upward through a dark tunnel drawn by a beautiful light at the end of the tunnel. Near the end of the tunnel, they meet Jesus, an angel, or relatives and friends who have died. The light is so filled with love, acceptance, nonjudgment, and peace that they have had trouble turning back to Earth to re-enter their bodies. Often they have to be convinced to return by the beings of light or they are told that they must return because their time to die has not yet arrived.

Is this light heaven? Yes and no. Whatever mansion of light we end up in after we die is heaven for us, a place that is perfect for us in accordance with our spiritual evolution. All the realms of light are indeed heavenly. But the mansions of light to which most of us go after death are not what I am calling the Kingdom of Heaven in this book or the place Jesus called the Kingdom of Heaven. The Earth is surrounded by many invisible realms. I will attempt to describe the principal ones.

Just as the etheric body surrounds and interpenetrates the physical body, so too the physical Earth is surrounded and interpenetrated by an etheric body. Some people do not end up "anywhere" after death; that is, they fail to make the transition to their proper after-death home. They get lost in the Earth's etheric plane. They may remain attached to the physical plane even though they are dead (a fact they often fail to realize). Usually this happens with persons who have extreme emotional attachments to Earth, whether to other humans, a home, sex, or even to a substance like alcohol. These are the souls occasionally glimpsed as ghosts.

These souls can also, on occasion, attempt to possess (magnetically attach themselves to) another person in an attempt to keep experiencing physically. This can happen if the living person has emotionally damaged soul parts that vibrate like the damaged parts of the discarnate entity. For example, a ghost with alcoholic energies may hang around bars in an attempt to attach itself to an alcoholic and thereafter "drink" through that person. These souls, as well as ordinary people who remain in the etheric plane for a few days because of ordinary attachments, (e.g., to see who comes to their funerals or to say goodbye to loved ones) need our prayers so they can find their way to their proper place in the Light. St. Teresa freed many such newly-dead persons by her prayers.[132]

---

[132]For an excellent book that recounts the experience of two real life "ghostbusters," a married couple who had a special mission to free up many ghosts into the light, see the book *Phantoms Afoot* by Mary Summer Rain.

The Earth's etheric body, in turn, is surrounded by the Earth's vast astral plane.[133] In the lower astral plane are found many hells, places of great darkness and negativity. People of great negativity end up here. They are surrounded only by people as vicious, treacherous and selfish as themselves. In addition, their "outward" environment, emotionally and mentally created by their own inner darkness, mirrors their own inner ugliness. Most souls in hell, ironically, are comfortable there. It is a place compatible with their own negativity, and most of them are used to it because, even while on Earth, they lived in inner hells of their own creation. We should pray for the souls in these hells so that, eventually, they will come to their senses, and if and when they do so, that they'll have a change of heart, seek the light, and make amends to those they've hurt the next time they're here on the physical earth.

Next come the various purgatories, places of greater but dimmed light. Purgatory is like a hospital for people who have had sudden traumatic deaths, for people who have experienced gruesome suffering on the Earth plane, for people who have committed suicide, and for others who need care and help before ascending farther into the light.

Next, but still in the astral plane, come the mansions of light. A person who dies and then goes through a tunnel to one of the mansions of light is bypassing the hells and the purgatories (which are "outside" the tunnel). There are thousands of mansions of light, starting with the dimmest and proceeding to mansions of dazzling beauty and light. Which one we go to depends upon our own spiritual level of evolvement, our ability to love. The degree of love or awareness is determined at the personal judgment upon one's entrance into the light, a judgement described by Jesus in Matt. 25:31-46 (see also the mystical experience of such a judgement in chapter 16).

---

[133]The Earth's etheric plane is more akin to the physical. It is also the immediate layer beyond the physical earth. The astral plane is higher and is the destination for most souls after death.

The personal judgment that occurs when one enters the light after death is not conducted by God. God does not judge. The judge and jury in such cases is *ourselves*. We see the whole of the life we have just lived with the light of our soul— "in a flash." In an instant we see with a deeper level of understanding and compassion where we have triumphed and failed in accomplishing *our own* expectations for the life just finished.

"Expectations" here refers to *spiritual* expectations. The soul does not care about what one has accomplished in a worldly sense except to the extent such worldly efforts and achievements fostered soul growth. In the case of people we hurt while we were on Earth, we *feel* what it was like for them when we hurt them, and we resolve to make karmic amends to them.

Everything on the astral plane has a finer vibrational makeup than the physical plane. Colors are richer, more dazzling; sounds are much more exquisite; smells are more intense. It is like the difference between an extraordinarily vivid dream and our drab-by-comparison everyday physical-plane life. On the astral plane we create our surroundings by thought and emotion. Actually, that is also the case on the physical plane, but on the astral plane it may become self-evident that this is the case because our surroundings can change with the speed of thought.

Above the astral plane is the causal plane. It surrounds and interpenetrates the planes below. In this plane reside only those who have come into Christ Consciousness, those who have learned how to love as Jesus did, those who have put on the Mind of Christ. As Jesus taught (e.g., John 3:3), the only people who enter here immediately after death are the saints, those few persons who, having put on the mind that was in Christ Jesus (Philip. 2:5), have *experientially* realized the Christ Consciousness. All of us are called to what our creed calls the Communion of Saints but, as we know well, few of us are completely ready when the hour of death comes (Matt. 25:13).

Beyond the causal plane is the plane of Spirit to which only those with nondual consciousness, the consciousness of the Kingdom of Heaven, are admitted. This is the Kingdom of Heaven that Jesus talked about and to which I have mapped the way in this book. Very few souls enter the Kingdom after death. On this point, every high mystical tradition on the planet agrees.

The Yaqui spiritual master, don Juan, related the following vision to Carlos Castaneda:

> The power that governs the destiny of all living beings is called the Eagle, not because it is an eagle or has anything to do with an eagle, but because it appears to the seer [of don Juan's tradition] as an immeasurable, jet-black eagle, standing erect as an eagle stands, its height reaching to infinity. . . .
>
> The Eagle is devouring the awareness of all the creatures that, alive on earth a moment before and now dead, have floated to the Eagle's beak, like a ceaseless swarm of fireflies, to meet their owner, their reason for having had life. The Eagle disentangles these tiny flames, lays them flat, as a tanner stretches out a hide, and then consumes them; for awareness is the Eagle's food.
>
> The Eagle, that power that governs the destinies of all living things, reflects equally and at once all those living things. There is no way, therefore, for man to pray to the Eagle, to ask favors, to hope for grace. The human part of the Eagle is too insignificant to move the whole. . . .
>
> The Eagle, although it is not moved by the circumstances of any living thing, has granted a gift to each of those beings. In its own way and right, any one of them, if it so desires, has the power to keep the flame of awareness, the power to disobey the summons to die and be consumed. Every living thing has been granted the power, if it so desires, to seek an opening to freedom and to go through it. It is evident to the seer who sees the opening, and to the creatures that go through it, that the Eagle has granted the gift in order to perpetuate awareness.[134]

---

[134]Carlos Castaneda in *The Eagle's Gift*, Pocket Books, New York, 1981, 1982, pp. 172-173.

Although this vision of after-death may seem frightening, it expresses several spiritual truths. First, the purpose of human life is growth in awareness or consciousness, for which "love" is another name, for how can we love if we are operating in ignorance of who we and others really are? Second, God (the Eagle) has created us so that God can experience spacetime through us. Third, by this spacetime experience, we grow in awareness, thus "feeding" God with the knowledge and vision of God's own face—His Son, the Christ. Fourth, it is not an easy thing to gain the Kingdom of Heaven, the freedom one is allowed to seek and gain. Most people, after death, though they've grown in awareness, have not grown enough to escape into their own "eaglehood" (divinity, self-perpetuating awareness). For them, more experience is needed. Some few souls do escape, becoming thereafter like eagles.

Jesus made no secret of the fact that it is *extremely* difficult for people to enter the Kingdom of Heaven. A great many of Jesus' parables and sayings express this difficulty. He said that "many are called but few are chosen," (Matt. 22:14) and he observed that, for rich people (rich in money, power, position, fame, learning), it is almost impossible to enter heaven (because of their ego-aggrandizing attachments)(Matt. 19:23-24).

Jesus told the parable of the sower, in which the vast majority of the seeds (the Gospel) fell upon ground that proved unsuitable (Matt. 13:3-23). He said that, unless our righteousness exceeds that of even the average priest or minister, "you shall in no case enter into the Kingdom of Heaven" (Matt. 5:20). He told the parable of the marriage feast (the Kingdom) to which *none* of those originally invited gained entrance (Matt. 22:2-7). And he said that, "Except a man be born again (by which he meant death and rebirth into Christ Consciousness), he *cannot* see the Kingdom of God" (John 3:3).

Jesus' mission was universal. In these sayings he was not speaking only about Jews, pagans, nonbelievers, or even "sinners" as some Christians have preferred to believe through the centuries. He was talking about *everyone*, Christians included, and, as always, what he said was true. Very few humans (and very few Christians) go to the heaven where Jesus dwells after death, *scarcely any* compared to the numbers on Earth. That, two thousand years later, remains the sobering reality. Eventually, of course, we will all arrive there, perhaps even in one lifetime if we work hard enough.

The Tibetan Buddhists tell the same story, but in another way. In their great classic, *The Tibetan Book of the Dead,* which is a guide to be read to those who are dying in the hope that this "Great Doctrine of Liberation by Hearing, which conferreth spiritual freedom on devotees"[135] will allow them, upon death, to "be set face to face with the *fundamental* Clear Light; and, without any Intermediate State, . . . obtain the Unborn."[136]

The Book of the Dead teaches that, upon death, the person comes before the *fundamental* or *primary* Clear Light (don Juan's Eagle, God for the Christian, and, in terms of consciousness, what I am calling the state of nondual awareness). If the person can recognize that light, that is, consciously identify with that Light as his or her own divine self, liberation from the cycle of rebirths is realized. If not, the person regresses to the secondary Clear Light of the "second bardo" (causal level, the level of the Christ Consciousness) and assumes a "shining illusory body." If he or she can awaken there, liberation is attained.

If not, the person regresses to the "third bardo" (subtle level of consciousness) where the person is confronted with all the angels and demons (peaceful and wrathful "deities") of that level. If the person is able to recognize these as his or her own thought-forms, the person can stay there. If not, the person regresses to the next lower level (the psychic or lower astral world), and from thence to rebirth in the physical.

---

[135]W.Y. Evans-Wentz, editor, in *The Tibetan Book of the Dead,* Oxford University Press, 1927, 1960, Third Edition p. 85.
[136]Ibid.

Will we be automatically enlightened after death? Yes and no. We will, freed from the denseness of matter, have a broader, more liberated perspective, but, otherwise, not much will have changed. Except for the initial "soul review" or judgement in the light of the soul, people are generally exactly the same after death as they were before death, with the same degree of consciousness, love, and realization. For those on the astral plane, only the physical body is missing. The astral body remains, and, if we want it to, looks exactly like the physical body.

Wherever we end up, there will be opportunities to grow spiritually. Nothing in God's universes stays static. But growth in the astral plane often proceeds at a much more leisurely pace than it does here on the physical plane. Here, because of our physical bodies and the inherent limits of spacetime, our choices generally have urgency, sometimes life or death urgency. We don't have a hundred years to float around mulling over our choices as we might on the astral plane. In spacetime, life is relentless in its everyday demands, and our constant responses to these demands, our choices, *can* result in very fast inner growth.

Normally, therefore, deceased persons, after a decent rest period, will want to return here to once again accelerate their growth and to resume the journey to the Kingdom of Heaven. So, with the help of their spirit guides and guardian angel, they choose new parents to be born to, a new life plan to help them grow, and they reincarnate. It goes on and on until one day they finally evolve enough to enter the Kingdom where Jesus dwells, and from which there is no longer a need to "go out" (Rev. 3:12).

Chapter 23

THE ESTABLISHMENT OF THE
KINGDOM OF HEAVEN ON EARTH

Christians believe in the resurrection of the physical body and the eventual establishment of the Kingdom of Heaven on Earth. That Kingdom, prayed for daily in the prayer that Jesus taught us to say, will come when all the inhabitants of this planet see and operate with the Christ Consciousness, an event that may occur sometime during (perhaps at the close of) the Age of Aquarius. St. Paul, St. Thomas Aquinas, and two medieval church councils, help us see a few of the possibilities for what the human body may be like at that future time.

The Scriptures tell us that, at some point in the future, the Kingdom of Heaven will be established on the Earth (2 Peter 3:13, Rev. 21:1). Whether this will occur by the gradual unfoldment of the consciousness of humanity, or whether the establishment of the Kingdom will come suddenly, accompanied by dramatic signs, or by a combination of the two, we do not know, nor do we know when it will come. Jesus did not know either (Matt. 24:36). But *that* this final fulfillment will eventually happen there is no doubt.

When the Kingdom is established upon Earth, everyone here will be spiritually developed to the point of living effortlessly in nondual consciousness. After all, there can be no external physical manifestation of the Kingdom unless the Kingdom has first been established within, in the consciousness of every human. The external Kingdom will come about as a natural expression of that inner Kingdom. In that Kingdom there will be no disease, no war, no suffering, no poverty, and no death. All humans will live in conscious union with God and with each other, each one manifesting Spirit in their own uniquely creative way (Matt. 13:52). This creativity will continually deepen and find ever new and wondrous ways of expressing itself, for there is no end to the depths and the riches of God, nor is there any end to the gifts God is prepared to shower on those who follow the path of love (1 Cor. 2:9).

Those who live in the Kingdom of Heaven on Earth will live in "resurrected" physical bodies, bodies with abilities far beyond the capacities of our present ones. The belief in the resurrection of the body, based upon the words of St. Paul in 1 Corinthians 15:39-44, has been a staple of the Christian Creed since the earliest times. Like most of the symbolic or mythic beliefs of the Creed, the resurrection of the body has several meanings. It is the same as with Jesus' parables which usually have dozens of truthful meanings, not all of which we have yet consciously realized. One of those meanings is in reference to the bodies of those who will live in this future Kingdom of Heaven on Earth.

In earlier chapters I have described what both the resurrection of the body and the ascension of body and soul into heaven mean *spiritually* in terms of the Christian's inner spiritual development. We are resurrected *bodily* when we emerge out of the Dark Night of the Soul into union with God; we ascend *bodily* into heaven when we are raised up spiritually into nondual consciousness. The key point is that these changes in awareness happen while we're still on earth. This spiritual meaning, however, in no way precludes the further meanings now being suggested.

The Christian tradition, based on 1 Corinthians 15:39-44, has also given a third meaning to the resurrection of the body. Someday some of the inhabitants of the after-death Kingdom of Heaven will also take part in an actual physical resurrection or return to Earth. St. Paul wrote:

> All flesh is not the same flesh. . . . So also is the resurrection of the dead. It [the body] is sown in corruption; it is raised in incorruption. It is sown in dishonor; it is raised in glory. It is sown in weakness; it is raised in power. It is sown as a natural body; it is raised as a spiritual body. There is a natural body and there is a spiritual body. [1 Cor. 15:39, 42-44]

Most of the "speculation" that has surrounded the belief in the resurrection of the body has concerned what St. Paul meant by a "spiritual" as opposed to a "natural" body. Speculation on that point has been abundant, from the early Church Father Origen to the great medieval scholars St. Albert the Great and St. Thomas Aquinas to many others. Some have speculated that St. Paul meant a *spirit* body as opposed to an actual *physical* body. The Church's Fourth Lateran Council in 1215 (confirmed by the Second Council of Lyons in 1274) rejected this idea, decreeing "All will arise with their own bodies which they now have."

The essential teaching of that Council, in using the words "the bodies which they now have," was that the body will be a physical one, not a spirit body. It did not mean, as some overly worried Christians today believe, that the body would be exactly the same one we have now with exactly the same organs, cells, molecules and atoms. I say "overly worried" because some Christians even oppose heart (and other) transplants because they fear that someone else will end up with *their* heart. That is silliness. As we all know, our bodies even now are in constant flux. We toss off millions of cells every twenty-four hours and incorporate millions of new cells, so much so that nearly every cell in our bodies is replaced every few years. There is no reason to suppose it will be any different in an earthly Kingdom.

St. Thomas Aquinas, writing between the two Councils just cited, stated that the body will be a spiritual body "not because it is a spirit" but "because it will be entirely subject to the spirit." Following St. Paul he gave his own ideas about how such a *spiritualized* physical body might differ from the bodies we "now have," saying "they will not be able to suffer anything that is harmful to them," that "the body will in its own way put on the lightsomeness of glory," and "[the body] will share in what is the soul's very own characteristics so far as possible, in the perspicuity of sense knowledge, in the ordering of bodily appetite, and in the all-round perfection of nature."[137] In these speculations, Aquinas concentrates solely on the gross physical body. He says nothing about increased mental and psychic abilities. Those too, presumably, will be considerably enhanced.

I am not going to add to the speculations of the past. I will say, however, that, in a century which has almost doubled physical life-expectancy, which sees new records set in dozens of sports every year, and which has only begun to study the physical benefits of meditation and spiritual healing practices, the future abilities of our present bodies alone is probably beyond our imagination.[138]

The "resurrection of the body" also refers to the ability of Jesus and other high spiritual masters to *consciously* create or resurrect, i.e., reform, their physical bodies at will. Jesus, as the Scriptures tell us, resurrected his physical body on the third day and appeared to many thereafter in bodily form. After the Resurrection, Jesus appeared, perhaps in the type of spiritualized physical body to which St. Paul refers (i.e., one that could pass through walls), or perhaps, more likely, in both his astral and his physical body. I suspect that it was in his astral body that he passed through the locked door of

---

[137]St. Thomas Aquinas, in *Summa Contra Gentiles 4.86,* as quoted by Michael Murphy in *The Future of the Body,* Jeremy P. Tarcher, Inc., Los Angeles, 1992, pp. 204, 203.

[138]For readers who are interested in pursuing the matter further I recommend *The Future of the Body* by Michael Murphy; *Ageless Body, Timeless Mind* by Deepak Chopra; and *The Ageless Body* by Chris Griscom.

the room where the disciples huddled (John 20:19). His physical body, however, had fully materialized when he invited St. Thomas to put his hands in the wounds (John 20:27).

Similarly, it was probably in his astral body that he met the disciples on the road to Emmaus, his appearance "veiled," (Luke 24:13-29), but he materialized in the breaking of the bread (Luke 30:31). He was materialized in his physical body when, as recounted by Luke, he ate a piece of cooked fish (Luke 24:42). It is not entirely clear in another account (John 21:4-14) whether Jesus fully materialized or not.

Normally, in apparitions (e.g., Mary's appearances at Fatima in 1917) the spiritual being appears only in the astral body. Normally too, the spiritual being has to raise the vibrations of those humans to whom he or she is appearing so that they can see and hear him or her. The spiritual being, however, can also veil his or her appearance so that the people seeing the vision do not recognize him or her.

In an account similar to those in the New Testament, the twentieth century Hindu spiritual master Paramahansa Yogananda has written of his personal experience of the physical resurrection of his guru, Sri Yukteswarji Giri.[139]

To a large extent unconsciously, we created our present bodies before we were born (John 6:63)(see chapter 9). There is no reason to suppose we cannot some day *consciously* create its like or another newer "model." It is reported, and in some cases documented, that many saints of every tradition have created an extra physical body when one was needed for purposes of bilocation. The eighteenth century Italian St. Alphonsus de Liguori, for example, left

---

[139]Paramahansa Yogananda, in *Autobiography of a Yogi*, Self-Realization Fellowship, Los Angeles, 1946, 1990, pp. 475-496. (I am pleased to say that I have received both shaktipat (conveyance of spiritual energy by hand), and initiation into the kriya yoga taught by Sri Yukteswarji, from another of Sri Yukteswarji's disciples and the greatest saint I have met so far in this life, Swami Hariharinanda.)

his body in a coma-like state for several days in order to minister, in a duplicate body, to a dying Pope at Rome. The books of Carlos Castaneda and Lynn Andrews, as well as *Beyond the Lodge of the Sun* by Chokecherry Gall Eagle, tell of bilocation by contemporary Native American masters. Spyros Sathi reports that he has bilocated on many occasions.[140] Some day the ability of humans to create such an extra body could become commonplace.[141]

Perhaps other meanings, now unknown, will also eventually attach to the resurrection of the body. As St. Paul wrote, "eye has not seen nor ear heard, nor has it entered into the heart of man, the things that God has prepared for those who love him" (1 Cor. 2:9). To which one can only say, "Amen."

---

[140]Kyriacos C. Markides, *The Magus of Stovolos, The Extraordinary World of a Spiritual Healer,* Penguin, London, New York, 1985, 1990, pp. 200-206.

[141]Normally, the astral body is the "vehicle" used for out-of-body "traveling", but, for example, you can't time travel because the astral body can't transcend time. You have to use the thought body for that. Many masters, however, can actually materialize a second physical body, either partially or fully.

AFTERWORD

WHERE DO WE GO FROM HERE?

Where Do We Go As Church?

What might be the future of Christianity in the twenty-first century? This is a huge topic and one I scarcely feel competent to address adequately given that the Church worldwide has about two billion adherents, hundreds of denominations and rites, and thousands of institutions. But I will offer a few thoughts.

That the Church, as the community of those who are trying to follow Jesus into the Kingdom of Heaven, will survive is certain. Jesus promised that it would, and that the very gates of hell would not prevail against it (Matt. 16:18). He promised that his own words similarly would be remembered for all of human history (Matt. 24:35). So I am not worried about the Church's staying power. What form or forms the Church will take is another question altogether. Even Jesus predicted that some day people would worship God "in Spirit and in truth"(John 4:23) rather than in temples.

In the late 1960s, the English-American nondual mystic Alan Watts, who for a while was an Episcopal priest, wrote an essay entitled, "What Shall We Do with the Church?" In his usual brilliant but compassionately humorous way, Watts suggested that the future of the Church lay in getting away from moralizing, proselytizing, mythology, fundraising, and endless rational-level chattering, and getting back to offering the one service it should have been offering but usually was not—genuine spiritual and mystical experience. He also suggested that the Church had much to learn from other religions such as Buddhism.

Watts was ahead of his time. His words were little heeded—except by a large number of spiritually starved young people who took his lead in exploring the mystical riches of the East. Though Watts was one of the greatest mystics the English-American Church has produced, he was seen as a gadfly, a man who hung out with beatniks and hippies in crazy California, his works treated as marginal.

The times are now catching up with Watts. What he called for may soon be what millions of churchgoers will be demanding, that the Church offer them something real: real spiritual healing, real spiritual power, real mystical experience, real contact with the Communion of Saints, and real practical and knowledgeable assistance in getting to inner God realization. Those churches that respond will survive.

The Church as an institution is the servant of the servants of God, and Americans know that, in a service economy with empowered consumers, a service organization must provide what its customers want and need or the customers will go elsewhere. Nor can an organization supply a service, in this case spiritual and mystical expertise, if it lacks the ability to perform that service, i.e., if it lacks spiritual realization itself.

Watts ends his essay by saying "Of course, there is a good argument for just letting obsolete institutions fall apart, since 'no man putteth new wine into old wineskins'" (Matt. 9:17). That too may happen, and in today's accelerating global change, it could happen faster than people think.

In the next few years the Roman Catholic Church in America will be devastated by the rapid dying-off or retirement of what few, mostly elderly, clergy remain. Mainstream American Protestant churches have been losing membership for years. Church attendance in many Christian nations, such as England, Sweden, and France, is already extremely low. Throughout Latin America millions of people, whose spiritual nourishment has been neglected for decades, are converting to more experiential forms of Christianity at a dizzying rate. The Church in Russia and Eastern Europe, now without an atheistic state to fight, and now open to the influences of the West, will change profoundly in the twenty-first century. The so-called new age movement is burgeoning all over the world, particularly among Christians. Even the fundamentalist parts of the Church are undergoing ever accelerating change; many of its American members, ironically, are learning how to think and operate at the rational level by learning to practice politics in a pluralistic society.

So, what the twenty-first century holds for the Church as institution is anybody's guess. But one thing seems sure: the *form* of the Christian church, despite attempts to hold onto the past, may well be almost unrecognizable a hundred years hence.

Where Do We Go as Individuals?

First, before we "go" anywhere, we should first assess where we are. In the spiritual path we cannot jump steps. We must start exactly where we are now. Where we are now is perfect. It is perfect for the lessons the Holy Spirit wants us to learn. It is perfect in providing us with mirrors, that is, other people who reflect back to us our level of consciousness, our fears, and our strengths, perfect for our own future unfolding.

Second, we must listen to the "small still voice" of the Spirit within (Ps. 46:10). Most of us are very good at talking, even at talking to God in prayer and asking God questions. But most of us are not good at listening, at quieting the mind through meditation so the Holy Spirit can direct us and answer our questions. Failure to listen to the Holy Spirit is the only mistake that, as Jesus said, cannot be "forgiven" (Luke 12:10). If we pass up on, or fail to listen to, a grace or inspiration from the Holy Spirit, it passes us by. It's gone. It can't be undone, i.e., "forgiven."

Third, we must work hard on ourselves. Chogyam Trungpa has called the spiritual path "manual labor." Jesus likened it to putting the shoulder to a plow (Luke 9:62). In some ways the path can be brutal. Jesus said that, if our eye is holding us back from heaven, pluck it out (Matt. 18:9). If our hand is holding us back, cut it off (Matt. 5:30). If our family or other relationships are in the way, leave them (Luke 9:61). Only those of us who place God first with all our hearts and souls and minds (Matt. 22:37), and who are willing to sacrifice anything or any relationship that gets in the way, are likely to realize the Kingdom. People routinely make such sacrifices to win a gold medal at the Olympics or to try to win the Presidency. We must at least be as dedicated (2 Tim. 4:7; 1 Cor. 9:24). We have to be willing to go all out, day after day, for a lifetime.

Fourth, we must be patient. The spiritual path takes years. Heaven can't be stormed overnight, nor can we completely change ourselves overnight. Only the ego works violently, always wanting to push and shove, to hurry, to force. War is ego at its extreme, the effort to violently force things to go our way, and many of us are in a perpetual state of war within ourselves.

The Spirit works very gently, never by force. Its movement within us is subtle and delicate. As Bernadette Roberts says, spirit "grows us" from within naturally and gradually. The best spiritual practice is to do a little each day: pray, meditate, go to church, receive Holy Communion *each day*. Keep a daily journal, keep track of dreams, go for a quiet walk.

Fifth, we should find a community of people who think as we do, who are as serious about the spiritual path as we are, and who can pray with us and support us. As Jesus said, two or three gathered in his name are far more effective than going it alone (Matt. 18:20).

The best practice is probably what Wilber calls an "integral practice." In integral spiritual practice we exercise, on a daily basis, all the parts of ourselves with an eye to spiritual growth. We do something for the body (e.g., yoga, running, weightlifting), something for the emotions (e.g., psychotherapy, dreamwork, emotional release), something for the mind (e.g., spiritual reading), and something for the soul (e.g., meditation). This keeps the whole of ourselves attuned every day to inner growth and keeps the various parts of ourselves in balance.

Finally, we should remind ourselves daily who we are. We are already perfect in God's eyes. We are already God's beloved sons and daughters (Rom. 8:16). We are already sinless (1 John 3:9). We are already heirs with Jesus of the Kingdom (Rom. 8:17). Our essence is Love (1 John 4:7-8). We are already saved (1 John 2:2). We are already immortal (1 Cor. 15:54). The spiritual path is not designed to "get" any of these things for us; in truth, we do not now lack any of them. It is merely to help us gradually become *conscious* of who we already are, and to make ourselves more perfect vehicles for the manifestation of the Love of God on Earth. I pray we all become perfect vehicles for expressing God's Love so that, through us, the Kingdom of Heaven will come on Earth just as it already is in Heaven.

BIBLIOGRAPHY

Allport, Gordon. 1955. *Becoming.* New Haven, CT: Yale University Press.

Andrews, Lynn. 1981. *Medicine Woman.* San Francisco: Harper & Row.

―――. 1984. *The Flight of the Seventh Moon.* New York: Harper Collins.

―――. 1985. *Jaguar Woman.* New York: Harper Collins.

Aquinas, Thomas, St. 1969. *Summa Theologiae.* New York: Doubleday/Anchor.

Arieti, Silvano. 1955. *The Intrapsychic Self.* New York: Basic Books.

Bailey, Alice A. 1971. *Rays and the Initiations, A Treatise on the Seven Rays.* New York: Lucis Publishing Co.

Bateson, Gregory. 1979. *Mind and Nature, A Necessary Unity.* New York: Bantam

Benner, Joseph S. 1916. *The Impersonal Life.* Marina del Rey, CA: De Vorss & Co.

Berry, Thomas. 1988. *The Dream of the Earth.* San Francisco: Sierra Club.

―――. 1992. *The Universe Story: From the Primordial Flaring Forth to the Ecozoic Era.* With Brian Swimme. San Francisco: HarperCollins.

Boswell, John. 1980-81. *Christianity, Social Tolerance and Homosexuality.* Chicago and London: University of Chicago Press.

Bruteau, Beatrice. 1997. *God's Ecstasy: The Creation of a Self-Creating World.* New York: Crossroad.

―――. 1974. *Evolution Toward Divinity, Teilhard and the Hindu Tradition.* Wheaton, IL: The Theosophical Publishing House.

―――. "Symbiotic Cosmos," in *The Roll, Newsletter of the Scola Contemplationis.* Philosopher's Exchange (December 1993): 3425 Forest Lane, Pfafftown, NC 27040-9545.

Burrows, Ruth. 1980, 1st American ed. 1976. *Guidelines for Mystical Prayer.* Denville, NJ: Dimension.

―――. 1981, 1st American ed. 1975 by Daniel Mullins. *Before the Living God.* Denville, NJ: Dimension.

Campbell, Joseph. 1959-68. *The Masks of God*, Vols. 1-4. New York: Viking.

————. 1968. *The Hero with a Thousand Faces*. New York: World.

Castaneda, Carlos. 1968. *The Teachings of Don Juan: A Yaqui Way of Knowledge*. New York: Pocket Books.

————. 1972. *A Separate Reality, Further Conversations with Don Juan*. New York: Pocket Books.

————. 1977. *The Second Ring of Power*. New York: Pocket Books.

————. 1981. *Eagle's Gift, Losing the Human Form*. New York: Pocket Books.

————. 1984. *The Fire From Within*. New York: Pocket Books.

Catherine of Siena, St. 1991. *Dialogue of St. Catherine of Sienna*. Designed by Algar Thorold. Rockford, IL: Tan Books.

Cavallini, Giuliana. 1996. *Things Visible and Invisible: Images in the Spirituality of St. Catherine of Siena*. Translated by Sister Mary Jeremiah. New York: Alba House.

Chaisson, Eric. 1989. *The Life Era: Cosmic Selection and Conscious Evolution*. New York: W. W. Norton & Co.

Chopra, Deepak. 1993. *Ageless Body, Timeless Mind*. New York: Random House.

————. 1994. *The Seven Spiritual Laws of Success: A Practical Guide to the Fulfillment of Your Dreams*. San Rafael, CA: Amber-Allen, New World Library.

Clement of Alexandria, St. 1992. *Fathers of the Church: Clement of Alexandria: Stromateis, Books One to Three*. Washington, DC: Catholic University of America Press.

The Cloud of Unknowing. 1973. Edited by William Johnston. New York: Doubleday.

Da, Adi. 1972. *The Knee of Listening*. Middleton, CA: The Dawn Horse Press.

————. 1991. *The Dawn Horse Testament*. Clearlake, CA: The Dawn Horse Press.

de Chardin, Teilhard. 1961. *The Phenomenon of Man*. New York: Harper Torchbooks.

————. 1964. *The Future of Man*. New York: Harper Torchbooks.

DeRohan, Ceanne. 1984. *Right Use of Will, Healing and Evolving the Emotional Body.* Santa Fe: Four Winds.

Dionysios, St. 1997. *Dionysius the Areopagite, The Divine Names and the Mystical Theology.* By C. E. Rolt. Kila, MT: Kessinger.

Eckhart, Meister. 1981. *Meister Eckhart, The Essential Sermons, Commentaries, Treatises, and Defense.* Translated by Edmund Colledge, O.S.A. and Bernard McGinn. New York: Paulist Press.

———. 1986. *Meister Eckhart, Teacher and Preacher.* Edited by Bernard McGinn. New York: Paulist Press.

———. 1980. *Breakthrough: Meister Eckhart's Creation Spirituality in New Translation.* By Matthew Fox. Garden City, NY: Image Books.

Eisler, Riane. 1987. *The Chalice and the Blade.* San Francisco: HarperSanFrancisco.

———. 1996. *Sacred Pleasure: Sex, Myth, and the Politics of the Body—New Paths to Power and Love.* San Francisco: HarperSanFrancisco.

Eliade, Mircea. 1958. 1963. *Patterns in Comparative Religion.* New York: Sheed & Ward. Novato, CA: New American Library.

Emerson, Ralph Waldo. 1993. *Self-Reliance and Other Essays,* Unabridged. New York: Dover.

———. 1986. *Emerson on Transcendentalism.* Edited by Edward L. Ericson. New York: Ungar.

Ereira, Alan. 1992. *The Elder Brothers.* New York: Alfred A. Knopf.

Erikson, Erik H. 1950. *Childhood and Society.* New York: Norton.

Erigena, John Scotus. 1998. *Treatise on Divine Predestination.* Translated by Mary Brennan. South Bend, IN: Notre Dame University Press.

The Essential Gay Mystics. 1997. Edited by Andrew Harvey. Edison, NJ: Castle Books. (By arrangement with and permission of HarperCollins Publishers, NY.)

The Essential Piaget. 1995. Edited by H. Gruber and J. Voneche. New York: Basic Books.

Ferguson, Marilyn. 1980. *The Aquarian Conspiracy: Personal and Social Transformation in Our Time.* New York: Jeremy Tarcher.

Ferrini, Paul. 1995. *Love Without Conditions: Reflections of the Christ Mind.* Greenfield, MA: Heartways Press.

————. 1996. *The Silence of the Heart: Reflections of the Christ Mind.* Greenfield, MA: Heartways Press.

————. 1997. *Miracle of Love: Reflections of the Christ Mind.* Greenfield, MA: Heartways Press.

————. 1998. *Return to the Garden: Reflections of the Christ Mind.* Greenfield, MA: Heartways Press.

Fitzhugh, Elisabeth Y. 1987. *The Orion Material.* Takoma Park, MD: Synchronicity Press.

Flavell, J. 1963. *The Developmental Psychology of Jean Piaget.* Princeton, NJ: Van Nostrand.

Fox, Matthew. 1991. *Creation Spirituality, Liberating Gifts for the Peoples of the Earth.* San Francisco: HarperSanFrancisco.

————. 1983. *Original Blessing, A Primer in Creation Spirituality.* Santa Fe: Bear & Co.

————. 1988. *The Coming of the Cosmic Christ: The Healing of Mother Earth and the Birth of a Global Renaissance.* San Francisco: HarperSanFrancisco.

————. 1980. *Breakthrough: Meister Eckhart's Creation Spirituality in New Translation.* Garden City, NY: Image Books.

Frankl, Victor. 1985. *Man's Search for Meaning.* New York: Washington Square Press.

Fromm, Erich, with D.T. Suzuki and R. Martino. 1970. *Zen Buddhism and Psychoanalysis.* New York: Harper & Row.

Gall Eagle, Chokecherry. 1997. *Beyond the Lodge of the Sun.* Rockport, MA: Element Books.

Gebser, Jean. 1985. *The Ever-Present Origin.* Translated by Noel Barstad. Athens, OH: Ohio University Press.

Ghose, Aurobindo. 1982. *The Future Evolution of Man.* Pondicherry, India: Sri Aurobindo Association.

————. 1984. *The Synthesis of Yoga.* Pondicherry, India: Sri Aurobindo Association.

————. 1998. *Beyond the Human Species: The Life and Work of Sri Aurobindo and the Mother.* By Georges Van Vreckham. New York: Paragon, Omega Books.

————. 1984. *Sri Aurobindo or the Adventure of Consciousness.* By Satprem. Translated from the French by Luc Venet. New York: Institute for Evolutionary Research.

Gilligan, Carol. 1993. *In a Different Voice: Psychological Theory and Women's Development*. Rev. ed. Cambridge, MA: Harvard University Press.

Goswami. 1993. *The Self-Aware Universe*. New York: G.P. Putnam's Sons.

Gregory of Nyssa, St. 1961. *From Glory to Glory, Texts from Gregory of Nyssa's Mystical Writings*. Edited by S. J. Jean Danielou and S. J. Herbert Musurillo. New York: Charles Scribner's Sons.

Griscom, Chris. 1992. *The Ageless Body*. Galisteo, NM: Light Institute.

———. 1987-88. *Ecstasy is a New Frequency*. London and New York: Simon & Schuster.

———. 1988-90. *The Healing of Emotion, Awakening the Fearless Self*. London and New York: Simon & Schuster.

———. 1986-88. *Time is an Illusion*. With Wolfing Von Rohr. London and New York: Simon & Schuster.

Grof, Stanislav, M.D. 1988. *The Adventure of Self-Discovery: Dimensions of Consciousness and New Perspectives in Psychotherapy and Inner Exploration*. Albany, NY: State University of New York Press.

Habermas, Jurgen. 1971. *Knowledge and Human Interests*. Boston: Beacon.

———. 1973. *Theory and Practice*. Boston: Beacon.

———. 1975. *Legitimation Crisis*. Boston: Beacon.

———. 1979. *Communication and the Evolution of Society*. Translated by T. McCarthy. Boston: Beacon.

———. 1984-85. *The Theory of Communicative Action*. Translated by T. McCarthy. 2 vols. Boston: Beacon.

Harner, Michael. 1982. *The Way of the Shaman, A Guide to Power and Healing*. New York: Bantam.

Hay, Louise. 1984. *You Can Heal Your Life*. Carson, CA: Hay House.

Holmes, Ernest. 1997. *The Science of Mind*. New York: Putnam.

Horney, Karen. 1950. *Neurosis and Human Growth*. New York: Norton.

Houston, Jean. 1997. *The Possible Human: A Course in Enhancing Your Physical, Mental and Creative Abilities*. New York: Jeremy P. Tarcher.

Hubbard, Barbara Marx. 1998. *Conscious Evolution: Awakening the Power of Our Social Potential.* San Rafeal, CA: New World Library.

———. 1995. *The Revelation: A Message of Hope for the New Millennium.* Novato, CA: Nataraj.

———. 1982. *The Evolutionary Journey: A Personal Guide to a Positive Future.* San Francisco: The Evolutionary Press.

Huxley, Aldous. 1944. *The Perennial Philosophy.* New York: Harper and Row.

Isaac the Syrian, St. 1977. *Mystical Writings of St. Isaac the Syrian.* Willits, CA: Eastern Orthodox Books.

John of the Cross, St. 1991. *The Dark Night, The Ascent of Mt. Carmel, The Spiritual Canticle, The Living Flame of Love in The Collected Works of St. John of the Cross.* Translated by Kieran Kavanaugh, O.C.D. and Otilio Rodriguez, O.C.D.. Washington, DC: ICS Publications, Institute of Carmelite Studies.

Jampolsky, Gerald, M. D. 1988. *Love is Letting Go of Fear.* Millbrae, CA: Celestial Arts.

———. 1984. *Teach Only Love.* New York: Bantam.

———. 1990. *Out of Darkness into the Light: A Journey of Inner Healing.* New York: Bantam Doubleday Dell.

———. 1985. *Good-Bye to Guilt: Releasing Guilt Through Forgiveness.* New York: Bantam.

———. 1991. *Love is the Answer: Creating Positive Relationships.* With Diane V. Ciricione. New York: Bantam Doubleday Dell.

John Paul II, Pope. 1994. *Crossing the Threshold of Hope.* New York: Alfred A. Knopf.

Joy, W. Brugh. 1979. *Joy's Way.* New York: Jeremy P. Tarcher.

Julian of Norwich, Dame. 1999. *Revelations of Divine Love.* Translated by Elizabeth Spearing. New York: Penguin Classics, Penguin USA.

Jung, Carl. 1957. *The Undiscovered Self.* New York: Mentor.

———. 1964. *Man and His Symbols.* New York: Dell.

———. 1971. *The Portable Jung.* Edited by J. Campbell. New York: Viking.

———. 1961. *Analytical Psychology: Its Theory and Practice.* New York: Vintage.

———. 1969. *Synchronicity: An Acausal Connecting Principle.* Princeton, NJ: Princeton University Press.

Keating, Thomas, OCSO. 1994. *Invitation to Love: The Way of Christian Contemplation.* Rockport, MA: Element.

———. 1996. *Intimacy with God.* New York: Crossroad.

Kellerman, Jonathan, M. D. 1985. *When The Bough Breaks.* New York: Signet.

Keyes, Ken, Jr. 1975. *Handbook to Higher Consciousness.* 6th edition 1982, reprint of 5th edition, copyright 1975 by Living Love Center. Coos Bay, OR: Living Love Publications.

Kierkegaard, Soren. 1953. *Fear and Trembling and The Sickness Unto Death.* New York: Anchor.

Kohlberg, Lawrence. 1981. *Essays on Moral Development.* San Francisco: Harper.

———. 1981. *The Meaning and Measurement of Moral Development.* Worchester: Clark University Heinz Werner Institute.

Laszlo, Ervin. 1987. *Evolution: The Grand Synthesis.* Boston and London: New Science Library, Shambhala.

———. 1996. *The Whispering Pond: A Personal Guide to the Emerging Vision of Science.* Rockport, MA: Element.

Loevinger, Jane. 1977. *Ego Development.* San Francisco: Jossey-Bass.

Louth, Andrew. 1996. *Maximus the Confessor (Early Church Fathers).* London and New York: Routledge.

Maharshi, Ramana. 1962. *Self-Realization: Life and Teachings of Sri Ramana Maharshi.* By B.V. Narasimha Swami, 6th ed. revised from 3rd ed. Epilogue by S. S. Cohen, 7th ed. Tiruvannamalai, India: Sri Ramanaasramam.

Markides, Kyriacos C. 1985. 1990. *The Magus of Strovolos, The Extraordinary World of a Spiritual Healer.* London. New York: Penguin.

———. 1987. Homage to the Sun, *The Wisdom of the Magus of Strovolos.* London, New York: Penguin.

———. 1990. *Fire in the Heart, Healers, Sages and Mystics.* New York: Paragon.

Maslow, Abraham. 1993. *The Further Reaches of Human Nature.* New York: Penguin/Arkana.

————. 1982. *Toward a Psychology of Being.* 2nd ed. New York: Van Nostrand Reinhold.

May, Rollo. 1969. *Love and Will.* New York: Norton.

————. 1977. *The Meaning of Anxiety.* Rev. ed. New York: Norton.

Maximos the Confessor, St. 1985. *Maximus Confessor, Selected Writings, Classics of Western Spirituality.* Edited by George C. Berthold. New York: Paulist Press.

————. 1996. *Maximus the Confessor (Early Church Fathers).* By Andrew Louth. London and New York: Routledge.

Modi, Shakuntala, M.D. 1997. *Remarkable Healings.* Charlottesville, VA: Hampton Roads.

Murphy, Michael. 1992. *The Future of the Body, Explorations into the Future Evolution of Human Nature.* Los Angeles: Jeremy P. Tarcher.

Peck, M. Scott, M.D. 1978. *The Road Less Traveled, a New Psychology of Love, Traditional Values, and Spiritual Growth.* New York: Simon & Schuster.

————. 1983. *People of the Lie, The Hope for Healing Human Evil.* New York: Simon & Schuster.

Pennington, M. Basil, OCSO. 1982. *Centering Prayer: Renewing an Ancient Christian Prayer Form.* New York: Image.

————. 1995. *Call to the Center: The Gospel's Invitation to Deeper Prayer.* Hyde Park, NY: New City Press.

Piaget, Jean. 1990. *The Child's Conception of the World.* Lanham, MD: Littlefield Adams.

————. 1997.*The Moral Judgment of the Child.* Translated by Marjorie Gabain and William Damon. Glencoe, IL: FreePress.

————. 1972. *The Psychology of the Child.* Translated by Helen Weaver and Barbel Inhelder. New York: Basic Books.

Plotinus. 1988. *Plotinus with an English Translation: Enneads, Books 1-5* (Loeb Classical Library # 445). Translated by A. H. Armstrong. Cambridge, MA: Harvard University Press.

————. 1989. *Plotinus with an English Translation: Enneads, Books 6-9* (Loeb Classical Library # 468). Translated by A. H. Armstrong. Cambridge, MA: Harvard University Press.

The Portable Jung. 1971. Edited by J. Campbell. New York: Viking.

Quantum Questions, Mystical Writings of the World's Great Physicists. 1985. Edited by Ken Wilber. Boulder, CO and London: Shambhala.

Richardson, Lawrence. *An Introduction to a Higher Reality, The Art of Contemplating the Holy Spirit, The Spiritual Mentor and the Fire of the Holy Spirit* and *Contemplative Prayer Q&A,* all in *A Christian Mystic's Outreach* at www.Chrmysticaloutreach.com on the World Wide Web.

Roberts, Bernadette. 1985. *The Path to No-Self.* Boston and London: Shambala.

———. 1984. *The Experience of No-Self.* Boston and London: Shambhala.

Roberts, Jane. 1977. *The "Unknown" Reality.* Englewood Cliffs, NJ: Prentice-Hall.

———. 1979. *The Nature of the Psyche, Its Human Expression.* San Rafael, CA: Amber-Allen.

———. 1976. *Psychic Politics.* Englewood Cliffs, NJ: Prentice-Hall.

Rogers, Carl. 1961. *On Becoming a Person.* Boston: Houghton Mifflin.

Rolt, C.E. 1997. *Dionysius the Areopagite, The Divine Names and the Mystical Theology.* Kila, MT: Kessinger.

Roszak, Theodore B. 1992. *The Voice of the Earth.* New York: Simon & Schuster.

Sanford, John A. 1989. *Dreams, God's Forgotten Language.* San Francisco: HarperSanFrancisco.

———. 1979. *Dreams and Healing.* New York: Paulist Press.

———. 1982. *Evil: The Shadow Side of Reality.* New York: Crossroad.

———. 1984. *Invisible Partners: How the Male and Female in Each of Us Affects Our Relationships.* New York: Paulist Press.

———. 1987. *The Kingdom Within: The Inner Meaning of Jesus' Sayings.* San Francisco: HarperSanFrancisco.

Saraydarian, Torkom. 1994. *Christ, the Avatar of Sacrificial Love.* Cave Creek, AZ: T.S.G. Publishing Foundation, Inc.

Satprem. 1984. *Sri Aurobindo or the Adventure of Consciousness.* Translated from the French by Luc Venet. New York: Institute for Evolutionary Research.

Smith, Huston. 1976. *Forgotten Truth.* New York: Harper & Row.

———. 1989. *Beyond the Post-Modern Mind.* Wheaton, IL: Quest.

————. 1991. *The World's Religions.* San Francisco: HarperSanFrancisco.

Spangler, David. 1984. *Emergence: The Rebirth of the Sacred.* New York: Doubleday.

————. 1991. *Reimagination of the World.* With William Irwin Thompson. Santa Fe: Bear & Co.

————. 1996. *A Pilgrim in Aquarius.* Scotland: Findhorn.

————. 1995. *Everyday Miracles, The Inner Art of Manifestation.* New York: Bantam.

————. 1975. *The Laws of Manifestation.* Scotland: Findhorn.

————. 1981. *Reflections on the Christ.* 3rd ed. Scotland: Findhorn.

————. 1976. *Revelation, The Birth of a New Age.* Middleton, WI: Lorian.

Summer Rain, Mary. 1993. *Phantoms Afoot, Journeys into the Night.* Charlottesville, VA: Hampton Roads.

————. 1993. *Spirit Song, The Visionary Wisdom of No-Eyes.* Charlottesville, VA: Hampton Roads.

————. 1993. *Dreamwalker, The Path of Sacred Power.* Charlottesville, VA: Hampton Roads.

Suzuki, Daisetz Teitaro. 1986. *Essays in Zen Buddhism, First Series.* New York: Grove Press.

————. 1991. *An Introduction to Zen Buddhism.* New York: Grove Press.

————. 1956. *Zen Buddhism, Selected Writings of D.T. Suzuki.* Edited by William Barrett. Garden City, NY: Doubleday, Anchor.

Swami, B.V. Narasimha. 1962. *Self Realization: Life and Teachings of Sri Ramana Maharshi.* 6th ed. Revised from 3rd ed. Epilogue by S.S. Cohen, 7th ed. Tiruvannamalai, India: Sri Ramanaasramam.

Teachings of the Christian Mystics. 1998. Edited by Andrew Harvey. Boston: Shambhala.

Teresa of Avila, St. 1976. 1980. *The Interior Castle,* in *The Collected Works of St. Teresa of Avila.* 2 vols. Translated by Kiernan Kavanaugh, O.C.D. and Otilio Rodriquez, O.C.D. Washington, DC: ICS Publications, Institute of Carmelite Studies.

Teresa, Mother. 1990. *Compassion in Action, in For the Love of God.* Edited by Benjamin Shield, Ph.D. and Richard Carlson, Ph.D., 1990, 1997, Novato, CA: New World Library.

Thoreau, Henry David. 1988. *Walden.* New York: Konemann.

The Tibetan Book of the Dead. 1927. Edited by W.Y. Evans-Wentz. Oxfordshire, England: Oxford University Press.

Trungpa Rinpoche, Chogyam. 1988. *Shambhala: The Sacred Path of the Warrior.* Boston: Shambhala.

———. 1973. *Cutting Through Spiritual Materialism.* Boulder, CO and London: Shambhala.

———. 1976. *The Myth of Freedom and the Way of Meditation.* Boston: Shambhala.

Underhill, Evelyn. 1910. *Mysticism.* New York: Doubleday.

van Vreckhem, Georges. 1998. *Beyond the Human Species: The Life and Work of Sri Aurobindo and the Mother.* St. Paul, MN: Paragon, Omega Books.

Walsch, Neale Donald. 1995. *Conversations with God: An Uncommon Dialogue, Book One.* New York: G.P. Putnam's Sons.

———. 1997. *Conversations with God, Book Two.* Charlottesville, VA: Hampton Roads.

———. 1998. *Conversations with God, Book Three.* Charlottesville, VA: Hampton Roads.

Watts, Alan. 1968. *Cloud—Hidden, Whereabouts Unknown, A Mountain Journal.* New York: Vintage, Random House.

———. 1991. *Nature, Man and Woman.* New York: Vintage.

———. 1951. *The Wisdom of Insecurity, A Message for an Age of Anxiety.* New York: Vintage.

———. 1966. *The Book: On the Taboo Against Knowing Who You Are.* New York: Vintage, Random House.

———. 1963. *The Two Hands of God, The Myths of Polarity.* New York: G. Braziller.

———. 1989. *The Way of Zen.* New York: Vintage, Random House.

Webb, James. 1999. *Pathways to Inner Peace, Life-saving Processes for Healing Heart-Mind-Soul.* Minneapolis: Prism.

Wilber, Ken. 1996. *A Brief History of Everything.* Boston and London: Shambhala.

———. 1995. *Sex, Ecology, Spirituality, the Spirit of Evolution.* Boston and London: Shambhala.

————. 1980, 1996. *The Atman Project*. Wheaton, IL: Quest Books.

————. 1977. *The Spectrum of Consciousness*. Wheaton, IL: Theosophical Publishing House.

————. 1997. *The Eye of Spirit*. Boston and London: Shambhala.

————. 1986. *Transformations of Consciousness, Conventional and Contemplative Perspectives on Development*. With Jack Engler and Daniel P. Brown. Boston and London: Shambhala.

————. 1985. *No Boundary, Eastern and Western Approaches to Personal Growth*. Boston and London: Shambhala.

————. 1999. *The Marriage of Sense and Soul, Integrating Science and Religion*. New York: Broadway.

————. 1999. *One Taste, The Journals of Ken Wilber*. Boston and London: Shambhala.

————. 1996. *Eye to Eye, The Quest for the New Paradigm*. Boston and London: Shambhala.

Williams, Paul. 1982. *Das Energi*. Encinitas, CA: Entwhistle Books.

Williamson, Marianne. 1997. *The Healing of America*. New York: Simon and Schuster.

————. 1992. *A Return to Love, Reflections on the Principles of a Course in Miracles*. New York: HarperCollins.

Yogananda, Paramahansa. 1975. *Man's Eternal Quest*. Los Angeles: Self-Realization Fellowship.

————. 1946. *Autobiography of a Yogi*. Los Angeles: Self-Realization Fellowship.

Zukav, Gary. 1989. *Seat of the Soul*. New York: Simon and Schuster.

Index

Page numbers in italics refer to entries found in footnotes.

A

abortion, 244
Abraham, 254
Adam and Eve, 237-239
Adam as androgynous, *236*
Adi Da, 158
Age of Aquarius, 125, 259-260, 263-264
Age of Aries, 254-256
Age of Pisces, 249, 256-263
Age of Taurus, 252-254
aggression, 161
alcohol, abstinence from, 76
ananda, 198
ancestor worship, *82*
angel of the true self, 109
angelic energies, 110
anger, 94
angst, 65-66
animal sacrifice, 254-255
Apostles, 223
apparitions, 295
Aquinas, Saint Thomas, 201, 293-294
archaic consciousness, 33-35
archangels, 110
'ascended masters,' 221
Ascension, 197, 199, 200
'Ascension Initiation,' 209
Ascent of Mt. Carmel, The, *166*
astral body
  focal point of, 102
  nature of, 71, 73, 74, 78
  out-of-body travel and, *296*
astral level. *See* psychic consciousness
astral plane, 74, 78, 284-285
'at hand,' 2

attachments, 190
Augustine, Saint, 18, 223
auras, 72-74
avatar, 228

B

Bailey, Alice A., 148
baptism, 88
Baptism of Fire and the Holy Spirit, 52-53, 117, 174
beatific vision, 197, 198
beauty, 212
beginners, 88-89, 92-95
beliefs, magical, 38
Benner, Joseph S., 162
Beyond the Lodge of the Sun, 237-238
bilocation, 295-296
Birth of the Christ, 88
bodhisattva, 184
borderline personality, 35
breakthrough, 199, 202
breathing exercises, 89-90
Brief History of Everything, A, 16
Buddha, 221
Burrows, Ruth, *203*, 266

C

Castenada, Carlos, *83*, 174-175, 189-190
Catherine of Genoa, Saint, 166
'causal' body, 73
causal level of consciousness
  ascent to, 138-140
  challenges after achieving, 194-195
  character of, 185-186
  compassion in, 187-189
  darkness/void of, 185-187
  defined, 183-184
  detachment in, 189-192

315

Z

ABOUT THE AUTHOR

Jim Marion is a rare combination of Christian mystic and public policy lawyer. A contemporary American mystic who has followed the Christian spiritual path since childhood, Marion spent eight years studying for the priesthood and pursued divinity studies at Hartford Seminary Foundation. After leaving monastic life, he was active in political arenas and received a law degree from Boston University. Since then, Marion has pursued a public policy career in Washington, D.C., where he now lives. Since his pivotal mystical experience as an adolescent, Marion has never ceased to explore the issues, requirements, and challenges of authentic Christian spirituality and inner development. This is his first book for Hampton Roads.

Hampton Roads Publishing Company

... for the evolving human spirit

Hampton Roads Publishing Company
publishes books on a variety of subjects,
including metaphysics, health, integrative medicine,
visionary fiction, and other related topics.

For a copy of our latest catalog, call toll-free
(800) 766-8009, or send your name and address to:

Hampton Roads Publishing Company, Inc.
1125 Stoney Ridge Road
Charlottesville, VA 22902

e-mail: hrpc@hrpub.com
Website: www.hrpub.com